P9-CIT-861

The Presidential Election and Transition 1960-1961

THE PRESIDENTIAL ELECTION AND TRANSITION 1960-1961

PAUL T. DAVID

PAUL TILLETT

STANLEY KELLEY, JR.

CHARLES A. H. THOMSON

HERBERT E. ALEXANDER

V. O. KEY, JR.

JOHN M. HIGHTOWER

LAURIN L. HENRY

EUGENE J. McCARTHY

THRUSTON B. MORTON

Brookings Lectures and Additional Papers
Edited by Paul T. David

THE BROOKINGS INSTITUTION
Washington, D.C.

© 1961 by

THE BROOKINGS INSTITUTION

Published October 1961

Library of Congress Catalogue Card Number 61-18112

Printed in the United States of America
George Banta Company, Inc.

Foreword

THIS VOLUME on the 1960-1961 presidential election and transition offers an appraisal of the political developments of the last election. It is one in a series of studies Brookings has conducted in recent years on nominating and election politics. The series grew out of the monumental study of *Presidential Nominating Politics of 1952* by Paul T. David, Malcolm Moos, and Ralph M. Goldman for the American Political Science Association, and with the cooperation of Brookings, published by the Johns Hopkins Press.

Subsequently the Institution published several volumes on aspects of the general subject. They included, among others, *The Politics of National Party Conventions* (1960), by Paul T. David, Ralph M. Goldman, and Richard C. Bain; *Presidential Transitions* (1960), by Laurin L. Henry; *The 1956 Presidential Campaign* (1960), by Charles A. H. Thomson and Frances M. Shattuck; *Political Campaigning: Problems in Creating an Informed Electorate* (1960), by Stanley Kelley, Jr., *Convention Decisions and Voting Records* (1960), by Richard C. Bain, and *Television and Presidential Politics: The Experience in 1952 and the Problems Ahead* (1956), by Charles A. H. Thomson.

The preoccupations of the present volume are those of the student of politics and government. Four of the ten authors teach political science at as many different universities: Paul T. David, Virginia; Stanley Kelley, Jr., Princeton; V. O. Key, Jr., Harvard; Paul Tillett, Rutgers. Three others are professional political scientists on the staffs of research institutions: Herbert E. Alexander, Citizens Research Foundation; Laurin L. Henry, The Brookings Institution; Charles A. H. Thomson, RAND Corporation. One author, John M. Hightower, is the distinguished Department of State correspondent of the Associated Press. Two of the authors, active participant observers of the subjects on which they wrote, are members of the United States Senate: Eugene J. McCarthy,

Democrat, of Minnesota; and Thruston B. Morton, Republican, of Kentucky.

Seven of the twelve chapters were prepared initially as lectures given in the 1960-1961 series of the Brookings Institution. Several of these were extensively revised and up-dated for publication, as indicated in notes at the beginning of the respective chapters.

The plan for the lecture series and the added chapters that comprise the present book was developed for the Institution by Dr. David in collaboration with George A. Graham, Director of Governmental Studies at Brookings, and Dr. David served as editor for the volume. The reader will note that many of the events discussed in this book are viewed from differing perspectives by two or more of the contributing authors. In the final chapter, the editor has identified possible changes in political habits and customs, which are to be discerned in the events reviewed by the authors.

The Institution wishes to record its gratitude to the authors and editor for their several contributions, to A. Evelyn Breck for editing the manuscript for press, and to Virginia Angel for preparing the index.

The Institution is indebted to the Edgar Stern Family Fund and to the Ford Foundation for financial support that made the lecture series and the preparation of this volume possible. The views expressed are those of the authors and should not be interpreted as necessarily reflecting the views of the Brookings trustees, officers, or other staff members or of the foundations providing financial support.

ROBERT D. CALKINS
President

July 1961

Contents

1

The Presidential Nominations

PAUL T. DAVID[1]

ON JANUARY 20, 1961, when President-elect John F. Kennedy was inaugurated, a Republican President was replaced by a Democrat. The new President was the first born in this century. He was the youngest man ever elected President of the United States, and he replaced the oldest man who ever served in the office. The transfer of power to a new generation was associated with the change of political parties in the administration, but the consequences of the change in generations may be even greater than those inherent in the change of parties.

Much of this prospect for change had become inevitable long in advance, under our system for selecting presidential candidates and electing one of them. Under the Twenty-second Amendment, President Eisenhower was not eligible for another term. The Republican party was therefore required to choose a successor candidate, and it also seemed likely that the Democratic party would choose a successor to the twice-defeated Adlai Stevenson.

In other respects the preconditions were such as to lend interest to the nominations in each party. Democratic strength was resurgent in the congressional and state elections of 1956 and 1958.

[1] Professor of Political Science, University of Virginia.

In its earliest form, this chapter was read as a paper at the meeting of the American Political Science Association in September 1960. With substantial revision, it was given as a lecture at the Brookings Institution in December 1960. It was revised for publication in April 1961. The author is indebted to various readers and critics for their assistance in maturing the content of the chapter.

Prospects for a Democratic victory in the presidential election of 1960 were excellent. The Republican party retained the advantage of White House incumbency, and was widely credited with the possibility of winning the Presidency in 1960 with Richard M. Nixon as its candidate even if it lost both houses of Congress.

Throughout, there were the imponderables of the world situation and the complexities of their domestic impact. Difficulties abroad seemed to favor the Republican party in presidential politics during most of the period, until May and June of 1960. The failure of the summit meeting in the aftermath of the U-2 incident and the later cancellation of the President's visit to Japan were undoubtedly harmful to Republican prospects. Previously, the Gallup Poll had reported more than once that the voters were inclined to prefer a Republican administration as the custodian of foreign policy. Up to the end, it seemed possible that the election of 1960 might turn on events developing abroad as suddenly as the Suez crisis of 1956. For each party, this increased the risks inherent in the elections of 1960; and in each party it increased the need for nominees with strong nerves, a flair for the appropriate response, and a shrewd sense of timing—not to mention the more fundamental attributes of wisdom.[2]

The Chronology of Action and Events

The actual events leading to the nominations of 1960 can probably best be brought into focus by a concise review of the preconvention campaigns and the action at the conventions.

Preconvention Campaigns: Republican

In the Republican party, Vice President Nixon was solidly established as the heir apparent even before the election of 1956.

[2] A Gallup Poll published on May 29, 1960, reported that 57 per cent of the voters thought Nixon would do a more effective job than Kennedy in dealing with Russia's leaders; 34 per cent thought Kennedy would do a more effective job than Nixon; and 9 per cent saw no difference. On which would be most effective in keeping the United States out of World War III, the divisions

By March 1958, he had become the reported preference of 64 per cent of the Republicans. This was a standing, as of two years in advance of the convention, unmatched by any other prospective nominee in the history of the Gallup Poll. It nearly equaled the record of Governor Thomas E. Dewey in the spring of 1944, after his primary victories and the Willkie withdrawal.

The principal threat to the Nixon nomination emerged at the end of 1958 when Nelson Rockefeller was elected Governor of New York. Rockefeller's popularity slumped after he began to deal with the problems that beset every state governor.[3] Nevertheless, in the fall of 1959 he undertook one of the most extensive and highly organized preannouncement campaigns of modern times. This ended with his announcement, not that he would run, but that he would *not* run for the Presidency—a far more newsworthy statement. Yet he retained his large campaign staff, continued his efforts to influence Republican attitudes on issues of public policy, and continued to be available for a draft.[4]

The Republican preconvention campaigns were thus pitched at so low a tempo that they were almost imperceptible. The formal-

were Nixon, 45 per cent; Kennedy, 31; and no difference, 24. These results were based on a survey before the summit meeting.

A Gallup Poll published on July 18, 1960, based on a survey just before the Democratic national convention, found Kennedy leading Nixon in general voter popularity by 52 to 48 per cent, reversing Nixon's lead of 51 to 49 per cent in early June. The three-point shift in Kennedy's favor was attributed to voter reaction at the time the Eisenhower visit to Japan was canceled.

[3] On such problems and their contemporary effects, see Louis Harris, "Why the Odds Are Against a Governor's Becoming President," *Public Opinion Quarterly* (Fall 1959), pp. 361-70.

[4] At the end of Rockefeller's final tour and before his decision had been announced, an informal poll of the 21 newsmen accompanying him reportedly found that seven thought Rockefeller could win at the convention if he defeated Nixon in some of the primaries, ten predicted flatly that Rockefeller would win the nomination, and only four considered a Nixon nomination a certainty. Chalmers M. Roberts, "Rockefeller Ends Tour Acting Like Candidate," *Washington Post and Times Herald,* Dec. 19, 1959.

The Rockefeller campaign staff, according to an Associated Press dispatch as used in a story by Chalmers M. Roberts, consisted of some 70 persons, organized in the following six divisions: political; position (preparatory work for the governor's stand on issues); speech writing; image (concerned with how to project a desired concept of the governor to the public); logistics and transportation; publicity. There was no finance committee or division. *Ibid.,* Dec. 25, 1959. On the decision to retain the staff after the announcement of noncandidacy, see Associated Press story of Dec. 31, 1959.

ity of an announcement seemed unnecessary in Nixon's case. Nevertheless, he had to decide whether to enter some or all of the primaries. On January 9, 1960, an aide confirmed that Nixon was indeed a candidate and that he had willingly agreed to let his name be entered in the primaries of New Hampshire, Ohio, and Oregon. Nixon permitted his name to be used in the primaries in about the same way and for about the same reasons as an incumbent first-term President. The election results attracted interest mainly in comparisons of Republican and Democratic turnout, but most of these comparisons were inconclusive, with no contest on the Republican side. Nixon had anticipated that this would be the case, and refrained from open campaigning, preferring instead to develop his role as a hard-working public official.

With no opposition in the primaries, the delegates were usually pledged to Nixon. Action in the state party conventions was also overwhelmingly favorable. The Associated Press was thus able to issue a bulletin on May 24 to the effect that on that day, Nixon passed the majority mark in delegate strength needed for his nomination. When all 1,331 delegates had been selected, probably at least 80 per cent were committed to Nixon: the Associated Press made no final tabulation because Nixon's lead had become so top-heavy that it was no longer newsworthy. The principal hold-outs were New York, still in a position to support a Rockefeller draft if one should develop, and Arizona, South Carolina, and a few other areas where support for Senator Barry Goldwater was concentrated. The Gallup Poll reported in May 1960 that Nixon was the preference of 75 per cent of all Republican voters. His nomination had become a certainty long before the convention met.

Preconvention Campaigns: Democratic

In the Democratic party, the outstanding young man at the end of 1956 was Senator John F. Kennedy. He had come within forty votes of winning the party's vice presidential nomination in 1956,

when he first became a major subject of national attention.[5]
He was presumably a potential candidate for the 1960 presidential
nomination, but he had three strikes against him—his religion, his
youth, and his position as a senator in a party that had not gone to
the Senate for its presidential candidate since 1860. Because of
these handicaps, his nomination always seemed impossible to many
observers until it had occurred. The tendency to underestimate
Kennedy was so general that it undoubtedly was reflected in the
attitudes and strategies of the other candidates and their supporters.

The principal alternatives to Kennedy initially were Adlai Stevenson and Estes Kefauver, the ticket mates of 1956. For a time,
Stevenson was considered so completely out of the running that
he was not even included in the lists used by the Gallup Poll in
making its inquiries, but when he was included in a preference
list in 1958, it was discovered that he was the leading popular
choice and was ahead of Kennedy. Kefauver was also rated ahead
of Kennedy during the early months of 1957, but Kefauver's popularity as a possible future candidate was slumping badly by the
middle of 1957 and never recovered.

Stevenson was well aware of the disapproval with which most
party professionals viewed any possibility of giving him a third
nomination. He took the position throughout that he would neither
seek the nomination nor campaign for it, but would accept a draft
in the unlikely event that it occurred. With the open support of
Mrs. Eleanor Roosevelt and a few well-timed appearances, this
was sufficient to keep Stevenson in position as a major possibility
until the balloting was over at the convention. From mid-1958 to
the end of 1959 Stevenson alternated with Kennedy as the leading
preference of Democratic voters, as reported by the Gallup Poll.
Neither had a strong lead during this period; preference ratings in
each case were around the 25 to 30 per cent level.

Other possibilities were widely discussed. Three were gover-

[5] Richard C. Bain, *Convention Decisions and Voting Records* (The Brookings
Institution, 1960), p. 298.

nors: G. Mennen Williams of Michigan, Robert B. Meyner of
New Jersey, and Edmund G. (Pat) Brown of California. All
seemed to meet normal specifications of availability, but none was
able to demonstrate broad national appeal. Still others included
three senators: Hubert H. Humphrey of Minnesota, Stuart Symington of Missouri, and Lyndon B. Johnson of Texas. Humphrey
seemed likely for a time to inherit the Stevenson support. Symington was a potential compromise candidate, as he had been previously in 1952 and 1956. Johnson was generally considered the
most effective Senate Majority Leader in the party's history. He
was the only potential candidate, other than Kennedy and Stevenson, who seemed able to make a respectable showing in the preference ratings of the Gallup Poll, where he ran third among Democratic voters in 1958 and 1959.

The preconvention campaigns began officially in the Democratic
party with the announcements of candidacy by Humphrey on December 30, 1959, and by Kennedy on January 3, 1960. Humphrey indicated that he would enter the presidential primaries in
Wisconsin, the District of Columbia, Oregon, and South Dakota;
the decision to enter West Virginia came later. Kennedy said he
would enter the New Hampshire primary, and probably a number of others.

Both men approached the primaries with attitudes markedly
different from those of their principal potential opponents—
Stevenson, Symington, and Johnson, each of whom preferred to
stay out of primary contests. Humphrey had concluded that unless
he could make a substantial showing in the primaries, it would be
impossible to achieve serious consideration at the convention. Kennedy's problem was somewhat different. As the front runner in the
public opinion polls, he could expect to do well in the primaries,
but he also greatly needed evidence of vote-getting ability of the
kind that only the primaries could provide.[6]

[6] On the prior evolution of candidate attitudes toward the primaries, cf. Paul
T. David, Ralph M. Goldman, and Richard C. Bain, *The Politics of National
Party Conventions* (The Brookings Institution, 1960), pp. 276-78 and 296-97,
especially note 33.

The New Hampshire primary on March 8, Wisconsin on April 5, and West Virginia on May 10 all proved important. Humphrey refrained from entering the New Hampshire primary, candidly admitting that he would probably lose if he did. Kennedy managed nonetheless to produce a turnout of Democratic voters one third greater than that of the 1952 contest in which Senator Estes Kefauver had defeated President Harry S. Truman.

Kennedy's decision to enter Wisconsin was announced in Milwaukee on January 21. He commented: "Even though my chief competitors in the convention remain safely on the sidelines, hoping to gain the nomination through manipulation of the convention, I cannot follow the advice of those urging me not to enter this or other representative primaries."

A vigorous campaign ensued, at the end of which Kennedy polled 476,024 votes to Humphrey's 366,753. Humphrey was thus defeated in the state-wide vote, but carried four of the ten congressional districts and won one third of the delegates. It was estimated that 200,000 Republican voters, with no contest in their own primary, had crossed over to vote in the Democratic.[7] Many Catholic Republicans had voted for Kennedy and Protestant Republicans for Humphrey.

The West Virginia primary took on special importance because of the extent to which Kennedy's victory in Wisconsin was attributed to his religion. In the 14 Wisconsin counties where the population is 35 per cent or more Catholic, Kennedy carried all 14; in the 57 with populations less than 35 per cent Catholic, Kennedy carried 20, Humphrey, 37.[8] But in West Virginia the total population is only 5 per cent Catholic, against Wisconsin's 30; and both candidates looked to it as a test of whether Kennedy could win in an overwhelmingly Protestant state.

Two weeks before the West Virginia election, expert opinion, based in part on intensive public opinion polling, was to the effect that Kennedy would almost certainly lose the election. The

[7] *U.S. News & World Report,* April 18, 1960, pp. 43-46.
[8] *Ibid.,* p. 44.

Wall Street Journal reported on May 3, 1960, that the vote *against* him might go as high as 60 per cent. In the event, Kennedy won by 61 per cent of the vote to Humphrey's 39, and Humphrey withdrew as a candidate for the presidential nomination.

This remarkable upset seems to have been one of the rare cases in which the outcome of an election was changed by the campaigning of the candidates. Kennedy had found it necessary after Wisconsin to meet the religious issue head on, and he did so in his address before the American Society of Newspaper Editors on April 21, in grass roots campaigning throughout West Virginia, in his televised appearance with Humphrey on May 4, and in a special television broadcast in the state on the Sunday evening before the election. The Kennedy campaign was well-financed, and this seems to have been a factor, but no substantial evidence was found of improper expenditures on his behalf.[9]

In the aftermath of the West Virginia election, one party boss in New York commented: "We'd better get on the bandwagon or it will run over us." The West Virginia primary was the decisive point at which the Kennedy nomination became a near certainty. But there was no sudden capitulation of all of the other candidates. Symington continued to campaign actively. The Humphrey withdrawal put new life into the campaign to draft Adlai Stevenson. Lyndon Johnson continued his efforts in the Senate.

Kennedy won other primaries, defeating Wayne Morse in Maryland and Oregon. He was undefeated in any open contest and claimed new Democratic voting records in five of the primaries. He refrained from entering the primaries of Ohio, Florida, and California, but in circumstances such that he gained advantages. In Ohio, Kennedy agreed to stay out only after Governor Michael V. DiSalle had pledged the support of his delegation. In Florida, Kennedy left the field to favorite son Senator George Smathers with the understanding that he would enter if either Lyndon

[9] Edward T. Folliard, "Evidence is Missing in Vote-Buying Stories," *Washington Post and Times Herald,* May 31, 1960. For an analysis of the evolution of West Virginia voter opinion, based in part on current public opinion polling in the state, see the columns by Joseph Alsop in *ibid.,* May 6 and 13, 1960.

Johnson or Stuart Symington did so. In California, Kennedy had been faced with the threat that if he entered, Humphrey would do so also, with Governor Brown running as a favorite son in opposition to both. A series of negotiations ensued in which Kennedy pressed for assurances of neutrality if not support from Governor Brown, and secondly for the inclusion of a substantial number of his own supporters in the Brown delegation. Both of these objectives were achieved.

As usual, more than half of the delegates were selected in state conventions and through other party processes. The Kennedy strategy was to seek victories in the primaries to impress the delegates selected elsewhere and the leaders by whom they were influenced or controlled. The Kennedy forces also sought commitments at the state conventions, but in these arenas the other candidates were often successful in winning the delegates or in urging that they be left uncommitted until the convention.

The general result was a gathering consensus in which Kennedy became progressively stronger both in voter support and in delegate support, but without being able to demonstrate conclusive majorities in either case. The Gallup Poll, in its final pre-convention release on July 9, reported that Kennedy was the first choice of 41 per cent of the Democratic voters, Stevenson of 25 per cent, Johnson of 16, and Symington of 7—standings that had been relatively stable throughout May and June for Kennedy, but which represented substantial gains for both Stevenson and Johnson after Humphrey's withdrawal in mid-May.

As for delegate votes, the most noteworthy feature was the discrepancy between the published estimates of how the delegates would probably vote, and their known commitments. With 761 votes needed to nominate, Kennedy was credited respectively with 666½, 692, and 743 votes by three weekly magazines of massive circulation.[10] But the Associated Press, working more closely in terms of public commitments, credited Kennedy with

[10] *Life,* July 4, 1960, p. 27; *U.S. News & World Report,* June 20, 1960, p. 45; *Newsweek,* July 4, 1960, p. 19 (second ballot estimate).

only 546 votes on the Saturday before the convention opened, July 9. *Life* magazine gave Johnson 417½ votes on July 4, the Associated Press 235 on July 9.

The preconvention campaigns ended with two noteworthy events. Former President Harry S. Truman resigned from the Missouri delegation, saying that he had no desire "to be a party to proceedings that are taking on the aspects of a pre-arranged affair." He reaffirmed support for Symington but also urged the convention to give serious consideration to Lyndon Johnson.

The other event was Johnson's long-deferred announcement of his own candidacy. This occurred on July 5, two days after Congress had recessed for the conventions. Noting that he had stayed in Washington "to tend the store" while others campaigned, he predicted nonetheless that he would be nominated for President. He had the strong support of Speaker Sam Rayburn, who had announced the opening of a Johnson-for-President headquarters a month earlier.

Action at the Democratic Convention

When the Democratic national convention opened in Los Angeles on Monday, July 11, Kennedy seemed to have the nomination within reach, but the other announced candidates were all present and working hard. The Stevenson draft movement also seemed to be gathering a degree of popular support, especially in California. Over the week-end as the delegations assembled, Kennedy met with as many of them as possible. Other candidates did the same; even Stevenson began making the rounds. In many delegations an official poll of delegate preferences was conducted for the first time. The result was a dramatic increase in Kennedy's openly committed strength as reported by the Associated Press, which said on Monday morning that he had 620½ votes to Johnson's 273.

That same day, the Pennsylvania delegation gave Kennedy most of its votes; but when the California delegation was polled, his strength was less than anticipated, and there were minor defections elsewhere. By late Monday night, Los Angeles papers were carrying headlines to the effect that Kennedy was slipping, and he was worried on Tuesday and Wednesday, as he frankly admitted at his press conference on the following Saturday.

Tuesday produced three noteworthy events. The first was the so-called Johnson-Kennedy debate, in which the two men met before the Texas delegation. Despite Johnson's provocative behavior, Kennedy handled himself well. The second event was Stevenson's arrival at the convention hall to take his seat in the Illinois delegation. The arrival was a planned stratagem, but the resulting demonstration was remarkable for its apparent spontaneity and for the extent to which delegates became involved. The third event was the adoption of the platform after rejection of a minority report signed by most of the committee members from the southern states. Despite the strength of their objections, there was no threat of a bolt, not even a request for a roll-call vote. Both Kennedy and Johnson had endorsed the platform; and as long as Johnson remained in the running, southern strategy required a degree of moderation in attacking it.

On Wednesday, the convention heard nominating speeches, conducted demonstrations, and finally voted. In all, nine candidates were placed in nomination, with the number of favorite sons becoming a major nuisance. The voting did not begin until 10:07 p.m. in Los Angeles.[11] The anticipated Kennedy vote held firm on the first ballot, with minor increments as delegates previously uncommitted reached the point of decision. When Wyoming was reached, Kennedy achieved his majority. He had 806 votes at the end of the ballot to Johnson's 409, including the 21 votes of Kansas, which had passed initially.

The balloting that gave Kennedy his victory was highly sectional, as shown by the table on page 12. The Northeast and Middle West together gave Kennedy over three quarters of their votes,

[11] Log of convention chronology as published in *Congressional Quarterly Weekly Report,* July 15, 1960, pp. 1231-33.

TABLE 1.1. *Roll Call Vote On the Democratic Presidential Nomination, July 13, 1960*[a]

Region and State	Number of Votes	Kennedy	Johnson	Stevenson	Symington	Others
Northeast:						
Maine............	15	15	—	—	—	—
New Hampshire....	11	11	—	—	—	—
Vermont..........	9	9	—	—	—	—
Massachusetts.....	41	41	—	—	—	—
Rhode Island......	17	17	—	—	—	—
Connecticut.......	21	21	—	—	—	—
New York.........	114	$104\frac{1}{2}$	$3\frac{1}{2}$	$3\frac{1}{2}$	$2\frac{1}{2}$	—
New Jersey........	41	—	—	—	—	41
Delaware..........	11	—	11	—	—	—
Maryland.........	24	24	—	—	—	—
Pennsylvania......	81	68	4	$7\frac{1}{2}$	—	$1\frac{1}{2}$
West Virginia......	25	15	$5\frac{1}{2}$	3	$1\frac{1}{2}$	—
District of Columbia[b]	9	9	—	—	—	—
Canal Zone[b].......	4	—	4	—	—	—
Puerto Rico[b].......	7	7	—	—	—	—
Virgin Islands[b].....	4	4	—	—	—	—
Total...........	434	$345\frac{1}{2}$	28	14	4	$42\frac{1}{2}$
Middle West:						
Ohio..............	64	64	—	—	—	—
Michigan..........	51	$42\frac{1}{2}$	—	$2\frac{1}{2}$	6	—
Indiana...........	34	34	—	—	—	—
Illinois............	69	$61\frac{1}{2}$	—	2	$5\frac{1}{2}$	—
Wisconsin.........	31	23	—	—	—	8
Minnesota.........	31	—	—	—	—	31
Iowa..............	26	$21\frac{1}{2}$	$\frac{1}{2}$	2	$\frac{1}{2}$	$1\frac{1}{2}$
Missouri..........	39	—	—	—	39	—
North Dakota.....	11	11	—	—	—	—
South Dakota...	11	4	2	1	$2\frac{1}{2}$	$1\frac{1}{2}$
Nebraska..........	16	11	$\frac{1}{2}$	—	4	$\frac{1}{2}$
Kansas[c]..........	21	21	—	—	—	—
Total...........	404	$293\frac{1}{2}$	3	$7\frac{1}{2}$	$57\frac{1}{2}$	$42\frac{1}{2}$

Region and State	Number of Votes	Kennedy	Johnson	Stevenson	Symington	Others
South:						
Virginia...........	33	—	33	—	—	—
North Carolina.....	37	6	27½	3	—	½
South Carolina.....	21	—	21	—	—	—
Georgia...........	33	—	33	—	—	—
Florida...........	29	—	—	—	—	29
Kentucky.........	31	3½	25½	1½	½	—
Tennessee........	33	—	33	—	—	—
Alabama.........	29	3½	20	½	3½	1½
Mississippi.......	23	—	—	—	—	23
Arkansas.........	27	—	27	—	—	—
Louisiana.........	26	—	26	—	—	—
Oklahoma........	29	—	29	—	—	—
Texas............	61	—	61	—	—	—
Total...........	412	13	336	5	4	54
West:						
Montana.........	17	10	2	2½	2½	—
Idaho............	13	6	4½	½	2	—
Wyoming.........	15	15	—	—	—	—
Colorado.........	21	13½	—	5½	2	—
Utah.............	13	8	3	—	1½	½
Nevada..........	15	5½	6½	2½	½	—
New Mexico.......	17	4	13	—	—	—
Arizona..........	17	17	—	—	—	—
Washington.......	27	14½	2½	6½	3	½
Oregon...........	17	16½	—	½	—	—
California........	81	33½	7½	31½	8	½
Alaska...........	9	9	—	—	—	—
Hawaii...........	9	1½	3	3½	1	—
Total...........	271	154	42	53	20½	1½
Grand Total.....	1521	806	409	79½	86	140½

a In using this recapitulation of the roll call by regions and states, it should be recalled that in the actual event, the roll was called by states alphabetically, with the nonstate areas called last.

The vote can be found in alphabetical order, with complete details on the voting for "other" candidates, in *Congressional Quarterly Weekly Report*, July 15, 1960, p. 1228.

b Kennedy's majority was reached when the last state, Wyoming, voted, and these nonstate areas therefore voted after the outcome was already known.

c Kansas passed when first called and did not vote until after the outcome was known.

the West over half of its votes, and the South almost none. Johnson polled most of the southern vote, and hardly enough elsewhere to offset his defections in the South. Stevenson's vote was mainly found in the West, with only 2 votes in Illinois. States giving their votes to their favorite sons included Massachusetts, Texas, Missouri, New Jersey, Minnesota, Florida, and Mississippi.

The vice-presidential nomination occurred on Thursday and developed into one of the major surprises of the convention. Before the session, Kennedy announced: "After discussions with all elements of the Democratic party leadership, I have reached the conclusion that it would be the best judgment of the convention to nominate Senator Lyndon B. Johnson of Texas for the office of Vice President."

Opposition instantly developed among members of the liberal-labor bloc, but a floor fight was prevented by the absence of any willing alternative candidate who could be placed in nomination. At the convention, the rules were declared suspended by a voice vote, two thirds of the delegates having been said to have so voted, and the Johnson nomination was then put to a voice vote and declared carried.

The following day the candidates made their acceptance speeches, and there was a general closing of the ranks for the campaign. On Saturday, Kennedy held a press conference at which he discussed the events of the week with unusual candor. He then moved on to the organizing meeting of the new national committee, and a slate of Kennedy-chosen officers was installed with speed and efficiency in taking over the party machinery.

Action at the Republican Convention

Preparatory work for the Republican convention began at Chicago during the week following the adjournment of the Democratic convention. The platform committee was in session, beginning with two days of public hearings by the full committee. This innovation, copied from Democratic practice in 1956 and 1960, provided a forum for many of the party's public figures. These included Senator Barry Goldwater of Arizona, leader of the party's conservative wing, and Governor Nelson Rockefeller of New York. By Friday, July 22, the committee was beginning to release advance texts of a number of the platform planks. These showed little trace of the Rockefeller imprint; and from New York he repeated the need for provisions of greater strength on defense, foreign affairs, economic policy, and civil rights.

The possibility of a floor fight on platform in the convention—something that had not happened in a Republican convention since 1932—began to loom. There was not much chance that Rockefeller could win such a fight with his own resources, but there was great danger of an open rupture that would cost the party New York State in the November election.

At this point the Vice President went to New York for a conference with Governor Rockefeller that lasted into the early hours of Saturday morning. They agreed on a statement of 14 points that Vice President Nixon said would provide "a guide to our thinking for the consideration of the Platform Committee." The content seemed to indicate that the Vice President had gone most of the way in reaching agreement. The result was a public explosion at Chicago in which conservatives screamed "sell-out." Only an ominous silence was heard from Newport, Rhode Island, where the President was staying, but an intense struggle began for control of the convention's action on platform.

Over the week end as the convention assembled, the platform committee seemed disposed to stand firm, partly because the Rockefeller forces were unpopular and outnumbered, partly because there was great doubt concerning the Vice President's real views and intentions, partly because the committee's previous work had the President's approval, and partly because of the undoubted personal conservatism of most of the committee members. But on Monday, July 25, the day the convention opened, Vice President Nixon arrived in Chicago and immediately held a forty-minute press conference, where he gave notice that he would take the issues to the convention floor if necessary. The discussion centered mainly on civil rights; on defense and foreign policy issues, Nixon refused to be drawn into specifics. Nevertheless, the possibility of a floor fight, led by the party's principal candidate for the presidential nomination, had suddenly become real.

On Tuesday the committee capitulated. A rewritten defense plank was accepted without much difficulty after word was passed that it had the President's consent. On civil rights, the in-fighting occurred over the rules of parliamentary procedure. With Congressman Melvin R. Laird in the chair, a ruling that a majority vote (rather than two-thirds) would suffice to reconsider was upheld 55 to 41 and a motion to table was defeated 52 to 43. The committee voted 50 to 35 to reconsider and eventually adopted a revised civil rights plank by 56 to 28.

Meanwhile, Tuesday of convention week had been planned as Eisenhower day—unlike the unplanned Eisenhower day in San Francisco four years earlier—and he was given a rousing welcome by a million Chicagoans. Arriving at the Sheraton Blackstone, he expressed his warm appreciation, commented that "there is a political campaign on and we old fellows are supposed to be forgotten," and went upstairs to discuss platform problems and the choice of a vice-presidential nominee with Richard Nixon. At the convention that evening, the President made one of his most vigorous addresses. He referred to the "professional pessimists," whom he likened to Job's boils, defended the record of his administration at length, and asserted that "if we present the facts fervently, persistently, and widely, the next President of the United States will be a Republican—and that will be a blessing for America."

On the following morning, President Eisenhower addressed a breakfast meeting of 600 Republican candidates for public office. He noted that he would still be President for another six months, asserted that the platform draft had been brought into accord with his beliefs, and indicated his intention to take the initiative in dealing with Congress during its coming short session. That afternoon he left for Denver, leaving the stage vacant for the party's incoming nominee.

On the evening of Wednesday, July 27, the convention transacted most of its business in one four-hour session. The platform was approved, and Vice President Nixon and Senator Barry Goldwater were placed in nomination. Goldwater withdrew, urging all conservatives to rally behind Dick Nixon. Ten Louisiana votes stayed with Goldwater nonetheless, but all other votes, 1,321, were cast for Nixon. Nelson Rockefeller had announced for Nixon on the previous day, ending any prospect of a contest from that direction.

In the early hours of Thursday morning, Nixon met with more than thirty party leaders on the problem of the vice-presidential nomination. The choice had narrowed down to United Nations Ambassador Henry Cabot Lodge and party chairman Thruston B. Morton. Morton was the preference of many party officials, and especially those of the Middle West; but Lodge was deemed more likely to strengthen the ticket by most of those present. Nixon eventually stated his own reasons for preferring Lodge: the Republican party could only hope to win by concentrating public attention on the issues of foreign policy; and Lodge could make a greater contribution to this objective than any other potential nominee.

That evening the convention confirmed Lodge's nomination with no dissent. Both candidates then made noteworthy acceptance speeches, and the convention adjourned on a note of optimism considerably different from the defensive position in which it had begun four days earlier.

Interpretation and Assessment

The body of experience summarized in the previous narrative is subject to interpretation and assessment from many points of view. Here it is possible to deal only with a few salient aspects of some immediate interest.

The Performance of the Conventions

In choosing the candidates, both conventions ran true to form. As the party in power, the Republicans confirmed the nomination of their heir apparent with even less trouble than usually occurs in such cases. Nixon's 99 per cent of the vote can be compared with Hoover's 77 in 1928 and Taft's 72 in 1908. As the party out of power, the Democrats came to the balloting with four major candidates. They produced a deeply divided vote, and nominated the front runner with only 53 per cent of the total.

Some commentators thought the conventions were deficient as representative institutions because in each case they seemed to be accepting a predetermined choice. This was an interesting reversal of form; more often, the conventions have been criticized for opposite reasons. One can readily imagine the kind of criticism that would have occurred in this instance if either convention had rejected the candidate that it selected. When there is a visible mandate that is both valid and specific, the representative institution can make no other choice if it is to remain representative.[12]

The Republican party had given its mandate for Nixon long before the convention met to execute the decision. On the Democratic side, the case was not quite so clear, since Kennedy was not a majority preference of the whole party on a first-choice basis before the convention had acted. But the popular mandate for Kennedy was nonetheless very strong, and that for any other candidate was very weak. Johnson, despite his effort to outgrow his sectional origins, was still essentially the candidate of a single section of the country, as the convention voting clearly indicated. The Symington candidacy had never succeeded in getting off the ground. Stevenson remained as the probable choice if the convention proved unable to agree on anyone else, but had dropped well behind Kennedy in both voter and delegate popularity on a first-choice basis.

Some election theorists believe that when there are several can-

[12] Presidential nominating procedures have often provided examples of mandates that were specific without being valid and valid without being specific. Cf. David, Goldman, and Bain, *op. cit.*, Chaps. 10 and 11, especially pp. 218-19.

THE PRESIDENTIAL NOMINATIONS

didates, with no first-choice majority for any, any candidate should be preferred who could defeat each of his opponents if paired against them separately, one at a time.[13] The available evidence indicates that, on this basis, Kennedy was the majority choice of the Democratic party at the time of the convention.[14]

But the problem is always difficult when the decision lies between a candidate who has less than a majority on a first-choice basis, and a second-choice candidate who is generally acceptable to all major factions but is the first choice of none. In this kind of situation, the first-choice candidate is generally weak in second-choice support, as Kennedy certainly was at Los Angeles. Election theorists have often concluded that this kind of problem is mathematically indeterminate, even with full information about the total structure of preferences, because there can be no conclusive determination of how the second-, third-, fourth-, and more remote choices should be weighted.

The practical wisdom of the conventions has been generally to the effect that if the front runner cannot come into the convention with about 40 per cent of the vote on the first ballot, he should be rejected in favor of a compromise choice; but that if he has crossed the 40 per cent line and is clearly stronger than anyone else, he deserves the prize.[15] On this basis, Kennedy was entitled to the nomination before the convention met.

Usually the delegates are guided not only by indications of preference within the party, but also by their overriding mandate to

[13] Duncan Black, *The Theory of Committees and Elections* (1958), Chaps. 9 and 10; David, Goldman, and Bain, *op. cit.*, p. 315, note 24, and p. 489, note 7.

[14] In a series of tests of the preferences of Democratic voters when asked to make a choice on a two-man basis, the Gallup Poll reported on February 27, 1960, that Johnson was preferred to Symington by 47 to 28 per cent, with 25 per cent undecided; Kennedy was preferred to Johnson by 58 to 32 per cent, with 10 per cent undecided; and Kennedy was preferred to Stevenson by 50 to 43 per cent, with 7 per cent undecided. At the time, Kennedy was the first-choice preference of 35 per cent of all Democrats, but against either Johnson or Stevenson, the strongest of the other possibilities, he was already the majority choice of the party voters who had decided. He was probably even more firmly the majority choice on this basis by the time of the convention, when his first-choice preference rating was up to 41 per cent, as previously noted.

[15] The statistical basis for this observation can be found in David, Goldman, and Bain, *op. cit.*, Tables 17.3, 17.4, and 17.5.

pick a winner if they can see one. On this basis, the mandate for Kennedy was about as clear as any finding based on public opinion polling can be. For more than a year, he had been repeatedly identified in trial heat polling as the Democratic candidate most likely to be able to defeat Richard Nixon, who in turn had been regularly identified as the Republican candidate most likely to defeat any Democrat.

On the vice-presidential nominations, the ticket-leader made the choice in each party and the convention confirmed it. In a sense, the convention was abdicating its function of choice; but obviously neither convention could make a choice unless it could find at least two willing candidates for the vice-presidential office who were willing to accept consideration. The absence of alternative candidates at the point of action was the result of the consensus among party leaders that the presidential nominee should make the choice, after consultation and due deliberation. In 1960, both nominees were willing to accept the responsibility and able to discharge it.

The performance of the conventions can be appraised from many points of view in addition to their records as representative institutions in picking the candidates.[16] Even for this, it may be said that the only final test is the merit of the candidates themselves. Here it would be presumptuous to make any final attempt at assessment, but it can be noted that when the conventions were over, the impression was abroad in the land that both parties had managed to pick the strongest tickets available to them, and in each case to pick a presidential candidate who could safely be entrusted with the administration of the government if elected.

What was most noted by all the commentators was the striking change that was in prospect when President Eisenhower came to be replaced by either of the candidates. It seemed apparent that the time had come to move to a new generation and a new type of leadership. It cannot be said that this aspect of the decision was the result of a deliberate preference for a younger man on the part of either convention, but at least the conventions managed to

[16] See Chap. 2.

avoid putting any obstacle in the way of the major historical transition that has occurred.

The Functions Performed
by the Nominating Campaigns

If it is desirable to examine the record of the conventions, it may be even more important to examine that of the campaigns that preceded them, since what the conventions could do was already largely determined when they met. What functions were performed by the nominating campaigns; and how well did they perform them?

The manifest social function of any political campaign is to contribute to the basis for rational choice.[17] Presidential nominating campaigns can contribute to rational choice by helping to develop the issues, by testing factional strength and intensity, and most of all by testing the candidates themselves. The choices where rationality is needed include those by the party voters in determining their preferences, the similar choices by party leaders (who also study the voters), and finally the decisions by the delegates when they vote—with due regard for the views of their party leaders and constituents.

In the Democratic party, the nominating campaigns were important primarily for what they did by way of testing the candidates. In the course of this testing, Humphrey was knocked out of the running. The contest then settled down to one in which a rising younger man, Kennedy, was pitted against three older men, Stevenson, Johnson, and Symington, each of whom had attained positions of eminence at a considerably earlier period. It seems as certain as anything can be that Kennedy could not have been nominated without the kind of showing that he was able to make in the campaign. If the Kennedy choice was rational, it was the prior campaigning that made rational choice possible.

In the Republican party, the situation was different. There was

[17] Other functions also exist. Cf. Stanley Kelley, Jr., *Political Campaigning: Problems in Creating an Informed Electorate* (The Brookings Institution, 1960), pp. 1-7; David, Goldman, and Bain, *op. cit.*, pp. 297-99.

no open preconvention contest, and the most likely candidate, Nixon, was a man already well known. But there were some major questions concerning which party faction could most effectively claim his allegiance; and there were major issues concerning the general direction in which the party's course should be set. The internal struggle between the issue positions symbolized by Rockefeller, Eisenhower, and Goldwater eventually broke out into the open at the convention, but mainly because of the tactics pursued by Rockefeller and the responses that he provoked from his party colleagues. The preconvention activities were high in educative value for the Republican party and its leaders.

The Influence of Issues and Interest Groups

All of this suggests that in various latent ways, the influence of issues and interest groups on the outcome in each party may have been greater than was generally suspected.

By its mere existence, the Kennedy candidacy symbolized the issue that was also latent in the Al Smith candidacy of 1928: the rights of a citizen of the Catholic faith to run for office with an expectation of fair consideration by the electorate. This issue had to reach the kind of resolution that was represented by the West Virginia outcome before Kennedy could win at the convention, as it had to reach a somewhat similar resolution on a national scale before he could win in the election.

Other issues of civil rights were salient throughout the campaigns and at the conventions, in turn reflecting the extent to which Negroes have become a major factor in national politics as an organized interest group. Kennedy's strong line on civil rights was a necessary factor in mobilizing his convention majority; Nixon's similarly strong line was less related to nominating considerations, but equally important in preparing to compete for the electoral votes of several pivotal states.

Leaders in both parties were aware of the competition for public attention between the issues of foreign and defense policy, on the one hand, and those of domestic economic policy, on the other.

The Democrats, while strongly criticizing the record of the Eisenhower administration on foreign and defense policy, seemed mainly inclined to make their bid for popular favor on the basis of the party's relationship to domestic economic issues. All of the candidates for the Democratic nomination talked about foreign policy, but competence in this area never seemed to become effective as a criterion for choosing among the candidates. Among the Republicans, on the other hand, foreign policy considerations were credited with being decisive in the choice of Lodge for the vice-presidential nomination.

In the debating among the Democratic candidates, efforts were sometimes made to develop and clarify differences in regard to the issues of agriculture, labor, and welfare policy. Most of this discussion left no clear result, except in Humphrey's showing in the agricultural areas of Wisconsin, where his local victories seemed related to his past efforts on behalf of Midwestern agriculture.

At the conventions the problems of agriculture occupied much of the time of the two platform committees, but as usual, there was little clear evidence that the leaders of organized agriculture were making any special effort to influence the choice of nominees in either party. The business interests of the country also seemed to be relatively neutral in the nominating activities of 1960, unlike their heavy involvement in the Taft-Eisenhower struggle of 1952. Presumably, Nixon was acceptable to most of the business interests affiliated with the Republican party, while in the Democratic party, Kennedy, Symington, and Johnson all seemed to have their quotas of active support from segments of the business community.

Kennedy had long sought the support of organized labor in the contest for the Democratic nomination, with some success, and the labor group was again present at the Democratic convention much more fully than at the Republican.[18] Symington was acceptable to

[18] On events before the convention, see in particular two noteworthy stories in the *Wall Street Journal*, both by Roscoe Born. The first, on January 18, 1960, reported that leaders of the AFL-CIO had decided not to back any candidate for President in 1960, as a demonstration of the movement's annoyance over the treatment it had been receiving from the Democratic party. The second, on February 11, 1960, reporting on the meeting of the AFL-CIO general board

most of the labor leaders and was actively supported by some; Lyndon Johnson was the object of their special opposition. They did much to make Johnson's nomination for President impossible, and they could claim some credit for the Kennedy nomination. The labor leaders were not happy over the proposal to nominate Johnson for Vice President, but were consulted in advance of the announcement and recognized the merits of the combination that would result in the effort to win victory in November. They went along with the choice and took active steps to quiet the flurry of protest by labor delegates in several state delegations when the choice of Johnson became known.

The Strategies of the Candidates: Out-Party

Comment after the Democratic convention gave Kennedy top marks as a campaigner. He was greeted as a near-genius who had defeated the old pros at their own game, as one who had worked hard at his own candidacy from 1956 to 1960 without ever making a major strategic or tactical error.

The unanimity of this comment makes it reasonable to inquire whether any of the other candidates could have won the nomination by pursuing a different strategy. The answer can only be

at Miami Beach, indicated that Senator Kennedy had won a substantial victory by securing a reversal of the position reported in the first story, copies of which had been included in kits of material that were distributed when the Committee on Political Education began its sessions. See "Labor Sits It Out" and "Meany Predicts Labor Will Back Candidate in 1960."

At the convention, Roscoe Born reported in the *Wall Street Journal*, July 12, 1960, that labor leaders were "pressuring this Democratic convention in greater numbers, and with more organized efficiency, than any previous one." Their objective, he said, was to recast the Democratic party by provoking conservative southern elements into leaving the party; this was the reason for their concentration on the civil rights issue. Party realignment was seen as essential to a "longer-range strategy of putting a stop to election victories that turn into legislative defeats." See "Labor and Politics."

Victor Reisel's column as published in the Los Angeles *Citizen News*, July 5, 1960, reported an estimate from labor circles of at least 365 labor delegates and alternates at the Democratic convention, compared with 220 at Chicago in 1956, who in turn were said to have had about 125 votes. The labor voting strength at the Democratic convention of 1952 was about 100 votes according to David, Goldman, and Bain, *op. cit.*, pp. 102-04, 341-42, 517.

speculative, but it is nonetheless "no," except for Stevenson. Humphrey's strategy was probably the best available to him and still not good enough. The same could be said, for different reasons, of the strategies pursued by Symington and Johnson. Their antipathy to the primaries partly reflected their tendency to underestimate Kennedy and to assume that he could be defeated at the convention regardless of what happened in the primaries. But there is little reason to think that either Symington or Johnson could have improved his prospects by entering the primaries. In each case, their basic difficulty was their inability to awaken the enthusiasm of the rank and file in any of the forums where they made the attempt.

One of the oddities of the Johnson strategy was his decision, in collaboration with Speaker Sam Rayburn, to bring Congress back into session again after the conventions were over. Apparently, this was intended to strengthen the position in seeking support for the Johnson candidacy at the convention, as well as to give him a favorable forum in which to begin the campaign if nominated. To the extent that these were indeed the motivations, they seem to have reflected an erroneous judgment in both respects.

Stevenson's strategy was the most questionable in terms of any combination of rational goals. If he genuinely desired the nomination, an announced campaign beginning soon after the Humphrey withdrawal in May would have strengthened his popular support and increased his delegate strength, without making it necessary for him to undertake the burdens of campaigning in the remaining primaries, where filing dates were already past. Stevenson might then have been able to deadlock the convention long enough to emerge as the only possible majority choice. Conversely, if Stevenson believed that Kennedy was entitled to the nomination after his victories in Wisconsin and West Virginia, a view attributed to Stevenson by some at the time, he did little to assist in bringing the Kennedy candidacy to success. At the convention itself, Stevenson's behavior was sufficiently ambiguous to weaken his influence with the delegates and with many other party leaders.

If the two-thirds rule had still been in effect in the Democratic party, as it was until 1936, the strategy problems of all of the candidates would have been different. Kennedy would have found the divisive aspects of an active campaign in the primaries much more dangerous. He might have been pushed back to the kind of strategy used by Roosevelt in 1932, a strategy very similar to that followed in 1960 by Johnson and Symington with much less success. On this basis, Kennedy's chances of winning would have been much poorer, and Stevenson, even without much effort on his own behalf, might have become the only possible alternative in the end.

The Strategies of the Candidates: In-Party

In the Republican party, the strategic decisions of the potential candidates were controlled by two basic expectations, first that Nixon would win the nomination easily even if given a contest, and second that despite his skill as a candidate, he would have an extremely tough fight in trying to win the election. It was the combination of the two expectations that led Rockefeller, Goldwater, and Nixon to behave as they did. Rockefeller and Goldwater concentrated on trying to influence Nixon's position, and that of the party, on platform issues because they saw no hope of defeating Nixon for the nomination. After the platform struggle had been completed, Rockefeller and Goldwater then let Nixon have his nomination with their support and on a near-unanimous basis in order to begin closing ranks for the difficult election contest in prospect.

Nixon was indebted to both Rockefeller and Goldwater for giving him the opportunity to clarify his own middle-ground positions in a publicly dramatic way, which in turn gave him the opportunity to emerge as his own man in a situation where it can be assumed that he was in conflict with many of the prior positions of the Eisenhower administration. Nixon used the opportunities with consummate skill, never withdrawing his support for what the Eisenhower administration had done in the past while always putting his emphasis on the possible changes that would need to be made in the future.

Behind all this, many commentators saw a basic change in Nixon strategy for winning the election, a change that they believed took place when Lyndon Johnson was added to the Democratic ticket. At that point, it is argued, Nixon gave up his previous hopes for carrying much of the South and became far more intent than before on carrying New York and other northern states. This, it is said, is what made his 14-point agreement with Rockefeller necessary.

In making the agreement, however, Nixon was merely returning to a long standing pattern in his own behavior in preferring strategies directed at the northern vote when the issue came down to a hard choice. If this is so, the main effect for Nixon of the Johnson nomination may have been simply a clarification of the problem that he could use in discussing the situation with the President.

Prospects for Reform in the Nominating Process

Future years seem likely to see a further consolidation in the styles of out-party nominating campaigns that were developed in the Willkie campaign of 1940, the Dewey campaign of 1948, the Eisenhower campaign of 1952, the Stevenson campaign of 1956, and the Kennedy campaign of 1960. All of these out-party nominating campaigns had major elements in common. Kennedy could not have been nominated without the kind of preconvention campaign that the recent previous experience had indicated; and his campaign, like some of the others, would not have been possible in the absence of the state presidential primaries that provided so many strategic opportunities.

In their cumulative effect, the nominating campaigns of recent years mark a profound change from the patterns of campaigning and candidate selection that prevailed from 1832 to 1932. In general, they reflect a shift to a more open politics, to a politics less subject to any sectional veto, and to a politics more compatible with the expectation that the entire national electorate will be permitted to influence the processes of nominating choice.[19]

With the processes of change having come so far, it would seem reasonable to conclude that the presidential primaries are here to stay. Their potentialities for developing the prospects of a front runner are not likely to be underrated again to the extent that they were by so many Democratic political leaders in 1952, 1956, and 1960. But whether the existing primary systems will be improved or their number increased before 1964 or 1968 is not so certain. The area remains one in which too many would-be reformers disagree on what ought to be done. The disagreement is reflected in the widely variant schemes that have been introduced for consideration by members of the present Congress.

The number and variety of those schemes, however, does indicate a revival of interest in Congress in finding new solutions to an old problem. The congressional response undoubtedly reflects the kind of sentiment that developed in many constituencies as they looked at the conventions in July and waited out the revision of the election returns in November and December. For many voters, the conventions and the electoral college had become equally archaic, although electoral college reform undoubtedly seemed more urgent than convention reform when Congress met in January 1961.

Among the several proposals, the most interesting were those by Senator Mike Mansfield, the Senate Majority Leader. On January 9, 1961, he introduced a proposed constitutional amendment to abolish the electoral college and provide for direct election of the President; and he also introduced two bills to deal with the nominating process for President. One bill, modeled in part on the Douglas-Bennett bill to provide federal aid for presidential

[19] Cf. David, Goldman, and Bain, *op. cit.,* Chap. 12, "The Changing Character of Nominating Campaigns."

primaries,[20] would establish a federal board to receive petitions on behalf of candidates for the presidential nominations and provide for placing their names on the ballot in states holding presidential primaries on an agreed basis. Each candidate would forfeit a bond of $25,000 if he failed to poll at least 3 per cent of the vote in the states holding approved primaries. Those candidates who did receive more than 3 per cent of the vote would be reimbursed for their nominating campaign expenses up to a limit of $250,000 from federal funds.[21]

The proposal involves a number of problems for which satisfactory answers are not yet available, most notably in connection with its probable tendency to make it difficult or impossible to operate a draft. Had it been in effect in 1952, it might have eliminated both Eisenhower and Stevenson as candidates. It is nevertheless the most flexible of the proposals so far introduced for federal action and would doubtless be modified considerably before enactment if it should become the principal vehicle for congressional action in its field.[22]

The second Mansfield bill would provide reimbursement for the radio and television broadcasting expenses of each of the major parties in presidential campaigns, up to a limit of $1,000,000, provided the national convention of the party concerned was held in accord with certain stipulations: (1) after September first of the election year, in order to make the election campaign shorter, and

[20] The Douglas-Bennett proposal was discussed in Paul T. David, Malcolm Moos, and Ralph M. Goldman, *Presidential Nominating Politics in 1952,* Vol. I (Johns Hopkins Press, 1954), pp. 217-24.

[21] S. 228, 87 Cong. 1 sess., in *Congressional Record,* daily ed., Jan. 9, 1961, p. 337.

[22] My own views and those of various associates on desirable types of presidential primary were spelled out in David, Moos, and Goldman, *op. cit.,* Vol. I, Chap. 6 and pp. 240-42; Paul T. David, *Specifications for a Model State Presidential Primary Law,* Brookings Institution Reprint No. 11, April 1956 (a reprinting of the memorandum proposing the model law enacted in Florida in 1955); and David, Goldman, and Bain, *op. cit.,* Chap. 10 and pp. 489-93.

At hearings on June 28, 1961, before the Senate Committee on the Judiciary, Subcommittee on Constitutional Amendments, the writer favored the use of federal legislation to encourage a greater number of states to adopt legislation similar to the Florida law of 1955. See *Nomination and Election of President* and *Vice President and Qualifications for Voting,* Hearings, Pt. 2, 87 Cong. 1 sess., p. 420.

(2) under provisions such that each state would have the same number of delegates that it has senators and representatives in Congress, with no fractional voting permitted, thus providing a convention with fewer than 550 voting members.[23] This direct attack on the problems of convention size that underlie so many infirmities in convention behavior is unique among the congressional proposals.

President John F. Kennedy is the first to attain the office who is himself the beneficiary of an active out-party campaign in the primaries under his own leadership. He seems likely to differ rather strikingly from his predecessors in the extent to which he may bring positive views to the reform of the party conventions and the nominating process.[24] If the proposals for legislation are given active consideration by Congress and the President, the basis may eventually be laid for a series of reforms that would go well beyond changes in the primaries—reforms that could make the conventions more effective in the performance of their nominating and other functions, while also authorizing and stabilizing a greater degree of popular participation in the whole process.

[23] S. 227, 87 Cong. 1 sess., in *Congressional Record,* daily ed., Jan. 9, 1961, pp. 336-37.
[24] At the hearings referred to in footnote 22, Assistant Attorney General Nicholas de B. Katzenbach discussed pending presidential primary proposals, but indicated that the administration had not yet developed a specific position. See *Nomination and Election of President and Vice President* . . . Hearings, Pt. 2, pp. 363-91.

2

The National Conventions

PAUL TILLETT[1]

As EVERY SCHOOLBOY SHOULD KNOW, the quadrennial national conventions of major political parties in the United States perform three major functions besides nominating the candidates, which was discussed in Chapter 1: they adopt the platforms, act as the governing bodies of their national parties, and serve as the first campaign rallies for party workers assembled from all over the nation. In the act of carrying out these functions, the national conventions reshape the parties they represent.

The parties began as nationally significant groupings when the convention replaced the caucus. The conventions remain as potent devices for nationalizing the parties. Looking back on the Republican and Democratic national conventions of 1960, it appears that despite boredom, confusion, and virtually foregone conclusions, long-term forces were at work strengthening the conventions as instruments of the national parties.

Drafting and Adopting the Platforms

The platforms received more serious consideration at both conventions than has been customary in recent presidential contests. Both parties departed from tradition in the 1960 conventions with respect to the drafting of their programs. Usually congressional

[1] Assistant Director, Eagleton Institute of Politics, Rutgers University.

leaders dominate the formulation of the platform of the party out of power, in this case the Democrats. In 1952 and 1956, Representative John W. McCormack of Massachusetts, Majority Leader of the House of Representatives, was chairman of the Democrats' platform committee. Senator Eugene Milliken, Republican of Colorado, headed the Republican committee in 1952, and four years later Senator Prescott Bush of Connecticut took over. In 1960, the Democrats named Representative Chester Bowles of Connecticut as Chairman of the Committee on Platform and Resolutions. Bowles was not a congressional leader; he was a freshman member of Congress. At the time of his appointment, it was known that Bowles favored the nomination of Senator John F. Kennedy, the successful aspirant.

The party in power generally has a platform presented to it by the incumbent. Apparently everything went according to tradition for the Republicans until the Nixon-Rockefeller meeting the Friday before the convention; then the platform drafted by Robert Merriam and Malcolm Moos, of the White House staff, was abandoned in favor of the 14 points on which Rockefeller and Nixon declared themselves to be in complete agreement. These 14 points represented considerable departure from practice and philosophy of the White House during the preceding eight years. Before they were finally incorporated in the party program, the resolutions committee had to be dealt with by Nixon himself.

Both Democrats and Republicans seem to have taken steps away from drafting platforms that everyone in the party could "live with." Each platform tended to fit less than some of its predecessors with Wendell Willkie's classic characterization of party platforms as "fusions of ambiguity." To the consternation of logical positivists and others, however, platform pledges that simply and directly said what they meant seem to have proved no more meaningful than masterpieces of fudging.

With some exceptions, the strategy of both parties appeared to be that of yielding almost completely to the demands of the most powerful voice on any given issue.[2] Neither party was completely

[2] The interested reader may find illuminating a comparison of the various planks in the Democratic platform dealing with civil liberties and civil rights

successful in muffling dissent, though given the emotional intensity aroused by the civil rights planks in both platforms, the
leaders must be credited with high achievement on this score.

Democratic Civil Rights Plank

The evolution of the Democratic civil rights plank is of considerable interest in marking stages of development in opinion
and strategy on this issue. In 1948, a strong civil rights pledge
was adopted—651½ to 582½. The minority was large enough to
encourage the unsuccessful Dixiecrat revolt of that year. Eight
years later, a minority of the resolutions committee contended for
a stronger plank, but lost. In 1960, the resolutions committee
adopted the position urged on it by the NAACP, avoided acri-
monious exchanges between northern spokesmen and southern
firebrands, maneuvered a mild debate on the floor, and obtained
approval of the plank and the platform without a great deal of
struggle. A somewhat similar procedure was followed by the
Republicans at Chicago. There the dispute in the committee over
how to word the pledge to eliminate racial discrimination in employment and how to endorse "sit-ins" caused some controversy
and provided the single open dispute in that convention.

The Democratic platform as a whole grew naturally and normally from the work of the Advisory Council to the Democratic
National Committee appointed following the 1956 campaign.[3]
Between 1956 and 1960 the Advisory Council issued policy
papers which formed a background to "The Rights of Man," as
the 1960 Democratic platform was called. The work of the Advisory Council influenced the resolutions committee despite the
absence from the council of the congressional leaders in the party
and in spite of the fact that on several issues, such as agriculture,

and a document called "Program for Civil Rights—1960" prepared by the
Leadership Conference on Civil Rights, an *ad hoc* coalition of civil rights and
civil liberties groups formed to influence the national platforms in 1960.

[3] The value of the work of the Council received recognition when the national
committee approved its continuation, July 14; a decent respect for the relationship between the committee and a Democratic President was shown March 11,
1961, when the new national chairman, John Bailey, announced that the Council
had been abolished.

the position of the council was opposed by the party congressional leader in that area.

Formal preparations for the work of the platform committee began in April with the appointment of Bowles. He had previously been a member of the Advisory Council's committee on foreign policy; and the vice chairman of the platform committee, the late Philip B. Perlman, had been deputy chairman of the Advisory Council. In May, Bowles undertook to consult with party leaders, representatives of interested groups, sectional leaders, civic associations, and individuals, by means of regional hearings, personal conversations, and correspondence. Hearings were held in Philadelphia, Detroit, St. Louis, Minneapolis, Denver, Salt Lake City, and Los Angeles, in order, Bowles said, to provide all groups, sections, and interests in the Democratic party and the nation with an opportunity to express their views more completely than would be possible in the hectic week of hearings by the platform committee just prior to the national convention. It was Bowles's hope that through adequate consultation, the platform committee assembled in Los Angeles could be handed a draft as the basis for the platform that would be no more than 3,000 words in length. His reach exceeded his grasp, though it must be said his aim was noble.

The drafting work began several weeks before the first Los Angeles meeting of the platform committee. The drafting committee, including Professor Abram J. Chayes of the Harvard Law School, James Sundquist of Senator Joseph Clark's staff, Thomas Hughes, legislative assistant to Representative Bowles, and William Welsh, formerly research director of the Democratic National Committee and in 1960 administrative assistant to Senator Philip Hart, considered abstracts of the regional hearings, reports by the various committees of the Democratic Advisory Council, and the gleanings from Bowles's conversations with various party leaders. Senator Kennedy was directly effective when, during the drafting process, he made the recommendation that the civil rights plank replace pious generalizations of the 1952 and 1956 planks with specific recommendations.

Careful planning and preconvention work by the drafting committee and by Bowles appeared to have been largely wasted when the platform committee first assembled in Los Angeles. A typical member of the committee received from the National Committee before his arrival in Los Angeles only a few of the reports of the advance hearings, along with an invitation to appear for further hearings on July 5 in Los Angeles, notification of reservations at the Biltmore Hotel, and a statement that the check for *per diem* expense allowance was enclosed. The checks arrived somewhat later, and arrangements for accommodations had to be made after arrival in Los Angeles. Again, despite the careful planning, it was necessary to go through the tedious business of listening to the representatives of pressure groups state their positions before the full platform committee.

Members of the committee were well-behaved beyond the call of duty, it seemed to this observer. They were not told until July 8 that the real chore of drafting the platform had been taken on by a twenty-man drafting committee, which received a draft from the Bowles group prior to its presentation to the platform committee on July 9. The members of the platform committee— 108 men and women—endured four days of hearings and listened to more than seventy witnesses present testimony which, when printed or mimeographed, weighed over thirteen pounds.[4] What the representatives of pressure groups said appeared to have little influence on the drafting committee (which did not listen to them), or on delegates who were members of the platform committee. Principally, those witnesses seemed to have enabled the Democrats to say that they had listened to all sides before drawing up their platform, and to satisfy the internal demands of pressure groups on their leaders; that is, to enable the leaders to give the impression of having attempted to sell the Democrats their point of view.

When the hearings concluded on Saturday, the platform committee met frequently until Monday, attempting to reach agree-

[4] For these facts and for much other information, I am indebted to Richard W. Taylor of Coe College, whose paper "Pressure Groups and the Democratic Platform of 1960" was prepared as a report on his observation as an Eagleton-Citizenship Clearing House Fellow to the Democratic National Convention in 1960.

ment on various planks in the draft submitted to them by the twenty-man subcommittee. These sessions were secret. Printed drafts were numbered and could not be taken from the room. One member reported that the platform committee made over one hundred changes in the draft, adding that these were mostly minor.

Two minority reports were submitted.[5] The minority report on civil rights was supported by ten southern delegations: Alabama, Arkansas, Florida, Georgia, Louisiana, Mississippi, North Carolina, South Carolina, Tennessee, and Virginia. Even the protest was well-controlled. The dissent merely asked that the "proposed civil rights plank" be repudiated by the convention.

When the platform came to the convention floor, its approval was a foregone conclusion. The minority reports were disposed of very simply. Virginia was given five minutes to urge a plan for repayment of the national debt and Chairman Chester Bowles took five minutes to reply to the attack. Then the southern point of view on civil rights was apportioned thirty minutes, divided into five six-minute speeches. The minority report was answered by five four-minute talks, and Bowles made a ten-minute speech to conclude the rebuttal. Minority reports were then voted on and defeated by voice votes, after which the question was put on the whole platform; and "The Rights of Man" was accepted.

The Republican Platform[6]

For the Republicans, too, the drafting of the platform was a serious and time-consuming business. The process had begun some years before with the designation of Charles H. Percy as the chair-

[5] In addition to the dissent from the civil rights plank, Virginia presented a minority report on the plank dealing with the national debt, even though the state could not secure the signatures required for a minority report from the delegations of other states on the platform committee.

[6] In what follows regarding the preparation of the Republican national platform, I have relied heavily on the report by Karl A. Lamb, Department of Political Science, The University of Michigan, "Civil Rights in the 1960 Republican Platform: A Case Study in Party Procedures and Party Leadership"; and that of John H. Kessel, Amherst College, "Political Leadership: The Nixon Version." Both were Eagleton-Citizenship Clearing House Fellows at the Republican National Convention, 1960.

man of the Republican Committee on Program and Progress. Late in 1958 this committee had issued several task force reports under the title, *Decisions for a Better America*. These reports had been published and given wide circulation throughout the country. Some weeks before the Republicans assembled in Chicago, the national committee named Percy chairman of the platform committee; and Gabriel Hauge, who had worked with the Percy committee, was appointed executive secretary. Nevertheless, it appears that the initial platform version was drafted by representatives of the administration, principally Robert E. Merriam, deputy assistant to the President for interdepartmental affairs, and Malcolm Moos, administrative assistant to the President. The Vice President was represented in preconvention discussions by George L. Grassmuck, political scientist on leave from the University of Michigan. A draft platform was prepared by the time the convention met in Chicago and had been approved tentatively by President Eisenhower and Vice President Nixon. Nevertheless, Republicans, too, went through the showcase hearing procedure. In this respect, they improved on the Democrats slightly by dividing the hundred-man platform committee into a series of subcommittees to deal with major plank categories.

The subcommittee procedure is time-honored in the Republican party and was not an innovation. Eight subcommittees were appointed. The committee members assigned themselves to subcommittees virtually on the basis of choice. However, Chairman Percy exercised some control when nearly every southern committee member sought to choose the civil rights and immigration subcommittee.

If the membership of the critical civil rights subcommittee was typical, it would appear that whether he could have done so, Mr. Nixon did not attempt to manipulate subcommittee membership for his own advantage. The chairman of this critical subcommittee was Joseph F. Carlino, Speaker of the New York State Assembly and a follower of Governor Rockefeller. Five southerners were seated on the subcommittee; and, although they were not of the Eastland-Colmer-Barnett pattern, they were a considerable distance from Chairman Carlino. One of them, John G. Tower of

Wichita Falls, Texas, a former teacher of political science and Republican candidate for the Senate seat of Lyndon Johnson,[7] became the informal leader of the subcommittee after the members had in effect rejected the leadership of Carlino. Only three subcommittee members seemed to share Carlino's interest in a strong civil rights plank—Mrs. Frances Bolton, the United States Representative from Ohio; J. Flipper Derricotte, District of Columbia, a Negro lawyer and teacher; and Bayard Ewing, Rhode Island national committeeman and attorney. Those who held the balance of power were the wife of a physician, more interested in socialized medicine than in civil rights, a northern woman sympathetic to the approach of the southern moderates, and a confused and overwhelmed new congresswoman who had inherited the seat from her late husband.

For a few days after the platform committee met in Chicago on the Monday preceding the opening of the convention, everything went smoothly. About Thursday, however, trouble began to be apparent. Members of the civil rights subcommittee decided to write a civil rights plank satisfactory to themselves. At the same time, the somewhat disgruntled members of other subcommittees began to understand that the real platform had been drafted elsewhere. On Thursday, deputy attorney general Edward Walsh came in from Washington with a sixteen-page brief containing draft civil rights planks and explanatory material. All of this had been approved by Vice President Nixon and Attorney General Rogers. On Friday night, Nixon and Nelson Rockefeller held their widely publicized meeting in New York, from which emerged the famous 14 points.

In the assignment to gain subcommittee approval for a civil rights plank acceptable to Rockefeller, Carlino had a difficult task at best; but he need not have lost the support of Mrs. John E. Wise of Wisconsin, President of the National Federation of Republican Women, and several others like her. In this subcommittee, the issue of what kind of platform became entangled with the issue of whose responsibility or privilege it was to formulate it. Members of the subcommittee like Mrs. Wise took their re-

[7] Mr. Tower was elected to the Senate May 27, 1961.

sponsibility seriously and were disturbed to discover that the platform was being drafted elsewhere. Carlino's attitude was that
when Nixon and Rockefeller had hammered out an agreement on
the shape of the civil rights plank they would "give us the word."
Mrs. Wise did not agree and expressed her disagreement by siding
with Tower.

Carlino stayed in touch with Percy and Hauge, but he did not
stay in touch with his subcommittee, which continued to meet
under the informal chairmanship of John Tower. When Carlino
finally presented the plank agreed on by Nixon and Rockefeller
Saturday night, he ran headlong into the objections southerners
had been voicing at subcommittee meetings that he did not attend
and that he had thought they were merely expressing for the
record. In his view, the members of the subcommittee were naive;
they had all been in politics long enough, he stated, to know that
the source of platform statements has to be the party candidate.
Matters were not made better by the fact that the subcommittee
was asked to approve a document it had been unable to read for
itself or to see before its adoption.

On Sunday, the subcommittee reconvened and Tower presented
substitute proposals acceptable to most members of the subcommittee. But Carlino would not permit amendments to be voted
on by the subcommittee. When the statement that had Nixon's
approval and for which he asked approval was read to the subcommittee Sunday evening, the subcommittee voted eight to seven
to reject the moderate civil rights program in favor of the language suggested by the southerners. Almost immediately, there
began a meeting of the full platform committee, which continued
until seven Monday morning. At this meeting, the full committee
formally rejected the civil rights proposal presented by Carlino
and embraced the southern substitute. This was the situation when
Nixon arrived in Chicago. Finally, on Monday afternoon, Chairman Charles Percy and Leonard Hall brought together fifteen
party leaders; each was assigned to delegations with whom he had
the greatest influence. They were given an amendment to the
plank on civil rights which reintroduced the substantive pledges of
the minority subcommittee report with a few verbal concessions

to the southerners. The amendment was not ready until the platform committee reassembled Tuesday morning. Each part of the plank was considered separately; seven votes were taken. The Nixon-Rockefeller language won out in four instances, while the southern language was approved for the remainder. In the end, neither Nixon nor the southerners on the subcommittee won, but a floor fight on the platform was averted, as in every Republican convention since 1932.

Television may have provided an added reason for so much struggle to achieve agreement on civil rights. It is likely, for example, that even had the southern proposal been adopted in its entirety by the subcommittee and the platform committee, it would have been overwhelmingly rejected in favor of the Nixon-Rockefeller language by the full convention had a floor fight taken place. As it was, the controversial plank went to the convention in a platform generally approved by the committee members. The program arranged for television by the Republican National Committee thus came off smoothly without extensive lobbying in the aisles, no uproar, confusion, or open display of disharmony.

The Meaning of Platform Action in 1960

The platforms, as usual, were considered and adopted before the nominations were made. Why the parties persist in such an order can readily be understood—the attention of all delegates and the increasingly "present" television viewers centers on the presidential nomination—all interest in the platform might evaporate if it were presented for adoption after the nomination. Then, too, a platform adopted after the candidate had been named might be presumed to have his backing. His later inability or unwillingness to act on it or to enact its pledges would be difficult to explain and embarrassing in any case. As matters stand, candidates enjoy the best of both worlds. Both Senator Kennedy and Vice President Nixon played important roles in the formation of the platforms of their respective parties. Mr. Nixon, personally, took special pains with the platform. Whether by mere good fortune or prearrangement, Senator Kennedy had a strong supporter at the head of the platform committee. The product presumably represented to a large extent what the Senator thought it was necessary to promise to various organized groups and the voters at large in order to win the election. He won the election, perhaps, on the strength of the platform (the Democratic civil rights plank drew Negroes back to the party and, irony of ironies, in several key southern states, Negroes supplied the margin of victory); but as this is written, major portions of the platform seem in danger of being jettisoned by its beneficiary. Many clauses perhaps cannot be implemented, given the narrow margin of Kennedy's victory, the reduced Democratic majority in Congress, and the continued effectiveness of the bipartisan conservative coalition.

In all this, there is more than a suggestion that the Democrats cynically manipulated their statement of intentions to promise the greatest boons to the greatest number; or, at best, took the common view that platforms are meaningless anyway. (In these matters, as in the election, Nixon and his party ran a close second.) But surely, those portions of the electorate informed enough to know and care about the content of the platforms are also sophisticated enough to realize that no promise to an electorate more impersonal and less oracular than General Eisenhower's "I will go to Korea" can create an enforceable contract.

For all that, such pledges are not written in snow. Where the nominee is concerned, they create legitimate expectations that insofar as the promises can be personally performed, they will be performed; and, insofar as they require the cooperation of others with lawful authority, the candidate, if elected, will try to obtain that cooperation by every legitimate means. But by this time everyone concerned must know that the nominee cannot speak for every member of his party, and if he is elected President, he cannot speak for Congress even if his party "controls" it. The platforms simply keep the goad in the politicians aspiring to be responsible to them—they rarely embarrass those who are determined not to heed them.

This is something more than saying that those who take platforms seriously do take them seriously, because not all who do take the pledges seriously do so out of conviction, much less enthusiasm. Many representatives, however, are subject to electoral discipline and desire to respond to popular demand. For such legislators, the platforms crystallize the demands of important groups— and for the leaders of the groups involved, the pledges provide a prod, a measuring standard, and a rallying cry.

National party platforms, then, may be important to the people who draft them, to pressure groups or organized interests in the electorate, and to officials and lawmakers wishing to know in a general way what the incoming President will support, including the members of the new administration. More significantly, innovations made in the platform drafting procedure of both parties in 1960 suggest that the drafting process is now established as one of the major tools of the national party, and can be used to subordinate and moderate sectional opinion rather than to represent it.

Governing the Parties

The essential actions of party governance were not visibly taken in 1960 by the conventions, with the possible exception of the Kennedy nomination. Some formal decisions taken in advance were controlling. These included the choice of convention cities, which was past change when each convention met, and the choice of convention leadership. Democratic National Chairman Paul Butler's final influence lay most clearly in the choice of Los Angeles[8] and the slate of convention officers. So far as the Democrats were concerned, there was obviously a preconvention understanding that the party would not suffer an open rupture at Los Angeles. No doubt both Kennedy and Johnson were in accord with the understanding, but probably neither could have produced it without the other's consent, express or tacit. Evolving sentiment in the South since Little Rock, and reaction in the North, made it possible. Butler, in turn, had doubtless become aware of the under-

[8] On this see Paul T. David, Ralph M. Goldman, and Richard C. Bain, *The Politics of National Party Conventions* (The Brookings Institution, 1960), pp. 337n, 388n, 389n.

standing and was compelled to accept it as the basis of convention planning, whether he agreed with it as policy.

The fact that each party was passing through a leadership crisis was also basic to the behavior of both conventions. Nobody had firm control because the previous leaders were lame ducks and the new leaders had not yet been fully chosen, much less invested with full authority. Butler and Eisenhower were the most conspicuous lame ducks, but not the only ones; others included, for example, some considerable percentage of the membership of each national committee.[9]

The Convention Officers

At neither convention were there contests over the election of temporary or permanent chairmen, or other convention officers chosen in advance.

One of the most striking characteristics of both conventions was the almost complete absence, among convention officials, of the elder statesmen. Of course, Herbert Hoover gave his speech; but Harry Truman did not even leave Independence. President Eisenhower had his "day" at Chicago, but mostly stayed out of the way. Mrs. Roosevelt was in evidence much of the time at Los Angeles. While she was treated politely, courteously, and ceremoniously, she was used only once—to clear the aisles after a Stevenson demonstration.

Sam Rayburn refused the convention chairmanship and gave himself over entirely to Lyndon Johnson's campaign. He was represented in spirit on the rostrum by Representative Clarence Cannon, the convention parliamentarian. In Rayburn's customary

[9] There would seem to be little significance to the personnel changes on the national committees selected in 1960. The Republicans, with a larger over-all committee, replaced fewer individuals in fewer states than did the Democrats. Among the 148 members of the Republican National Committee, 30 new faces appeared in 23 states; the Democrats made 46 changes in the 108 seats on their committee, the new members coming from 32 of the 54 subdivisions represented. (*Convention Guide,* supplement to June 24, 1960, p. 17 *et seq.,* p. 30 *et seq.; Congressional Quarterly Weekly Report,* Aug. 12, 1960, pp. 1440-41.) This appears to be about par for the Democrats, insofar as the matter could be determined from examination of the *Proceedings* of the 1956 convention when 30 states sent 42 new members to the national committee. *Official Proceedings of the Democratic National Convention, 1956,* pp. 812-16, 838-50.

place as permanent chairman stood the young, attractive, and impartial Governor of Florida, LeRoy Collins.

Collins had a great deal to do—at least he had a great deal more to do than Charles Halleck, his Republican opposite number. Halleck simply had the duty of reading from the script, which he did very well. Collins had to rule, for example, on the voice vote concerning the civil rights plank of the Democratic platform; he had to rule again on the right of a favorite son candidate like Herschel Loveless of Iowa to withdraw his name from nomination; and he had to rule on the voice vote to make the nomination of Lyndon Johnson unanimous by acclamation. This is the one time, on television, when Sam Rayburn got into the act. Collins seemed to hesitate for a moment as the voice vote was taken (to at least one disinterested observer it seemed that the ayes and nays were evenly balanced); Rayburn could be seen on the screen shouting "rule! rule!" while Collins turned to Cannon for a ruling, and the ancient parliamentarian seemed to delay.

The Democratic Loyalty Question

When planning for the Democratic convention got underway, it seemed likely that the out-party would face a renewal of the controversy over limiting the right to participate in the convention to those pledged to support the nominees and from states where the convention choices would appear on the ballot under the Democratic label. The so-called "loyalty" controversy, however, had been settled before the convention began. In 1952, attempting to avoid a repetition of the 1948 Dixiecrat revolt, the committee reported and the convention adopted the pledge that bound each delegate to use every honorable means to ensure that the convention nominees would appear on the state ballot in the place reserved for the Democratic party. Delegates from Virginia, Louisiana, and South Carolina refused to make such pledges. They were ruled ineligible to vote, but finally were seated. In 1956, at the recommendation of the national committee and the rules committee, the convention adopted a modification, continued in 1960.

The call of the convention, signed by Paul Butler, contained the loyalty rule recommended by the Democratic National Committee, September 16, 1959:

It is the understanding that a state Democratic Party, in selecting and certifying delegates to the Democratic National Convention, thereby undertakes to assure that voters in the state will have the opportunity to cast their election ballots for the presidential and vice presidential nominees selected by said convention, and for electors pledged formally or in good conscience to the election of these presidential and vice presidential nominees, under the Democratic Party label and designation;

It is understood that the delegates to the Democratic National Convention, when certified by the state Democratic Party, are bona fide Democrats who have the interest, welfare, and success of the Democratic Party at heart, and will participate in the convention in good faith, and therefore no additional assurances shall be required of delegates to the Democratic National Convention in the absence of credentials contest or challenge;

It is the duty of every member of the Democratic National Committee to declare affirmatively for the nominees of the convention, and his or her failure to do so shall be cause for the Democratic National Committee or its duly authorized subcommittee to declare his or her seat vacant after notice and opportunity for hearing.

The national committee also recommended the 1956 unit rule under which some states bind all delegates to vote as the majority of the delegation decides.

The loyalty rule apparently had been reaffirmed at the September 1959 meeting in order to provide a warning to those states which were, at that time, toying with the "free elector" proposals. The "free elector" movement was countered by a threat from Chairman Paul Butler in May 1960, to unite "loyal" elements in southern states to send rival delegations to the convention. What actually happened at Los Angeles, however, was a far cry from the difficulties that were threatened by southerners and by northern party militants desiring to curb southern rebels. Either north-south party tensions were only pallidly reflected in the work of the rules committee, or they had subsided considerably by the time the convention began. The latter interpretation may be correct. At least this was the inference that could be drawn from the statement by Governor Collins on June 7 that he did not expect any southern delegations to walk out or be ejected from the convention. As it turned out, Collins was in the chair during the convention as the permanent chairman. As late as the end of June, Butler was reported to be considering challenges to southern delegates known to have supported Eisenhower publicly, but it is also possible to regard the preconvention maneuvers as merely a war of nerves which Butler had mounted and maintained for a year or more against dissident southerners. In any event, by early July 1960, high Democratic leaders of every persuasion were radiating "peace and harmony."

The rules committee of the convention recommended the so-called loyalty oath compromise rule, and the convention ratified this decision without debate and without negative votes. As in 1956 the new national committee then required all its members to sign a pledge to support the 1960 national ticket as a condition of being seated on the committee. The pledge read:

> In the performance of my duties as a member of the Democratic National Committee, I hereby affirmatively declare my support of John F. Kennedy and Lyndon B. Johnson, the nominees of the 1960 Democratic National Convention, for offices of President and Vice President of the United States, respectively.

Everyone but the committeeman from Mississippi signed this pledge at the postconvention meeting of the new national committee. He was seated with the expectation that he would be authorized to sign by the state committee within a week. In late February 1961, it was learned that the delegate in question had not signed the pledge, but no action had been taken against him, and he still represented Mississippi on the committee.

Action on Credentials

As it turned out, none of the party leaders, nor the liberals serving on the credentials committee of the Democratic convention, nor the representatives of candidates participated in the "challenges" that took place at the convention.[10] A dispute involv-

---

[10] The Republicans, as the "in-party," had no credentials problems.

ing Puerto Rican representation revealed or concealed no major political issue, and the committee handled it with solon-like wisdom by recognizing elements of both contesting delegations and splitting the honors evenly between them. But Frank C. Vaughan, a delegate from Virginia, who had been a member of the Richmond Democratic committee, was challenged because he had been a principal organizer and leader of Virginia Democrats for Eisenhower and had campaigned for the Republican national ticket in 1952 and 1956. Moreover, he refused to commit himself to the support of the Democratic nominees in 1960. Taken together, these things demonstrated, it was contended, that he was not a "bona fide" Democrat participating in the 1960 convention in "good faith." The challenge was made by the Virginia delegate Virgil E. Goode. But the challenge originated with a Virginia lawyer, Graham Morrison, who was not a delegate. So far as could be learned, Goode and Morrison acted on their own initiative for reasons of their own.

The challenge came at the last minute and surprised almost everyone. The protest against Vaughan was filed with the national committee and with the credentials committee. The national body ruled that he should be seated temporarily but took no position on the merits. Kennedy backers sought to avoid a clash over Vaughan and challenges to more prominent southerners—Governor Price Daniel of Texas, Senator Strom Thurmond, arch-segregationist Leander Perez—and discouraged efforts to bar delegates from states with free electors.[11] By the time the credentials committee convened to consider the challenge, Governor Almond of Virginia had convinced Goode that Vaughan would support the nominees of the party and had persuaded him also to withdraw his challenge. Morrison would not withdraw, however, and under questioning it turned out that the assurance given by the Governor of Virginia that Vaughan would support the party's nominees meant simply that Vaughan would be bound by a state oath to support nominees of the party at the state and local level. Finally,

[11] *New York Times,* July 9, 1960.

the vice chairman of the committee, Leonard Woodcock of the United Automobile Workers, persuaded the credentials committee to look on the question as one of "personal honor." As he declared:

> If Governor Almond's statement of this morning is to mean any-thing at all, to me it seems that we are being given assurances that as a matter of honor, not as a matter of law and binding commit-ment . . . that the people who participate in the decisions of the convention will also carry out those decisions . . . made by the re-quired majority of the convention, and I would assume that the committee can take this assurance of the Governor of Virginia on its face value as I interpret it, and I assume that we are acting, all of us, as men of honor and bound by our honor to our country and our party.

Vaughan's representative wanted to continue the fight and observed that Woodcock was "not authorized to put words in our Governor's mouth. The statement stands just as he said it." But neither the committee nor Morrison had the stomach for further struggle, and the challenge was withdrawn.

The committee did not resolve another question connected with Morrison's challenge to Vaughan: "Could a person not a delegate challenge a delegate's qualifications?" Counsel to the committee, Harold Leventhal, who was also counsel for the convention, and the co-chairman of the credentials committee, Camille Gravel of Louisiana, took the position that a person who was not a delegate did not have a direct interest and therefore did not have standing to challenge the credentials of another delegate. However, the chairman lent a sympathetic ear to Morrison's contention that the committee ought not to decide the issue in the heat of controversy, and the matter of standing was left unresolved.

The Rules Committee[12]

In some respects, the conventions are prisoners of their pasts, and although the importance of certain activities has been en-

---

[12] For the material on the development of the conflict over the loyalty oath in the rules committee, I am indebted to Abraham Holtzmann, North Carolina

hanced in recent years, a great many people continue to behave as though these activities were unimportant. This was especially apparent in the attitude of the Democrats toward the business of the rules committee. While nothing interesting happened in this committee at the Republican convention, at Los Angeles the work of this group under Governor Herschel C. Loveless of Iowa contained several potential points of conflict and growth.

By and large the rules proposed were those adopted by previous conventions, supplemented where necessary by the rules of the House of Representatives. A preconvention skirmish over a proposal by Stephen A. Mitchell, counsel to the rules committee, to bar any state from changing its vote on nominations during a roll call was apparently won by forces supporting the candidacy of Senator Kennedy. The change was calculated to prevent the withdrawal of favorite sons and minor candidates and to forestall a stampede to the leader on the first ballot. Robert Kennedy announced his group's opposition to the proposed change;[13] supporters of Johnson did not seek the change; and Stevenson's workers were reported to be concerned about the possible effect of switching, but without a firm position.[14] However, the rules committee suggested several changes in the rules, at least one of which had some bearing on the continuing attempt under the leadership of Paul Butler to enhance the national committee by increasing the prestige of the national committeemen.[15] In this instance, the Democratic National Committee in its call for the convention exercised authority granted it at the previous convention to modify the number and distribution of delegates "without affecting proportionate distribution in order to enhance effectiveness of the next convention."[16] At its meeting September 16,

State College, whose study of the loyalty oath compromise within the Democratic Party, 1954-1960, will be published as one of the series of case studies in practical politics, sponsored by the Eagleton Institute of Politics.

[13] *New York Times,* July 6, 1960.

[14] *Ibid.,* July 7, 1960.

[15] Sidney Hyman, "The Collective Leadership of Paul M. Butler," *The Reporter,* Dec. 24, 1959, p. 8.

[16] The operative text of the resolution adopted in 1956 follows: ". . . the present system of determining the number of delegates and the distribution

1959, the national committee decided to give each national committeeman and national committeewoman one-half vote and provided that the national committeeman and committeewoman, when voting, would not be bound by the voting of their respective state delegations, whether this was done under instructions as a result of a primary election or because a delegation was following the unit rule.

This move was recognized for what it was by southern representatives at the meeting of the rules committee, and a considerable controversy ensued. No one from northern states or from other areas which might be interested in strengthening the national party was prepared to discuss or to defend the new rule. Stephen Mitchell, who sat with the rules committee as its counsel, and who was presumably informed about the new rule, would only say that it was thought that these men and women were on the national committee, and they stood on a different basis from other delegates, without explaining why it was thought to be desirable to give them an independent vote or any vote at all. In the circumstances, the proposal appeared an unjustified power grab. But at the time, no one raised this issue or questioned the desirability of permitting members of the national committee to vote in the convention. Everyone's attention went solely to the problem of how these votes were to be exercised. On the motion of the delegate from Alaska, the sense of the proposed rule on this point was reversed, and each national committeeman and committeewoman was given one-half vote to be exercised subject to the discipline of the state delegation of which they were parts.

The rules committee also demonstrated the casual nature of the preparation for the convention. (Here surely is an area where the national committees could move without giving offense to the congressional committees, political moguls, or to anyone else.)

---

thereof among the several States, Districts, and Territories shall continue, except as the same may be modified by action of the Democratic National Committee without affecting proportionate distribution in order to enhance effectiveness of the next convention, and except as the Committee may determine bonus delegates and delegates from Territories." *Official Proceedings of the Democratic National Convention, 1956,* p. 424.

Mitchell stated at the Monday morning meeting that copies of the rules had been available since Saturday morning at the rules committee headquarters at the Biltmore Hotel. Only a handful of the members of the committee had received those copies, however, and Mitchell's observation was made in response to a query why the rules had not been made available in advance of the meeting.

Among the Democrats there was also some controversy about reducing the length of nominating and seconding speeches for the convenience of the television audience; that is, to make the visual product more palatable. The Democrats ultimately yielded to progress, overruling southern pleas that the convention was a showcase, and the party would be well-advised to permit its heroes to speak at length on a national television hook-up.

The Conventions as Campaign Rallies

A major function of the conventions is to position the parties for the long campaigns to November and to act as gigantic campaign rallies for the candidates selected by the parties. In this respect, both conventions of 1960 must be judged successes, although to an outsider it appeared in late July that the Republicans had the better of the cause.

The Party Images Conveyed

Although the out-party, the Democrats came to Los Angeles with considerable reason to expect victory in the fall. In fact, some of them thought that victory was assured. The events at Los Angeles did not win many recruits to this point of view. The Republicans arrived in Chicago dispirited and somewhat fearful of the future, uncertain that anything could be done to assure victory in November. They left enthusiastic, convinced that they had selected the correct candidate and that he could lead them to victory in November. On the last day in Chicago, even Senator Goldwater's convention backers seemed reconciled, and the candidate himself seemed warmed by the manifest enthusiasm about him. More importantly, Nixon had already chosen the battleground for the campaign where it was thought he was the stronger—international affairs.

The Republicans also ran a tidier convention. They were perhaps wiser in their choice of meeting place, in that a far smaller number of seats were available than at Los Angeles and the seats were nearly always filled. They were much more efficient in their handling of the problems of getting credentials to delegates, to alternates, to newspapermen, and to other convention camp followers.

The Republicans were probably correct in judging that one of the principal impressions left on the public by the Democratic convention was that the Democratic delegates were undisciplined and impolite, not seriously dedicated to the work of a national party convention. Only one speech at the Democratic convention —that of Senator Eugene McCarthy of Minnesota—seemed to rise to the level expected of a speaker at a national convention, and this speech was for Stevenson, who hardly figured in the convention. On the other hand, the Republicans came dangerously close to creating the image of a convention of sheep led around by a teleprompter. At both conventions, the non-spontaneity of the "spontaneous" must have been obvious even to the viewer in Des Moines. Only the first demonstration for Stevenson when he appeared on the floor of the convention at Los Angeles on Tuesday evening as a delegate from Illinois could have been spontaneous, and there was considerable doubt about the self-starting nature of that wild demonstration. The demonstrations for Mrs. Roosevelt were genuine and spontaneous, but not uncalculated.

This writer has the impression that the Republicans were rather more successful in presenting the platform at the convention than the Democrats. The measure of this is not, I think, the disputes over the adoption of the platforms, but the effectiveness of the presentation or the unveiling of the platforms on television at the conventions. The film narrated by Chester Bowles did not project an image of the party as sharply as that produced by Charles

Percy and his associates. The film of the Democrats was too diffuse and dealt at length with issues remote from the campaign. It also was far too didactic, filled with good things that the Democrats and no one else could do. Few who saw the film must have been able to believe the line. The Republicans, on the other hand, had the experience and built on the precedent of their Cabinet discussion and comment on the platform at the 1956 convention. The final product Percy presented went down much more smoothly than the opus produced by the Democrats.

In both parties, the controversy over the platform seemed to serve the same basic purpose; that is, straightening the lines of the coalition that were being forged at the convention for conducting the election campaign. The opponents of the major principles embodied in the platforms were revealed to the majority in Los Angeles and Chicago to be small in number, weak in leadership, and almost powerless. From this, each party majority may have gained strength. At the same time, paradoxically, the revolts or pseudo-revolts over civil rights in both parties served the other function of free speech, of permitting the opponents and dissidents to have their say and to leave the convention with the feeling that they had been unable, after a fair opportunity, to persuade a majority. Probably the naming of Johnson as Kennedy's running mate drew much of the heat from southern opposition, and led most southern leaders to believe they should support decisions of the convention. Despite some noises heard in July and August from the swamps and bogs at the mouth of the Mississippi River, this was the net effect of the rumblings over the Democratic platform.

But while southern delegates choked down deeply felt antagonism over the civil rights plank, northern liberals who had their way with the platform were handed something bitter to swallow in the vice presidential nomination. Such violent disagreements silently arrived at, such tarnished prizes awarded each faction, left many delegates and their leaders attempting to mutter and chew at the same time. The contrast at Chicago two weeks later could not, in my judgment, be missed.

The Effect of Television

The most marked changes in convention procedures and methods of carrying on business have resulted in recent years from the presence of television cameras in and about the convention halls. For television's sake, the delegates at the Republican national convention were instructed as follows: "be on time, sit quietly, wear subdued clothing—preferably not white." In meetings of state caucuses, the delegates at Chicago were exhorted to be on their best behavior and to give the nation a dignified contrast to the behavior of the delegates at the Democratic national convention in Los Angeles. Just to make sure, at the Republican convention the aisles were narrowed so that demonstrations could be controlled and the marchers could be held to two abreast. The floor was ruled by professional ushers whose duty it was to hold demonstrations to a prescribed maximum, and who calmly directed groups of chanting supporters, even those demonstrating for Nixon, off the floor, down the aisles and out into the streets.

Both parties attempted to hold down the length of their conventions. Even so, both of them had more television time than they could profitably fill. The performance at Los Angeles by the Democratic nominees and scattered artists and entertainers from Hollywood and elsewhere on the last day of the convention was quite possibly one of the most boring spectaculars ever scheduled in this exciting new political medium. Both conventions were scheduled for the convenience of the television audience and were aimed at securing the best and largest audience in the prime evening hours. The Republicans slipped up in one respect and held an official short session on the morning of the first day. After that, all sessions began early in the evening on eastern daylight saving time. The length of speeches was curbed and a whole day's worth of speeches customarily given on "ladies day" was ruthlessly hacked out of the convention format by both Republicans and Democrats in 1960.

Television commitments have put a premium on avoiding floor fights and the possibility of lengthy roll-call votes to settle them.

The effort to put on a "good show," to avoid the appearance of disunity, and to use the convention as a campaign rally not alone for delegates but for partisans all over the nation militate against such controversy, but do not make it impossible, at least in the out party. The Republicans gave an observer the impression that the convention was organized for split-second TV timing, even if it was not rigged.

One suspects that television coverage of the conventions reached its highwater mark in 1960 and that unless drastic changes are made in the format of the conventions the networks will not again attempt to cover the proceedings in as great detail as they did in 1952, 1956, and 1960.[17] This development would not be wholly without salutary effects. While it must be conceded that the camera reporters were agile, inventive, and ubiquitous, the television newsmen were almost beside themselves in their effort to create news. They rushed to the side of the one delegate who held out against the unanimous nomination of Lodge on the first ballot, demanding to know why he had voted against Lodge. At first he said "it's because I just don't like him"; but when pressed said "it's none of your business." Governor Christopher Del Sesto of Rhode Island (a Republican) must have spoken for millions when he scolded several reporters for the nauseous repetition of the question about the influence of Catholicism on the campaign and the election. At both conventions the television newsmen gave far more credence to rumor and paid far more attention to minority—in fact, distinctly minor movements—than they deserved. At the Democratic convention the attention given the Stevenson demonstrations and demonstrators could perhaps have been excused because of the illustrious nature of his support and of the man himself. It could also be accounted for on grounds of television reporters' inclinations, biases, and interests. No such excuses are available in the Republican convention, where television reporters erred considerably in magnifying the strength and amplifying the noise of Goldwater and his supporters.

[17] Cf. Charles A. H. Thomson, *Television and Presidential Politics* (The Brookings Institution, 1956), pp. 107-12; and Chap. 4 of this book.

Restructuring Leadership
for the Campaign and After

A national flavor tainted the proceedings at both conventions. The head men were not regional men, nor were the vice presidential candidates selected only for their regional flavor. Johnson, obviously named to placate the South, did not make it as a typical southerner, but as a nationalized southerner who understands that the Confederacy is submerged in the Union.

The platforms were shaped by national considerations, and steps were considered by the Democrats to make the party program binding. The very idea is obnoxious to powerful forces in both parties. Senator Thomas J. Dodd, shortly after the 1960 election, declared that the "concept that a convention platform is binding on elected representatives in the Congress is absolutely inimicable to our system of government." In his opinion it would be "the worst betrayal of trust" for a President and Congress "to accept whole hog the convention platform of a victorious party and to subordinate the four-year deliberative process of the President and the Congress to the four-day drafting process of non-elected members of a party platform committee."

Probably revolts of the kind seen at both conventions in 1960, and especially the Republican convention, are endemic in the convention process and will be repeated. The revolt of John Tower of Wichita Falls, Texas, probably represents the resentment of the "little man" at being pushed around. Undoubtedly such opponents of the "machine" will continue to rise and express the frustration and resentment that delegates feel in having no real task to perform at the convention. For several conventions civil rights may continue to be the lightning rod for revolt. The encouragement in all this, it seems, is that the long-heralded, long-awaited breakup of the "solid south" is at last at hand.

3

The P   ign

°

_____

...s are waged to make marginal changes in
...ents. The campaigner, in the short time in which
...o work, has a very limited ability to change popular attitudes toward parties, candidates, and public policies or to alter the
scope and efficiency of political organizations. He must take as
given some of the most important determinants of an election's
outcome and lay his plans accordingly. Even then he may expect to
see events arise during the course of the campaign that will have
an impact on public opinion largely beyond his control.

This account of the 1960 campaign will be guided by the conception of campaigning just outlined. The subjects discussed will
include, first, the political facts of life as they presented themselves
to party strategists in late July and early August; second, the
organizations and strategies they constructed in response to these
facts; and third, the events of the campaign that seemed to have
been important in deciding who won.[2] Hopefully, this discussion
will help to explain why the campaigners acted as they did, will
cast into relief some new departures in campaigning, and will be
of some use in evaluating the 1960 campaign's contribution to

[1] Assistant Professor of Politics, Princeton University.

[2] I wish to thank W. H. Lawrence for access both to his files and his views on
the 1960 campaign. I am grateful also to the editors of Holt, Rinehart, and
Winston for allowing me to draw upon some of the materials I used in an
article on the 1960 election written for The *American Government Annual,
1961-62.*

the desire and ability of voters to make wise choices at the polls. Perhaps I should state that I think the 1960 campaign did give voters a greater opportunity to make a rational choice between candidates than most previous ones have.

The Context of the Campaign

Among the "givens" with which campaigners had to come to terms in 1960, none was more important than the status of the two major parties. The Democrats were clearly the majority party. About five adults of voting age considered themselves Democrats for every three who thought of themselves as Republicans. The Democratic party controlled the Senate 66 to 34, the House of Representatives 280 to 152. Democratic governors sat in 33 of the nation's 50 gubernatorial offices. In the more than 170 of the nation's 450 largest cities that have partisan executives, Democratic mayors outnumbered Republican mayors by about 3 to 1. The Democratic party, as these data suggest, had a great deal to offer its candidate in both organizational strength and voter appeal. Republicans could take comfort only in the fact that their party retained control of the federal executive and that their party's adherents were less likely to be nonvoters on election day than were those of the opposition.

Dr. Gallup's early polls, however, showed that the Republican presidential candidate's standing with voters was considerably better than that of his party. This was a fact that Republican strategists could find encouraging and of which Democratic strategists had to take note. Just before the Democratic convention opened in Los Angeles, Kennedy had led Nixon 52 per cent to 48 per cent in a Gallup poll trial heat. The first postconvention poll showed the situation more than reversed: the Nixon-Lodge ticket led the Kennedy-Johnson ticket 53 per cent to 47 per cent. Dr. Gallup also found Nixon's "enthusiasm quotient" (E.Q.)[3] to be slightly

[3] Gallup's E.Q. is that percentage of persons who, on a ten-point scale ranging from "extremely favorable" to "extremely unfavorable," give a candidate at least a "highly favorable" rating.

higher than his rival's—43 to 42. Nixon's running mate, Henry Cabot Lodge, drew an E.Q. of 45—15 points higher than Lyndon Johnson's.

Senator Kennedy's religious affiliation had to be taken into account by campaign strategists on both sides. That it would influence voting was evident. How to treat it as an issue was not. Practical politicians knew that Nixon would win some votes from normally Democratic Protestants and that Kennedy would attract some from normally Republican Catholics. They could be reasonably sure that anti-Catholicism and Catholic bloc voting would be interdependent; that is, that an increase in one would be likely to lead to an increase in the other. They knew that the distribution of both Catholics and anti-Catholics would be of great importance in determining the effect of the religious issue on the election's outcome. Only a little over 20 per cent of the nation's population is Catholic, but the Catholic proportion of the population runs considerably higher than that in a number of states ordinarily classed as doubtful in presidential elections. Among these are Massachusetts, Connecticut, New York, New Jersey, Pennsylvania, and Illinois. How anti-Catholics would be distributed, no one could say for sure.

The state of the nation's affairs, both internal and external, was a factor certain to be important on election day. All polls showed foreign policy to be a major concern of the nation's voters, if not their major concern. In the months preceding the conventions, the cold war had become colder. In May the summit conference had collapsed. In June President Eisenhower's visit to Japan was canceled in the face of widespread riots there protesting the new Japanese-American security treaty. In July the Russians shot down an American RB-47 reconnaissance plane, charging that the United States had resumed espionage flights over Russian territory. Two trouble spots were full of potential dynamite for the best-laid campaign plans. One was Cuba, where the Castro regime had become increasingly strident in its anti-Americanism. The other was the newly independent Congolese nation, already beginning to dissolve into warring factions. Russia's Premier Nikita Khrushchev had given belligerent support both to Castro and to the Lumumba faction in the Congo.

The nation's economy had its trouble spots, too. During the summer the Federal Reserve Bank of New York had described the economy as "on a high plateau." In June, employment was at its highest point in the country's history, but unemployment had risen as well. In July, steel production fell to less than half of capacity. Farm income showed little sign of recovery. Richard Mooney reported to the *New York Times* that "Few authorities say with certainty that either a resurgence or a recession is imminent. Rather they point to strengths and weaknesses that might lead to one or the other."[4]

The party strategists, finally, were faced with a postconvention session of Congress. Such a session had played an important and— for the Democrats—helpful role in the presidential campaign in 1948. In 1960 the return to Washington offered no clear advantage to either party. It was simply an embarrassing necessity, a consequence of Lyndon Johnson's unsuccessful attempt to win the Democratic presidential nomination. With bills still pending in Congress that would affect powerful interest groups allied to the Democratic party, trade unions in particular, he had probably hoped to make such groups think twice before opposing his candidacy too vigorously. With the conventions over, however, the two presidential candidates had to return to roles that were hardly suitable for party leaders. Kennedy once again became the junior senator from Massachusetts, Nixon the silent and powerless presiding officer of the Senate.

The Organizations

Planning and the execution of plans require organization. In 1960 both Senator Kennedy and Vice President Nixon had developed highly efficient (by political standards) personal organ-

---

[4] *New York Times,* July 24, 1960.

izations long before the national conventions of their respective parties had chosen them as candidates. After the conventions their task became one of merging these with the more permanent headquarters machinery of the two parties.

Top management positions in the Kennedy campaign organization were held by Senator Henry M. Jackson, the National Committee Chairman; Robert F. Kennedy, the candidate's brother and campaign manager; Larry F. O'Brien, a Massachusetts public relations man who became director of the National Committee; and Byron White, who assumed leadership of the National Citizens for Kennedy-Johnson. Robert F. Kennedy seems to have been the manager of these managers, second in command only to the candidate himself. O'Brien took over executive control of the National Committee staff while Jackson was the committee's public spokesman.

The modern campaign organization has a complex, if sometimes chaotic, division of labor. Among the specialists to be found there, professional propagandists have assumed an increasing prominence. In the Kennedy camp were O'Brien, who had previously worked with the candidate in his senatorial campaigns; Pierre Salinger, the candidate's press secretary; Samuel Brightman, the publicity director of the National Committee; J. Leonard Reinsch, adviser on television and radio; and the staff of Guild, Bascom, and Bonfigli, a San Francisco agency retained to handle advertising. Pollsters, like propagandists, are increasingly common figures in campaigns. Louis Harris served Kennedy in this capacity. He took repeated polls to determine the public image of the two parties and candidates, the issues uppermost in the voter's mind, and the voting inclination of various population groups and in various geographical areas. Among other specialists attached to the Kennedy organization were George Belknap, a political scientist with survey experience, and Blair David McCloskey, an adviser on diction and delivery.

Policy advisers to Kennedy—his braintrust—were numerous and distinguished. Chief among them was Theodore C. Sorensen, a member of the Senator's Capitol Hill staff. Harvard law professor Archibald Cox was the academic coordinator of a contingent of part-time or full-time professorial advisers that may have numbered as many as one hundred. Among them were historian Arthur Schlesinger, Jr., economists Paul Samuelson, John Kenneth Galbraith, Seymour Harris, Richard Lester, and Willard Cochrane; and law professor Abe Chayes. The *Wall Street Journal* reported in August that the professors would help to prepare position papers on some 120 different policy problems.

In the Nixon campaign organization, top-level responsibilities were divided among three men: Senator Thruston Morton, Chairman of the Republican National Committee; Leonard Hall, general manager of the campaign; and Robert Finch, a Los Angeles lawyer and campaign director. Heading the Volunteers for Nixon-Lodge was Charles S. Rhyne, a former president of the American Bar Association. Finch was regarded by some as the number two man of the organization, counting Nixon himself as number one.

The Nixon organization had much the same sort of specialists as its counterpart had on the Democratic side. Claude Robinson was the chief pollster. The Vice President's braintrusters included Arthur F. Burns, former chairman of the Council of Economic Advisers; Gabriel Hauge, former economic adviser to President Eisenhower; Harvard law professor Lon Fuller; Harvard government professor William Y. Elliott; and physicist Edward Teller. The Vice President's stable of public relations advisers was impressive: Hal E. Short, serving as executive assistant to Chairman Morton; L. Richard Guylay, in 1960 (as in 1956) the Republican National Committee's Public Relations Director; Richard Bean, on leave from Lockheed Aircraft; and Herbert Klein, serving as the candidate's press secretary.

Something new in campaigning in 1960 was the Republican National Committee's founding of its own advertising agency. Heading this "house" agency, "Campaign Associates," was Carroll Newton, a vice president of Batten, Barton, Durstine, and Osborn. He had been BBDO's account executive for the Republicans in 1956. Edward A. (Ted) Rogers, Nixon's television adviser at the time of the famous "Checkers" speech, was also associated as an original owner of the agency. The venture was designed to make it easier for top talent from competing agencies to unite efforts on behalf of the Republican ticket. The agency's staff of about fifty handled all varieties of advertising media except billboards.

The Strategies

Having considered the context in which strategists for the 1960 campaign formulated their plans and the headquarters organizations they constructed to carry them out, the discussion can turn now to an examination of the plans themselves. I cannot claim to have inside information on what was said in strategy sessions or to have had access to any strategy blueprints. The main outlines of what Democratic and Republican campaigners were trying to do, however, can be inferred with reasonable confidence from what they did and from bits and pieces of information that members of the two entourages leaked to the press.

Registration Drives

First, both parties clearly felt that efforts to mobilize already committed adherents should be given a high priority in allocating their resources. In Los Angeles Robert F. Kennedy, according to a *Wall Street Journal* report, presented each Democratic state chairman with a brochure containing population figures for his state's counties with a place for registration figures left blank.[5] These were to be filled in by the chairman and returned to Kennedy. Nor did the Democratic high command rely solely on this not too subtle prodding to encourage the registering of potential Kennedy voters. Soon after the convention Representative Frank Thompson of New Jersey was appointed to head a national task force to stimulate and supplement local work, and eight regional conferences were scheduled with state and local leaders, where Robert Kennedy again emphasized the importance of registration

[5] *Wall Street Journal,* July 18, 1960.

drives. Thompson's group concentrated its efforts in large cities in pivotal states and, within these cities, in lower middle class and working class neighborhoods. It was given substantial help by a Citizen's Non-Partisan Registration Committee of the AFL-CIO and by the same organization's Committee on Political Education (COPE). Apparently, these efforts were at least moderately successful. The Democrats took credit for some 100,000 new registrants in Los Angeles, 20,000 in San Francisco, and new registrations that were favorable by 5-3 margins in Pittsburgh and 2-1 margins in Philadelphia.[6]

The Republican registration drive was described by *New York Times* correspondent Cabell Phillips as "a determined but somewhat less ambitious effort," than that of the Democrats.[7] If this were true, it was not because the Republicans attributed less significance to such drives; indeed Vice President Nixon was later reported to feel that the inability of the Republicans to match the trade union-Democratic efforts was one of the more important factors in his defeat.[8] A small field staff from the national Republican headquarters organized telephone campaigns in some 500 heavily Republican counties, and some corporations also supplemented party efforts. A highly placed Republican public relations man observed after the campaign, however, that businessmen, used to giving orders to paid personnel, are as yet no match for either politicians or union leaders in the effective use of volunteer labor.[9] In the end, the Republicans had to rely chiefly on their local organizations to get new registrants, and these organizations were often weak in the very areas where work was most needed.

The Basis for Choice

If strong emphasis on mobilizing party adherents in registration drives was a common element in the strategies of both parties,

[6] William L. Rivers, "The Margin of Victory," *The Reporter*, Oct. 27, 1960, p. 21. On who was helping who in the registration drive, see also Chap. 5.
[7] *New York Times*, Sept. 11, 1960.
[8] *U.S. News & World Report*, Jan. 30, 1961, pp. 40-41.
[9] In an interview with the writer.

their strategies differed completely in another respect. The difference, put simply, was this: Vice President Nixon tried to induce the voter to make a choice between men. Senator Kennedy strove to make his choice one between parties as well as candidates. Nixon's non-partisanism was a standard feature of his basic speech[10] and found typical expression in an address delivered in Portland, Oregon:

> . . . I am not going to begin by saying to those who are Republicans in this audience, "Vote for me because I'm a Republican and you're a Republican."
>
> I believe that when we select a President of the United States that our history tells us that the American people look not just to party labels. They look behind them. They look to the man. They look to what he stands for, and they try to determine what kind of leadership America needs, and they say, "Will this man provide the leadership America needs, and does he stand for the positions that I believe in?"
>
> So, today, to all of you here . . . I say: Consider both of the candidates for the Presidency and the Vice Presidency as well; consider their records; consider their backgrounds and their experience, and then on November the 8th make the decision that you feel will be best for America—not simply on a party basis, not on some collateral issue that should not affect your decision, but on the issues that will best affect the future of America and the free world.[11]

Kennedy's contrasting approach is clear in a statement he included in a speech in Buffalo on September 28: "No Democratic candidate for the President has ever run and said 'Parties don't matter,' because we are proud of our record. We want to be identified with it. We want to follow it."[12] Kennedy gave a somewhat more varied expression to this theme than Nixon did to his, but he was no less

[10] W. H. Lawrence has observed that "Mr. Nixon had a single 'basic speech,' which he delivered in town after town day after day with hardly any change in language, or, indeed, even in the timing and movement of his gesturing hands. Reportorial newcomers to the campaign trail constantly were amazed when veterans with the Nixon entourage began quoting the Vice President accurately several words ahead as his speech was being delivered."

[11] Senate Committee on Interstate and Foreign Commerce, *Freedom of Communications:* Pt. II, 87 Cong. 1 sess., pp. 86-87. Cited hereinafter as *Freedom of Communications.*

[12] *Freedom of Communications,* Pt. I, p. 399.

persistent in identifying himself as a Democrat than Nixon was in his attempts to denigrate the importance of party labels. Though Nixon often protested in his basic speech that it would be politically wise for him to say "Vote for me because I'm a Republican," it is difficult to believe him to have been so naive. Kennedy could mobilize Democratic votes and win, Nixon needed conversions.

The Frame for the Candidate's Image

Choices of issues and of alternative ways of presenting the candidate confront every campaign strategist. In political campaigns, it is possible to distinguish between the issues that are directed to the population at large and those that are directed at interest group audiences. Further, while it is usual to distinguish between "issues" and "candidate images" in the analysis of campaign propaganda, this kind of distinction is much less valid for the first kind of issue than the second. In appeals to the undifferentiated electorate, issue themes are woven into a plot in which the candidate can play the hero.

The plot that Kennedy and Nixon sketched out for their audiences shared many of the same elements: Americans live in a dangerous age. The chief source of the danger is the Soviet Union. America's stake in the struggle with the Communist world is no less than national survival. So much one might have learned by listening to either candidate.

Early in the campaign Nixon normally developed the plot from this point in the following manner: He would ask, "What is the important issue?" and, answering his own question, would say, ". . . it is this: It is the concern that America must find a way through its leadership to keep the peace without surrender in the years ahead and extend the cause of freedom without surrender." He would then point with pride to the successful record of the Eisenhower team: ". . . I say successful because when we came into office in 1953 the United States was at war. We have ended one war; we have avoided other wars; and today we do have peace and have it without surrender of principle or territory. . . ."

A record, however, the Vice President would go on, "is not something to stand on; it is something to build on." We must, therefore, always "examine our military posture, our economic strength, and the other areas of strength of this country—to be sure that we're doing our very best." Even strength, Nixon would admonish his listeners, was not enough: strength must be used wisely. President Eisenhower had provided an example of wise diplomacy at the Paris summit. He had not traded insults with Khrushchev. Neither had he apologized for the U-2 flights; and at this point Nixon, referring to a Kennedy statement on the U-2 flights, would observe that he hoped the time would never come "when any President—Democrat or Republican—feels that it is necessary to apologize or express regrets for attempting to defend the security of the United States." Summing up, the Vice President would modestly advance his own qualifications to offer the wise leadership the times demanded, and, less modestly, those of his running mate:

> And may I say . . . that I realize that the experience of the candidates, when you vote for President and Vice President, will have a lot to do with your decision. It would not be appropriate for me to talk about my experience as compared with that of my opponent; it is appropriate for me to talk about the experience of my running mate. And I would say that I am proud that he is on the ticket with me; I would further say that I don't know of any man in the world today who has done a better job of standing up against the men in the Kremlin and representing the cause of peace and freedom than he has. . . .[13]

The need for experienced leadership to keep the peace was clearly *the* theme that Republican strategists had decided on for their campaign, just as the experienced leader was the image they hoped to present of Nixon. Undoubtedly, it was this decision on a theme that played a large part in the choice of Lodge as Nixon's running mate.

[13] All quoted statements here are taken from Nixon's remarks at Grand Forks, N.D., Sept. 14, 1960. (*Freedom of Communications*, Pt. II, pp. 94-100 passim.) All were standard parts of the basic speech he used at the beginning of the campaign.

If Nixon's appeal to voters generally was almost entirely built around the word "experience," Kennedy's relied almost as heavily on the word "movement." The Republicans, the Democratic candidate charged, had allowed the country to drift:

> The Republican orators are fond of saying that experience in foreign policy is a major issue in this campaign. I agree. But the issue is not merely experience of the candidates. It is the experience which the whole nation has gone through in the last 8 years. . . . Never before have we experienced such arrogant treatment at the hands of our enemy. Never before have we experienced such a critical decline in our prestige, driving our friends to neutralism, and neutrals to outright hostility. Never before have the tentacles of communism sunk so deeply into previously friendly areas—in Iraq and the Middle East, in the Congo and Africa, in Laos and Asia, and in Cuba, 90 miles off our shores, and elsewhere in Latin America.
>
> Mr. Nixon is experienced—experienced in policies of retreat, defeat, and weakness.[14]

His campaign, Kennedy said, was "founded on a single assumption, the assumption that the American people are tired of drift in our national course . . . and that they are ready to move again."[15] Often Kennedy would add, "Mr. Nixon says 'We never had it so good.' I say we can do better."

The phrases, "I say we can do better" and "I say we need to move again" appear over and over in the Kennedy speeches. The Kennedy "movement" theme was clearly designed to tap popular frustrations borne of the cold war. It also helped to turn one possible flaw in the Kennedy image—his youth—into a virtue. As Kennedy himself put it: "I want Mr. Khrushchev and the world to know that a new generation of Americans is taking over, Americans who fought in Europe and in the Pacific to maintain our freedom in World War II and who are going to rebuild the image of America as a strong and vital society. . . ."[16]

[14] Address at Alexandria, Va., Aug. 24, 1960. *Ibid.,* Pt. I, pp. 44-45.
[15] Address to the International Association of Machinists, St. Louis, Sept. 14, 1960, *ibid.,* p. 228.
[16] Remarks at Elgin, Ill., Oct. 25, 1960, *ibid.,* p. 751.

Interest-Oriented Appeals

The interest-oriented appeals used by the candidates in 1960 support two common generalizations: First, that the policy stances of major party candidates for President rarely show more than moderate differences; and, second, that "the center of gravity of wealth is on the Republican side while the center of gravity of poverty is on the Democratic side. . . ."[17]

Kennedy argued for federal aid to the states for school construction and teachers' salaries. Nixon supported federal aid for school construction but not for salaries. Both supported loan programs for higher education. Kennedy wanted medical insurance for the aged financed by a social security payroll tax. Nixon said that the medical needs of those over 65 could be met by a program that would give them a choice between private and government health insurance. Kennedy called for the passage of a bill to aid depressed areas. Nixon agreed that such action was desirable, if it were not like the "pork barrel measures" that had been proposed by the Democrats in the past. Both candidates proposed liberalizing the social security laws. Kennedy called for a $1.25 minimum wage bill. Nixon gave almost no attention to the issue. Kennedy asked for a review of depletion allowances. Nixon flatly declared himself in favor of the 27½ per cent depletion allowance on oil. Both candidates declared themselves ready to use the full powers of government to fight either inflation or recession. Kennedy condemned the "tight money" policy of the Eisenhower administration, while Nixon defended it. Kennedy denied that his program would cost the $15 billion Nixon said it would, but he never denied that it would cost more than Nixon's. Nixon said that his own proposals meant greater federal spending, but that he would not try to outbid the Democrats with the taxpayers' money.

Northern Negroes, Southern whites, farmers, Catholics, and Protestants were clearly regarded by strategists of both sides as

[17] Charles Beard's characterization of the two parties, quoted in V. O. Key, Jr., *Politics, Parties, and Pressure Groups* (Thomas Y. Crowell, 1958), p. 235.

constituting special problems. On the civil rights issue, both sides adopted strategies that allowed them little margin for error. The Democrats wrote a stronger civil rights plank into their platform than did the Republicans, and Kennedy gave more emphasis than his rival to the civil rights issue in his speeches. The Democrats nominated Lyndon Johnson as Kennedy's running mate, however, in an obvious move to placate the South. The Republicans, on their side, obviously hoped to capitalize simultaneously on anti-Johnson sentiment among Negroes and on Southern resentment of the Democratic civil rights plank.

Nixon apparently decided quite early that he would have to disassociate himself from the highly unpopular (in agricultural areas) Benson farm program. He declared that the administration's farm policy had been wrong, and underlined his opposition to it by making Interior Secretary Fred Seaton, not Agriculture Secretary Benson, his chief adviser on the problems of the farmer. For the short run, Nixon advocated larger payments to farmers in a crash program to reduce agricultural surpluses; for the long run, he called for moving away from government subsidies. Kennedy roundly condemned the "Nixon-Benson" farm program and proposed stricter controls on the supply of agricultural products to strengthen the farmer's bargaining power in the market.

With respect to the religious issue, the strategies of the two organizations seem to have been about as follows: Nixon would refrain from any discussion of Kennedy's Catholicism and strive to get Kennedy to adopt a similar course of action. Kennedy stood ready to discuss his religious affiliation openly, as he had in the West Virginia primary, if he thought the situation merited a personal appeal. He would also depend heavily on his running mate, other leading Democrats, and Democratic campaign literature to explain his position on church-state issues and to make pleas for tolerance.

The Geographic Targets

Insofar as the geographic targets of the campaign strategists may be inferred from the manner in which the candidates allocated their time, two facts stand out: First, the similar way in which Kennedy and Nixon distributed their campaign time among the states; and, second, the contrasting roles that Johnson and Lodge played in the campaign. Kennedy spent about 74 per cent of his time in twenty-four doubtful states during the campaign and about 88 per cent of his time in the same states during its last three weeks.[18] He spent about 57 per cent of his time in the seven largest of the doubtful states,[19] and about 71 per cent of his time in these states in the final three weeks.

Though Vice President Nixon announced that "We intend to carry this campaign to every one of the 50 States . . . ,"[20] this did not mean that his pattern of campaigning differed markedly from that of his opponent. The figures on Nixon's allocation of his campaign time comparable to those just given for Kennedy were: Proportion of total campaign time spent in doubtful states, 74 per cent; proportion of campaign time spent in doubtful states in the final three weeks, 88 per cent; proportion of total campaign time spent in the seven largest doubtful states, 51 per cent; proportion of campaign time spent in the seven largest doubtful states in the final three weeks, 67 per cent. Kennedy concentrated his efforts in the larger states to a somewhat greater degree than Nixon. He also spent relatively more time in the Northeast in the final three weeks and relatively less in the Midwest than did the Vice President in the same period.

That Lyndon Johnson's primary assignment was to hold the

[18] Figures given here are approximate. They were derived from the *New York Times* reports of the candidates' schedules. Since the candidates sometimes visited several states in the same day, the proportion of their time spent in each had to be estimated. In this discussion the reader should also note that any state where the final vote showed the winning candidate not more than 6 per cent ahead of his opponent was classed as "doubtful." This is a somewhat stricter criterion than the familiar 45-55 per cent split of the two-party vote commonly used in classing states or congressional districts as marginal. It was adopted on the assumption that the private polls taken by the two candidates' organizations would have allowed them to make finer discriminations between "doubtful" and "sure" states than the 45-55 split does, but not much finer than the 6 per cent criterion used here. Any criterion must, of course, be arbitrary.

[19] New York, Pennsylvania, California, Illinois, Texas, Michigan, and New Jersey.

[20] *Freedom of Communications,* Pt. II, p. 60.

South for the Democrats shows up clearly in the way he allocated his campaign time (of course, that this was his assignment was evident from the moment he was chosen to be Kennedy's running mate). Nixon, Lodge, and Kennedy devoted roughly equal portions of their time to the Southern states (from about 15 to 20 per cent). Johnson devoted about 44 per cent of his time to the region. He gave about half of his campaign in the final three weeks to the South, about one quarter of it to Texas alone. Johnson's campaign efforts tended to supplement Kennedy's. Lodge's tended to duplicate those of Nixon, though he did spend somewhat more time in the Northeast than did his running mate, and somewhat less time in the West.

To Debate or Not to Debate

A strategy decision of great importance in the campaign—perhaps it appears greater in retrospect than it seemed in prospect—was that of the two candidates to debate each other. Since all evidence seems to show that it was Kennedy who benefited from the decision, there has been widespread speculation about why Nixon agreed to meet his opponent in the four joint encounters. All reports indicate that Nixon and his advisers never welcomed the idea—that they opposed the debates because they felt Nixon was better known and, in debating his opponent, would only help to advertise him. The reports are not all agreed in their explanations of Nixon's decision to debate in spite of these considerations. The *U.S. News & World Report,* in an "inside" story purporting to represent Nixon's views on the matter, held that three factors had decided Nixon: that the national chairmen of the two parties had all but committed their candidates to the debates before the conventions, that the Republicans needed the free air time, and that private polls taken between the conventions had shown Nixon trailing Kennedy by 10 per cent.[21] None of these explanations is convincing. The Republican National Chairman presumably would not have committed Nixon to the debates had Nixon opposed

[21] *U.S. News & World Report,* Jan. 30, 1960, pp. 42, 44.

them, even if he could have done so. The two parties were given a great deal of free air time quite apart from the debates. And if Nixon's private polls showed him to be trailing Kennedy badly between the conventions, one would think that their marked disagreement with publicly reported polls would have raised doubts about their accuracy.

A more reasonable explanation of the decision to debate would seem to be this: Each of the two candidates was confident of his ability as a debater. Neither wanted to be regarded as running away from a fight. That Nixon was better known than his opponent was an inducement for Kennedy to debate. That Nixon could gain something from the debates he could have gained in no other way—access to millions of Democrats and independents—should have been an incentive to him. As a candidate of the nation's minority party, this was a chance not lightly to be foregone.

The Postconvention Session of Congress

The plans they formulated for the postconvention session of Congress are final elements in the campaign strategies of the two parties that should be mentioned. The Democrats, controlling both houses of Congress by large majorities, were under a strong compulsion to deliver on at least some of their platform promises. Accordingly, Senators Johnson and Kennedy outlined a minimum program in a joint press conference on July 30. The program included bills designed to provide medical care for the aged, new public housing, new Mutual Security appropriations, aid to education, and an increase in the federal minimum wage to $1.25 an hour. The two Democratic leaders proposed no action on civil rights for the session. They could hardly have done so if they hoped to hold their North-South coalition together and avoid a Southern filibuster.

One would infer from what happened later that the Republicans had agreed on several points of strategy for the session. One was to seize the initiative from the Democrats by offering a presidential program for the session. A second was to aggravate Democratic intraparty differences by introducing civil rights legislation. A third was to delay action, where it was possible to do so without appearing obviously obstructionist. And a fourth was to place full responsibility for what happened, or did not happen, on the Democratic majority.

The Course of the Campaign

The 1960 campaign developed through five main phases: the first, from the close of the conventions until August 7, the day before Congress reconvened; the second, from August 8 until September 1, when Congress adjourned; the third, from September 2 to September 25, the day before the first of the Nixon-Kennedy debates; the fourth, from September 26 to October 21, the day of the last debate; and finally, from October 22 until November 7, the day before the election. In each of these periods a particular kind of campaign activity dominated.

The first was a period of organizing, planning, and fence mending. Fence mending was, of course, a greater problem for Kennedy, who had had to fight for his nomination, than it was for Nixon. The Vice President quickly secured promises of all-out campaign support from both Senator Barry Goldwater and Governor Nelson Rockefeller. Kennedy's leading opponent for the nomination, Lyndon Johnson, had been brought into the fold with the vice presidential nomination, but relations had to be repaired with other principals in the nomination fight. Former President Truman did not announce that he would campaign for Kennedy until after a conference with Johnson on July 29. Stuart Symington and Adlai Stevenson were both asked to campaign and both agreed. Stevenson, together with Representative Chester Bowles of Connecticut, was appointed as a Kennedy foreign policy adviser. Later, during the congressional session, Kennedy went to Hyde Park where he paid his respects to Eleanor Roosevelt and won her promise of support.

Insofar as preventing passage of Democratic sponsored legislation was a part of Republican strategy for the second period of the campaign, it was eminently successful. The so-called "bob-tailed" session of Congress was almost barren of legislative result. Of the measures Kennedy and Johnson had called for in their minimum program, only a bill for new Mutual Security funds was passed. The Kennedy plan for medical care for the aged was narrowly defeated. The Senate passed the $1.25 an hour minimum wage bill, but no bill on the subject was reported back from the Senate-House conference committee. The conservative Democratic-Republican coalition on the House Rules Committee prevented any further action on aid to education or housing bills. There is little evidence, however, that the Republican "victories" had an appreciable impact on voter opinion. The Gallup Poll showed Nixon and Kennedy running neck and neck both before the session convened and after it had adjourned.

The formal campaign, and the campaign's third phase, opened September 2. The "movement" theme, both in its international and domestic variations, became the keynote of Kennedy's campaign speeches. He charged repeatedly that Republican inaction had led to a decline in the nation's prestige abroad and to economic injustice at home. Nixon's basic speech, as has already been noted, made his experience and knowledge of foreign affairs its dominant theme. At this time the speech was distinguished by the relative softness of its sell: Nixon was folksy in delivery and avoided the presumption (his word) of discussing his qualifications as a candidate. Instead he gave high praise to those of his running mate.

Khrushchev at the United Nations

The Kennedy-Nixon dialogue on foreign policy in September and October was greatly complicated by events taking place simultaneously in the session of the United Nations General. Assembly. Most of the drama was provided by Russia's Premier Nikita Khrushchev. On September 23, he demanded the resignation of Secretary-General Dag Hammerskjold. The next day he renewed his attack on the Secretary-General, asking for Hammer-skjold's replacement by a three-man directorate. On September 29, he heckled Britain's Prime Minister Harold Macmillan as the latter spoke in the Assembly. On October 1, he told the General Assembly that it could avert a terrible atomic war only by admitting Red China to United Nations membership. On October 7, he threatened to make a separate peace treaty with East Germany. On October 8, he declared that "America is not winning but losing," as the General Assembly voted 42 to 34 not to discuss the admission of Red China to the United Nations. In an outburst on October 11, he shouted that rockets were pouring from Russian factories "like sausages." On October 12, he became so enraged at a speech of a Filipino delegate that he banged his desk with his shoe. On October 13, he left New York.

To try to explain what Khrushchev hoped to accomplish by these antics would go beyond the scope of this study. Nixon, however, clearly saw them as offering him an opportunity to put his opponent at a disadvantage. On September 2, he said that the candidates had a responsibility to avoid disparaging America in any way that would encourage Khrushchev. The next day he told an Indiana audience:

> And might I suggest that there are some things we should not do while Mr. Khrushchev is here. One, I do not believe that it serves the cause of peace or freedom to talk about America's weaknesses, militarily, to talk about America's falling behind economically, to indicate that America is losing the battle of ideas throughout the world and that our prestige is falling throughout the world. I'll tell you why that shouldn't be done. One, because it isn't true; but, too, there is another reason. At a time when we are pointing up the things that are wrong about the United States, and it is a responsibility to do so that we can correct them, let us never forget that when one who is also here pointing up what is wrong about the United States, it is up to us to point out the things that are right about the United States and that are strong about the United States as well.[22]

Senator Kennedy refused to change his strategy in response to this

[22] *Freedom of Communications,* Pt. II, p. 207.

challenge to it. He said that Khrushchev was encouraged enough "as he stands 90 miles off the coast of the United States" and went on: "I propose to discourage him . . . the most ominous sound that Mr. Khrushchev can hear this week is not in the debates of the United Nations, but a sound of a United States on the move again, of a country ready to move"[23] If either of the candidates gained from Khrushchev's appearance in the United Nations, it was probably Kennedy. The Russian leader's conduct seemed to support Kennedy's charge that the Communist powers never had been more arrogant in their attitude toward this country.

The Religious Issue

During the first and second phases of the campaign, Senator Kennedy's religious affiliation was largely a silent issue. Political leaders said little about it after the Democratic convention except that it should play no part in voters' decisions and that it should not be discussed. Then on September 7 a Protestant group under the leadership of Dr. Norman Vincent Peale issued a statement charging that a Catholic President would be under "extreme pressure" from the Catholic hierarchy to conform his policy views to those of the Vatican.

After this attack Kennedy accepted an invitation to answer the questions of Protestant clergymen from the Ministers Association of Greater Houston. This was one of the most dramatic occasions in the entire campaign. In his prepared remarks Kennedy thanked his audience for the opportunity they had given him to discuss the religious issue. Then he began systematically to state his views:

> I believe in an America where the separation of church and state is absolute . . . where no church or school is granted any public funds or political preference—and where no man is denied public office merely because his religion differs from the President who might appoint him or the people who might elect him . . . where no public official either requests or accepts instructions on public policy from the Pope, the National Council of Churches or any other ecclesiastical source. . . .

[23] From an address in Nashville, Tenn., Sept. 21, 1960. *Ibid.*, Pt. I, p. 303.

I would not look with favor upon a President working to subvert the First Amendment's guarantees of religious liberty . . . and neither do I look with favor upon those who would work to subvert Article VI of the Constitution by requiring a religious test. . . .

I ask you tonight . . . to judge me on the basis of my record of fourteen years in Congress—on my declared stands against an ambassador to the Vatican, against unconstitutional aid to parochial schools, and against any boycott of the public schools (which I have attended myself). . . .

I do not speak for my church on public matters—and the church does not speak for me.

Whatever issue may come before me as President—on birth control, divorce, censorship, gambling, or any other subject—I will make my decision . . . in accordance with what my conscience tells me to be the national interest, and without regard to outside pressures or dictates. And no power or threat of punishment could cause me to decide otherwise.[24]

In a tense question period after his address the Senator was asked to comment on statements of the Pope, of the Vatican newspaper *Osservatore Romano,* and of the Catholic Encyclopedia.

In Oregon the next day Vice President Nixon told newsmen that Senator Kennedy's statement of his views should be accepted without further question. Earlier he had suggested that a cut-off date should be set for discussion of the religious issue, and he now announced that neither he nor his staff would have anything further to say about Kennedy's religious affiliation. The Democrats filmed Kennedy's Houston appearance and distributed copies of it for showings in Protestant areas.

If Nixon and the Republicans were to maintain silence on the religious issue after the Peale incident, clergymen were not. The New York Board of Rabbis issued an official pronouncement that "Voting for a Presidential candidate because he is a Catholic or voting against him because he belongs to the Catholic faith is a sinister betrayal of the fundamental precepts of American democracy. . . ."[25] A day later one hundred prominent churchmen and scholars, including rabbis, archbishops of the Greek Orthodox

---

[24] *New York Times,* Sept. 13, 1960.
[25] *Ibid.,* Sept. 10, 1960.

and Roman Catholic churches, and bishops of the Protestant Episcopal and Methodist churches, joined in opposing all attempts to make religious affiliation a test of fitness for the Presidency. Still later the Rev. Dr. Reinhold Niebuhr and the Rev. Dr. John C. Bennett, Dean of the Faculty at the Union Theological Seminary, accused Peale of having "loosed the floodgates of religious bigotry." Peale tried at this time to disassociate himself from the attack on Kennedy.[26]

In the time that remained before the election, clergymen stated their diverse views on the religious issue both as individuals and as groups. Reporters speculated at length on its probable influence on voting. Attending this kind of discussion was one of the ugliest aspects of the 1960 campaign—the circulation of anonymous and grossly distorted attacks on Catholicism, Catholics, and the Kennedy candidacy. The Fair Campaign Practices Committee, headed by Charles P. Taft, reported in November that nearly 200 different publications of this sort were in circulation. Some of them had been used previously in the 1928 campaign against Al Smith, the first Catholic major party candidate for President of the United States.

The Debates

The four television debates dominated campaign discussion in the fourth phase. The debates are discussed in Chapter 4 of this book, but some points are worth making here.

First, the basic theme of Nixon's campaign, the need for experienced leadership to preserve the peace, was not an easy one to present forcefully in the debate situation. As an issue it did not lend itself to extensive discussion, and panelists asked few questions about it. Nor did it lend itself to black-and-white presenta-

---

[26] The September 7 attack had come as a statement from a group calling itself the National Conference of Citizens for Religious Freedom. Peale, according to the *New York Times,* had been the chief spokesman for the group when it released its statement and had been listed on its official program as its presiding officer. On September 15, however, Peale announced that he had severed all connections with the group and denied having participated in framing the conference statement. See *ibid.,* Sept. 16, 1960.

tion. In the first debate, the Vice President had to admit that his opponent's length of service in public life was comparable to his own. He needed to make no such admission, and did not, in his campaign speeches.

Second, the public response to the debates suggests that some new interpretations of the voters' normal indifference to campaign discussion are in order. In the 1960 campaign, as in previous campaigns, few speeches drew audiences more than half the size of the most popular commercially sponsored television show. The audience for the debates, however, far surpassed even that of the Sunday World Series game. The Nielsen Television Index found a total audience of 30,013,000 television homes (66.4 per cent of all United States television homes) and an average audience of 26,894,000 television homes for the first debate (59.5 per cent of all United States television homes).[27] The audience for the second and third dropped somewhat: The total audience for the second was 27,979,000 television homes (61.9 per cent), and its average audience 24,001,000 homes (53.1 per cent). The total audience for the third was 28,792,000 television homes (63.7 per cent), and its average audience 24,860,000 (55.0 per cent).[28] Comparable data are not available for the fourth debate, although a Nielsen special report for 24 market areas does show a larger television audience on the night it was held (Friday, October 21) than on either the preceding or succeeding Fridays. Obviously, public apathy does not extend equally to all forms of campaign discussion.[29]

[27] Nielsen Television Index, first report for October 1960, courtesy of the A. C. Nielsen Company. The Nielsen organization defines *total audience* as that number of homes which view a program for at least six minutes. It defines *average audience* as the number of television homes that were tuned to the program during the average minute. It measures both (1) in terms of the projected numbers of homes reached, and (2) in percentages of all United States television homes. Hereafter percentage figures used with Nielsen data will mean "percentage of all United States television homes."

[28] Nielsen Television Index, second report for October 1960.

[29] It might be argued that these enormous audiences were due solely to the fact that all three networks carried the debates. They had done the same for the proceedings of the two conventions, however; and, no half-hour portion of either convention ever reached more than 21,560,000 television homes. See Nielsen Television Index, second report for July 1960, and first report for August 1960.

Quemoy, Matsu, and Cuba

During the debate period, two foreign policy issues assumed great prominence. One concerned the islands of Quemoy and Matsu, the other our relations with Cuba. Neither issue was originally raised in the debates, though both were discussed there at length.

In December 1954, the United States had signed a treaty with Nationalist China which committed the United States to a defense of Formosa and the Pescadores, but not the off-shore islands of Quemoy and Matsu. In January 1955, President Eisenhower asked the Senate for the so-called "Formosa Resolution," which would permit him to use United States forces as he "deemed necessary" to protect both Formosa and the Pescadores, and the off-shore islands. Senator Kennedy had voted for this resolution. He had also voted for an amendment which would have limited the Senate's approval for the use of our forces only to the defense of Formosa and the Pescadores. In a television interview on October 1, he defended his vote for this amendment.

Kennedy was questioned about this defense in the second debate. He restated his stand: He thought we should have a clearly drawn defense perimeter, known to our enemies. He would not suggest withdrawal "at the point of the Communist gun." But he believed the islands strategically worthless and indefensible.

Nixon seized on the issue. He agreed the two islands were unimportant as pieces of real estate. But

> . . . It's the principle involved. These two islands are in the area of freedom. The Nationalists have these two islands. We should not force our Nationalist allies to get off them and give them to the Communists.
>
> If we do that we start a chain reaction because the Communists aren't after Quemoy and Matsu. They're after Formosa. In my opinion this is the same kind of wooly thinking that led to disaster for America in Korea.[30]

In speeches in the ensuing week, Nixon charged repeatedly that Kennedy's policy toward the islands was one that would lead to

[30] *New York Times*, Oct. 8, 1960.

war and surrender. Kennedy counterattacked by asserting that Nixon was "trigger happy."

By the time of the third debate, both men had retreated from their original positions. Nixon now identified his position with that of the administration, which was that the islands ought to be defended if an attack on them was part of a general attack on Formosa. Kennedy, too, asserted that his position was essentially Eisenhower's—that the United States would have to go to war if any military action in the area of the off-shore islands indicated an attack on Formosa. Neither man, however, would let the other forget his original statement, and the issue was carried into the closing weeks of the campaign.

In the meantime Kennedy had given Nixon a new issue by becoming overly specific in his proposals for dealing with Cuba. From the beginning of the campaign Kennedy had referred to Cuba as a Communist outpost ninety miles off the coast of the United States. He used it as a symbol of the administration's alleged tendency to drift. When the administration imposed an embargo on exports to the island republic, Kennedy denounced the action as another instance of too little and too late. He proposed a four-point program, the third point of which was ". . . we must attempt to strengthen the non-Batista democratic anti-Castro forces in exile, and in Cuba itself, who offer eventual hope of overthrowing Castro."[31]

Nixon was ready to spring when he was asked in the fourth debate the next day to differentiate his position on Cuba from that of Kennedy. He regarded Kennedy's statements, he said, as "probably the most dangerously irresponsible recommendations" made during the course of the campaign.[32] The action Kennedy proposed would violate five treaties the United States had concluded with Latin American countries. It would violate the Charter of the United Nations. It would be an open invitation for Russia to intervene in Latin America. Answering Nixon, Kennedy reiterated his charges that the administration had contributed to Castroism, that

[31] *Ibid.,* Oct. 21, 1960.
[32] *Ibid.,* Oct. 22, 1960.

the trouble for the United States in Cuba was only the beginning of our difficulties in Latin America, and that the recently imposed embargo was doomed to failure. This issue, too, was carried into the final rounds of the campaign, though Kennedy later said that he had never intended to advocate intervention in Cuban affairs in violation of treaty obligations.

Final Events of the Campaign

On October 18, during the period of the debates, a new focal point was provided for discussion of the religious issue. On that date, the three Catholic bishops of Puerto Rico drafted a pastoral letter in which they forbade Catholics to vote for Governor Luis Muñoz Marin and his Popular Democratic Party. The governor had opposed religious instruction in the schools and had refused to oppose artificial sterilization and birth control. The incident was seized on by some American clergymen as evidence that the Catholic hierarchy would similarly intervene in mainland politics. Boston's Cardinal Cushing, however, denounced the action of the Puerto Rican bishops as "totally out of step" with American traditions.

After the fourth joint encounter, both candidates returned to slightly modified versions of the basic speeches they had used in the period preceding the debates. For Kennedy this meant constant reiteration of the "loss of prestige theme" and predictions of an economic recession. United States Information Agency reports that were leaked to the press in the last week of October and the first week of November tended to confirm Kennedy's charges of declining American prestige abroad and thus to add force to his arguments. The administration's refusal to release these reports undoubtedly succeeded only in giving their contents greater news value.

Nixon's appeal for votes took on several new facets in the campaign's closing days. His attacks on Kennedy became increasingly personal and increasingly harsh; he began to accuse his rival of "barefaced lies." He gave greater emphasis to his association with

President Eisenhower and gave up his earlier hesitancy to discuss the importance of his own role in administration decisions.[33] Finally, he made a series of headline-grabbing proposals. On October 25 he promised a manned flight around the moon by 1966-69. The next day he pledged himself to a summit conference with Khrushchev if an East-West nuclear agreement was in sight by February 1. On October 27 he promised, if elected, to tour Eastern Europe to "carry the message of freedom into the Communist world." On November 6, he said that he would ask President Eisenhower to visit Eastern European countries, accompanied, if possible, by former Presidents Hoover and Truman.

Two other final aspects of the campaign's homestretch deserve mention. An effort was made to make Reformation Sunday (October 30) a Protestant "Stand Up and Be Counted" day—counted against the election of John F. Kennedy. The driving force behind the effort was the National Association of Evangelicals, a group of 28,000 conservative and fundamentalist churches, with about 10,000,000 members. Reformation Sunday did become a day for political sermons in many Protestant churches, and some were of the sort the leaders of the association had in mind. But some were not. Ministers in many Protestant churches urged their congregations not to make a Protestant religious affiliation a test of qualification for the Presidency.

The last week of October also saw Senator Kennedy take a daring gamble. At that time Reverend Martin Luther King, Negro leader in the fight for integration, was jailed for a traffic violation in Georgia. Kennedy telephoned King's wife to express his sympathy. Robert Kennedy inquired into King's right to bail. Later a statement by Kennedy on the King incident and endorsements of his candidacy by King's parents were widely distributed among Negro voters.

All of these actions were taken in the face of an extremely un-

[33] For example, the Vice President told a California audience on November 4 that "Cabot Lodge and I know the problem [presented by the Soviet Union]. For 7½ years we have worked with and understand the President. For 7½ years we have participated in the great decisions, and we both know Mr. Khrushchev." *Freedom of Communications*, Pt. I, p. 1025.

certain political situation in the South. Vice President Nixon had made no statement on the King incident. This may have been because he, too, was gambling for the votes of both Negroes and Southern whites and assessed the situation differently than Kennedy had. Or his inaction may have been due to what he had seen as the repercussions of his running mate's Harlem pledge that a Negro would be appointed to a Nixon Cabinet followed by a Virginia statement that he could make no such pledge.

New Departures

Genuinely new departures in campaigning are rare. Well documented accounts of campaigns as early as 1828 show them to have been surprisingly modern in spirit and technique. Most of the differences between campaigning in our early history and in the present day can be traced to changes in the interest group structure of society, the gradual disappearance of the old style boss, and to innovations in communications and transportation.

The role played in the 1960 campaign by public relations men and advertising agencies was not radically different from that they have played in most recent campaigns. The only truly new development was the Republican "house" advertising agency. Whether the experiment will be repeated appears doubtful. At least some of those high in the Republican organization were dissatisfied with the service they received and are convinced that such an *ad hoc* advertising agency cannot match the services of commercial agencies.

The use of private polls by the parties was not a first for 1960, either, although it appears to have been greater and more systematic than in any previous presidential campaign. It is evident that professional politicians are beginning to be less skeptical of survey research and better informed as to what it can do for them. It seems certain that it will play an increasing role in developing campaign plans in the future. The public opinion poll is in many ways the functional equivalent of the atrophying network of precinct workers, one of the purposes of which was to inform party leaders on public attitudes toward issues and candidates.

The "jet" age came to politics in 1960. The candidates still relied on propeller-driven aircraft for transportation most of the time, but the jets allowed the candidates extraordinary mobility. On the two days of September 2 and 3, for instance, Senator Kennedy spoke in Manchester, New Hampshire; Presque Isle, Bangor, and Portland, Maine; San Francisco, California; and Anchorage and Palmer, Alaska. As Nixon began his formal campaign in a jet aircraft, he spoke one morning in Baltimore, that noon in Indianapolis, that afternoon in Dallas, and that evening in San Francisco. This kind of mobility is in contrast to the earlier, more clearly defined "swings" through the nation by presidential candidates on tour.[34]

With respect to its manner, rather than its matter, the 1960 campaign was a novelty among recent campaigns mainly because of the role that the religious issue played in it. It is not likely to differ so radically in this respect from the campaign of 1964, though probably feeling on the issue will not run so high. For the rest, it is the similarity of 1960's issue content with that of other postwar campaigns that is most striking. Domestic economic issues continued to be overshadowed by foreign policy problems in campaign discussion. The debates in the United Nations General Assembly were a kind of counterpoint to the debates of the candidates, and served to underline this basic difference in prewar and postwar American politics.

The four televised joint encounters were undoubtedly the most fundamentally new departure in campaigning in 1960. They were applauded by most observers of the campaign. Only a few joined one editor in the opinion that they were "electronically contrived bad dreams" and that "the very fact of arousing the interest of

[34] I am indebted to Mr. Paul Conner for giving me access to a paper in which he compares mobility patterns in presidential campaign tours. Contrasting Kennedy's 1960 campaign with that of Truman in 1948, Conner notes that "In all Kennedy displayed over three times the regional mobility of Truman, moving from one section into another 31 times compared to 9 times for the President."

millions further lowe level of campaign oratory that is usually not too high wh ch candidate performs solo."[35] I concur
in the majority opinio his issue.

The debates did unusual interest in the campaign. In
1956, the Roper pol 46 per cent of its respondents expressing "very much inte the presidential campaign in September and 47 per cen ber. In 1960 the number of respondents expressing "ve much interest" in the campaign rose from
45 per cent before the first debate to 57 per cent after the fourth
debate. Certainly few would argue that this was a "bad" development per se.

And the evidence does not support the notion that discussion
in "solo" campaign performances is usually of a higher quality
than that which developed in the debates. Longer speeches *could*
be used to develop thoughtful presentations of issues, but they
are not. In the typical campaign speech candidates rarely acknowledge agreement on any issue and often attribute fictitious positions
to their opponents. Agreement was acknowledged frequently in
the debates and the candidates distorted each other's arguments to
a limited extent. Issues are rarely drawn clearly in campaign
speeches. In the debates Kennedy and Nixon exposed their differences on a number of issues quite clearly—particularly on federal
aid to education, medical care for the aged, the nation's defense
posture, and government intervention in the economy. In campaign speeches candidates avoid discussing many issues raised by
their opponents. In the debates they were unable to do so. I agree
with the editors of the *Baltimore Sun* that while the "great debates" were neither great nor true debates, they were the best political discussion to which the American public has been exposed
in a modern campaign.

[35] Max Ascoli, "Intermezzo," *The Reporter,* Nov. 10, 1960, p. 18.

4

Mass Media Activities and Influence

CHARLES A. H. THOMSON[1]

IN THE PRESIDENTIAL CAMPAIGN OF 1960, television came closer than ever before to confirming the hopes, if not the fears, of those who had predicted sovereign political power for it in the days of its infancy. The television debates between Vice President Nixon and Senator Kennedy provided the most important innovation in the political use of any medium of mass communication since the fireside chat and the open press conference. The heart of the innovation was bringing the candidates together before an enormous audience composed of more than partisans, where each candidate could air differences on issues and party positions with a chance for immediate reply from the other, thus allowing a decisive portion of the electorate to compare important aspects of their performance. This innovation affected more than electronic campaigning; it affected other crucial campaign aspects at the same time: finance, strategy, and tactics.

The first television debate gave neither candidate a clear margin, but by demonstrating, to the largest audience ever assembled for a campaign event, that the differences in the apparent qualifications of the two candidates were small, it heartened the Democrats, energized their organization, and gave them confidence in victory; while it shocked and disheartened the Republicans. Was this a demonstration of television's naked power? Hardly. The fears of television's detractors were confirmed, if at all, in reverse.

---

[1] Member of Senior Staff, Social Science Department, RAND Corporation.

Nixon, who had long and skillfully specialized in the technique of the medium, who had allegedly subordinated content to style and to the presumed requirements of a good show, lost vital points in the allegedly critical elements of image by virtue of makeup, perspiration, and visible nervousness, at least at the outset. Kennedy, who scorned makeup (probably after being advised that he would be better off without it), and who threw speech structure and timing to the winds in favor of an unrelenting, machine-gun-paced barrage of words, gained a small but decisive advantage that his opponent never overcame.

The press produced no major innovations comparable to the debates, although an impressionistic sampling of the major metropolitan newspapers, the news magazines, and a few examples of the suburban press suggests that editors and owners were much less partisan than usual, while the working press showed an increasing preference for Kennedy in the postconvention period. A more formal study of a small but well-selected sample showed that during the 1960 campaign, Kennedy and Johnson together got more and better space than did Nixon and Lodge, whether space was summed for both teams or the presidential or vice-presidential candidates were compared with one another. Most newsworthy of all was the fact that both major candidates, and both teams, ran well ahead of President Eisenhower in press coverage—and Eisenhower had dominated political press attention, month in and month out, since his successful campaign of 1952.[2]

The Legislative Background of the Debates

Before turning to a more detailed estimate of the performance of the candidates, the parties, and the mass media in 1960, it is

[2] See *New York Times,* December 3, 1960. Data for campaigns prior to 1960 were gathered for a privately-financed survey of a few key papers in the metropolitan press from the Eastern seaboard, the Middle West, and the Far West, that commenced during the campaign of 1952 and extended through the congressional campaign of 1958.

necessary to recall two legislative events that helped to set the
stage.

The Lar Daly Amendment

First was the so-called Lar Daly amendment to the Communications Act of 1934.[3] This clarified somewhat the application of
Section 315 of the Communications Act and helped to free television from some of the risks inherent in full coverage of the conventions as well as the campaigns.

In 1958, the Federal Communications Commission, in a literal
interpretation of the law and a not unexpected failure of regulatory nerve, had reversed its earlier practices and decided that the
appearance in a news show of Chicago's Mayor Richard J. Daley,
then a candidate for re-election, justified a demand for equal time
from his opponent, Lar Daly. Previously, the commission had been
chary of deciding that such an appearance would constitute a "use"
of TV-radio facilities, and thus open the way for equal-time demands from all other qualified candidates. Charitably, one might
conclude that, in so deciding in the Daly case, the commission read
the English language literally in order to force Congress to a
change of language that would relieve the regulatory agency of
the need to use its own discretion.

Under pressure from the political parties and from the broadcasting industry, Congress then provided that the appearance by a
legally qualified candidate on any (1) bona fide news broadcast;
(2) bona fide news interview; (3) bona fide news documentary
(if the appearance of the candidate is incidental to the presentation of the subject or subjects covered by the news documentary);
or (4) on-the-spot coverage of bona fide events (including but
not limited to political conventions and activities incidental there-
to) should not be deemed to be a "use" within the meaning of
Section 315. Congress prudently added that nothing in this amendment should relieve broadcasters in such programs from obligations to operate in the public interest and to afford reasonable

[3] 73 Stat. 557 (1959).

opportunity for discussion of conflicting views on issues of public importance. The new amendment, both in its general provisions and in its specific reference to conventions as a bona fide event, gave wider legislative scope than ever before to the broadcasters to cover the conventions in depth, interviewing politicians and candidates of every provenance and hue without having to worry about whether equal-time claims were going to be set up against local stations or network outlets throughout the country.

Authorization for the Debates

The second change was embodied in Senate Joint Resolution 207, passed late in August 1960, that exempted candidates for the offices of President and Vice President only from the operation of Section 315, during the period from their nomination until election day. This relaxation culminated a campaign, waged chiefly by the networks since 1952 against Section 315, which was featured by the broadcasters' offer of free time for television debates between the candidates of the major parties.

The legislative battle was not won easily, and debate in both the House and the Senate revealed a hard core of suspicion of the political behavior of the networks or broadcasters once Section 315 had been relaxed or abolished, even for the special purpose of debate between the chief candidates. Senator Jacob Javits supported the joint resolution vigorously and unequivocally; he asserted that there was no more searching means than television for bringing out the point of view of a man and for plumbing his character. He pointed out that provision for debates would take some of the strain of financing campaigns off the backs of the candidates, and he reported a two-hour debate at the Academy of TV Arts and Sciences with Paul Butler and Thruston Morton (the party chairmen), Averell Harriman, and representatives of the Columbia Broadcasting System, that led him to the conclusion that television was the best instrument "to acquaint the public with what they are buying."[4] Senator Mike Monroney, sponsor of earlier efforts

[4] *Congressional Record,* daily edition, June 27, 1960, p. 13427.

to provide for appropriate legislative sanction, supported Senate Joint Resolution 207 as the best he could get. Senator Ralph W. Yarborough proposed an amendment that would have required the candidates to debate. Several Republicans favored the resolution but opposed the restrictive amendment, questioning whether it was constitutional.

In the House, the matter was debated on August 22; the general temper of the debate suggested strongly that the networks were attempting to enter into a gentleman's agreement with the parties and the Congress to stage the debates in full and fair manner, if they were given a clear legal opportunity to do so. Representative Oren Harris, who led the debate, justified the move as an experiment for this election year only. He stressed that there was no relaxation in the requirements for over-all fairness and pointed out that the FCC would be required to survey political broadcasting and report to the Congress so that the experiment and fairness could be judged. He brought up lists of favoring organizations, from the Grange through the veterans' organizations to various newsmen's associations. He dealt with the question whether the law should sanction (or should mention) the propriety of commercial sponsorship for the debates, citing the stands of the major networks.[5] Even more to the point, he told Michigan's reluctant Representative John B. Bennett that if the debates were to be sponsored, there would be no need to relax the requirement, since it was doubtful that candidates of other parties could get up the money to buy equivalent time. Representative James Roosevelt introduced a memorandum opposing the relaxation on the ground that Section 315 should be repealed outright. California's Representative John Moss expressed serious reluctance over anything that might affect local stations and local campaigning adversely; he accepted the resolution as an expedient, needing further study. Harris, in concluding the debate, promised an extensive survey,

[5] ABC's John Daly said that the question of sponsorship should be left to the candidates; CBS's Frank Stanton said there would be no sponsorship, but the program would be carried as a CBS "sustainer"; NBC's Robert E. Kintner sided with Daly; MBS's Robert F. Hurleigh said such programs should be carried as a public service except where the political committees bought time.

careful study, and legislative review in 1961. The joint resolution passed by voice vote.

The new legislative situation, including the Lar Daly amendment, favored candidates over spokesmen. By offering them invaluable opportunities of access to voters, it influenced them toward presentations that would put a premium on their forensic rather than their administrative or policy-making skills.

The Media at the Party Conventions

How did the media measure up to their opportunities at the conventions? Given the constraints of having to follow the procedures and events set by the convention managers themselves, the broadcasters managed to do about as well in 1960 as they did in 1956. They were more responsive to considerations of internetwork competition, as measured by the battle of the contemporaneous ratings, than they were to new and imaginative ways of bringing the story of the conventions to their audiences. In the judgment of qualified critics, and according to some well-placed self-ratings, NBC won the battle, leading CBS and ABC in that order at the Democratic convention, where there was more uncertainty, more local color, and more of a story to be told.

The Prior Build-up

What sorts of images did the candidates bring into the conventions and the campaign? According to private studies made at the time, the Kennedy image was not widely known before the primaries. At the 1956 convention, he had appeared as the clean-cut young Catholic who almost took the vice-presidential nomination while proving that under some conditions, southern politicians would prefer a Catholic over another candidate who had not kept the faith with his co-regionists. As Kennedy moved through the primaries, the public image became one more widespread, better defined, and more favorable than the previous cliché—the rich

young man who desperately wanted to be President and was willing to work very hard for it. In the West Virginia primary, television was credited with high potency in transmitting the personal
appeal of a candidate who might otherwise have gone down to defeat on religious grounds. The fact that Kennedy had won the key
primaries was widely heralded before the conventions, and a new
facet was added to his list of imputed characteristics: the good
campaigner, the vote-getter, the potential winner.

Nixon, by contrast, came into the conventions without any
gruelling campaign experiences. He had set his image in earlier
days, and had had the advantage of nationwide exposure not only
during the 1956 campaign, but in the earlier presidential and
congressional struggles. The 1956 experience had gone far to confirm the notion of a new Nixon, more poised, more at ease, less
involved with technique, more concerned with serious issues, and
less concerned to win with any means and at any cost. Although
his work in 1958 as an uncompromising campaigner in behalf of
Republicans offset this image to some degree, he gained as a man
of strong party loyalty—and also put himself beyond effective
challenge for the Republican candidacy by the strength and in-
clusiveness of the political obligations he had laid on the organizational stalwarts of his party.

The vice-presidential candidates were less well known, although
Ambassador Lodge's well-publicized activities as anti-Communist
tribune at the United Nations had kept him before a politicized
sector of the public for some years. He might well have gone into
the campaign ahead of Kennedy as a known public figure. Of all
of the major candidates, Senator Johnson had the least in the way
of a public image. His stage had been the Senate, and he was much
better known to political professionals and to the politically concerned elite than he was to the public at large.

Much image-making remained to be done as the parties and the
candidates moved into their conventions. The main tactical setting,
especially at the Democratic party, was the effort of the television
networks to compete with each other. This, spurred on by the new
freedoms of the Lar Daly amendment, offered the political contenders ample opportunities to show themselves.

The Nature of the Coverage

The broadcasters were still not ready to provide a sharply edited coverage of each day's events. Their style called for a combination of coverage of activities in the convention—as they slowly progressed through platform to keynote to nominations to balloting to acceptances—with attempts to display the network celebrities as much as to bring political notables to predetermined spots on the floor of the convention halls. Here lenses focused from the wings would permit a brief interview, provided the monitoring editor decided to choose it over other fare.

Media commentary was as good as one could expect in 1960. To the connoisseur, radio provided some of the best commentary of all. NBC's TV team of Huntley and Brinkley received the warmest critical acclaim for their dry, penetrating, and timely interchanges. And they received the compliment of strenuous activities by the other networks to provide similar personalities—one network going to the length of importing an English commentator and bringing to bear one of its senior executives who had intended to play a backstage role in reporting the Democratic event. All the networks, especially the larger two, backed up their on-the-spot reporting with specially assembled strings of reporters able to investigate the various ramifications of particular events. The printed press in 1960 as before, tried less for the scoop and the latest intelligence, and concentrated on news analysis, commentary, and interviewing in some depth of the major actors.

In 1960, there were no stories of friction between party managers and broadcasters comparable to the Butler protest in 1956 over a network's omission of a full campaign film. On the contrary, the superficial impression was one of easy and good relations, as the management of both parties dealt with their media problems with awareness of media habits and preferences and also of some of the opportunities. The Democrats in 1960, as in 1956, outmaneuvered the Republicans in the treatment of their platform process, despite its inherent political liabilities. Under the shrewd guidance of Platform Chairman Chester Bowles, the Democrats started early and moved their "hearings" to various regional points throughout the country, months in advance of the convention and the formal hearings of the Democratic platform committee itself. Captured on tape and film, the platform hearing films were used later in the campaign to good effect. By contrast, the platform hearings at the convention itself were played down, and stress was put on the presentation of the platform to the convention and the country at large.

Audience Response

Audiences cooperated with the Democrats and the Republicans by tuning in at appropriate times in respectable numbers. Peak audiences for each day coincided with the major events. In the Democratic convention, the following tabulation gives day, event, percentage of total television homes tuned in, and average number of homes tuned in during the event (stated in millions):

	Percentage of All Homes	Average Number of Homes
Monday—Senator Church's keynote address	31.3	14.1
Tuesday—Platform (Senator Bowles)	30.0	13.6
Wednesday—Stevenson nomination (Senator McCarthy)	44.2	20.0
Thursday—Johnson nomination (Governor Lawrence)	32.7	14.8
Friday—Kennedy acceptance	38.9	17.6

The Republican record was similar, with the largest audience coming at the time of Vice President Nixon's acceptance speech, when 17.2 million homes were tuned in. The second highest audience was for President Eisenhower, with 16.7 million homes constituting the average-minute audience.[6]

The amount of viewing was almost identical for 1960 as for 1956. In 1960, one rating service estimated that 86 per cent of

[6] Figures from *Broadcasting*, Sept. 5, 1960, p. 44, citing Nielsen reports.

the total potential audience saw some part of the Democratic convention; the 1956 figure was 88 per cent. The amount of time
spent by the average home in looking at the event was 9 hours
and 28 minutes in 1960 against 9 hours and 39 minutes in 1956.
The largest audience for the Democrats came on Wednesday (the
day of nominations), when an estimated 32.7 million homes tuned
in at some time during the day; there was a substantial audience
of some 12.7 million homes at the late hour when Kennedy's victory finally registered on the totalizers.

If the Democrats failed to get the most out of their convention
broadcast audiences by failing to compress their convention procedures and to run smoothly through their various routines, they
nevertheless presented to the faithful viewer more conflict than
had been predicted over the Kennedy nomination. In the main
they showed themselves characteristically Democrats in convention assembled: turbulent, variegated, emotionally involved.

The Republicans in their planning faced the problem of what
to do about audience interest in a convention in which the major
nomination was a foregone conclusion, and the secondary nomination a matter of considerably less import and interest. Insofar
as production planning had anything to do with it, the Republicans did little to attack this problem directly; as a party they have
been characteristically better satisfied with a smooth and ceremonial production than with the outward expression of differences.
In the event, the ceremony went smoothly, with Republicans from
all corners of the country looking alike as they mounted the platform with identical manner and stride, and contributed to an impression of party homogeneity that remains striking in a nation of
regional differences. But the interest in the Republican convention
was enhanced by the issue-conflict between Governor Nelson
Rockefeller on the one hand and Senator Barry Goldwater on the
other, mediated by the delicate balancing between Nixon and
Eisenhower.

The central campaigning problem of the Republicans was to
maintain full credence in the remaining political potency of Eisenhower, while presenting Nixon as the man ready to add powerful

new offensives based on the territory consolidated by his predecessor. The immediate solution was Nixon's acceptance speech. For
whatever it was worth, the broadcast media and the printed press
carried it with full justice to its maker. Noteworthy in retrospect
was the collapse of the Republican efforts to produce issue interest
through the platform process at a time when the platform was the
central point of uncertainty behind the scenes, and therefore of
potential public attention. Also noteworthy was the eloquent appeal of Senator Goldwater to a convention made up of delegates
who might have preferred him to any other, if they could have
been given their free choice without reference to previous organizational decisions or primary outcomes. Yet Goldwater gave full
support to Nixon as a means of preserving a party in power that
could be remade more fully along conservative lines in later years.
Not to be overlooked was television's coverage of a Rockefeller
demonstrating the warmest friendship for a man over whom he
had supposedly won a smashing ideological victory only weeks
before.

The Campaign and the Debates

The development of the campaign—if not the amount of campaigning already done at the conventions—obscured the so-called
kick-off speeches. The Democrats traditionally opened their formal campaign, mildly enough, at Detroit's Cadillac Square on
Labor Day. It is difficult to remember without reference to docu-
ments what the Republican kickoff speeches were. Nixon was recovering from a wounded knee at the usual time for ceremonial
campaign launching. But in 1960, probably more than in any
previous year, the candidates were not going to do anything at
kickoff time that would make the heralded television debates in
any way anticlimactic.

The debates took place on September 26, October 7, October
13, and October 21. The format was decided on by the candidates
and their representatives. Disregarding the advice of the networks,
the candidates opted for a quiz-show format for two of the debates, in which representative newsmen (chiefly from broadcast-

ing) working under a moderator asked questions in turn, and the candidate to whom the question was addressed got two and a half minutes to answer, and his opponent a minute and a half to rebut. In the first and last debates, each candidate got eight minutes to make an opening statement, and three minutes to make a closing statement. For the balance of the time, the candidates responded to questions from newsmen, in the same sequence as in the second and third debates. The order of appearance was decided by a toss of a coin; the privilege of the last speech was decided by the clock.

Again by agreement between the candidates, it was decided to devote the first debate to domestic issues and turn to international affairs in the second, while the questions of the reporters and the development of the interchange would decide how time would be spent in the remaining two. In the event, this division of attention was more formal than real, for the first discussion soon turned to aspects of domestic issues of relevance to the international scene, although the topics ranged from the farm program through minimum wage legislation, financing of school construction and of medical care for the aged, to problems of fiscal probity and the sanctity of the dollar. The bridge from domestic to international occasioned no conflict between the contenders; both were happy to assess the domestic scene from the viewpoint of how domestic strength would enable the country and its leaders to stand up to Khrushchev and the Chinese Communists.

The First Debate

The first debate amassed the largest audience—variously estimated at some 75 million viewers in some 30 million homes. However large this audience and whatever its age (some estimates included only those over 12, others took in any viewer of whatever age) it possessed one new and vital characteristic: it included full coverage of Democrats *and* Republicans *and* third-party supporters and uncommitted persons. What did each of the contenders do with this unique opportunity to reach the other's supporters and the undecided?

Kennedy, who had won the toss and went first, used his opening speech to develop his theme that the United States as a country is not doing enough—not being great enough, powerful enough, creative enough, active enough; not producing as much as we could, allowing food to rot while four million people get government food packages, and so on throughout the range of standard issues.

In his opening remarks Nixon agreed and disagreed. He agreed that America, already ahead, should stay ahead and move ahead at home and abroad. He disagreed that the United States had been standing still, or that its growth rate was unsatisfactory, or that it was in a state of "retreat, defeat or stagnation." He insisted that the Eisenhower record of growth was better than the Truman record, seven and a half years for seven and a half years. And he disagreed on the means of achieving agreed goals, asserting that the old-hat Kennedy proposals would only stifle achievement.

The question period started with blunt and unflattering questions for both candidates. One newsman asked Kennedy whether he was immature, and why he thought people should vote for him. Another asked Nixon what major proposals he had made that the government had adopted. In reply to these questions bearing on experience and qualifications, Kennedy did well on points. He asserted that his governmental experience was as long as Nixon's, and qualified him equally; moreover, he pointed to program and party as of importance too, claiming progress under Democrats against years of retrogression under Republicans. Nixon was forced into the difficult position of justifying his claims to superior policy-handling skill in a situation where the President had left him out on a limb by telling newsmen in an earlier press conference that he couldn't think of a policy proposal Nixon had fostered that he had adopted. Nixon's position as vice presidential member of the administration and as merely an adviser to the Chief Executive made it difficult to claim policy initiatives as clearly his own.

The quality of the questions was adjudged only fair; the quality of the discussion (and the temper of the confrontation) was almost equally mediocre. Little fundamental divergence on issues became apparent, although Nixon claimed that the Democratic platform would cost the taxpayer as much as $18 billion more, while the Republican spending increase, if he were elected, would be under $5 billion more than the current rate.

Despite the limited divergence on issues, there was a dramatic comparison going on. Kennedy was drawing level. Nixon, who had gone into the debate intent on demonstrating superior experience, poise, and acquaintance with the requirements of highest office, looked tense, haggard, anxious. He misspoke himself more frequently than the triple-tonguing Kennedy. Kennedy never relaxed, never smiled in his effort to pound home his charges with unflagging intensity and determination.

What was the immediate overt response to the first debate? When questioned, the candidates still sparred cagily. Kennedy thought it had been "useful." Nixon said it was a "good sharp exchange." Their campaign managers were more revealingly explicit. Robert Kennedy was "tremendously pleased" at this "extremely helpful" event. Herbert Klein thought it "came out very well," and gave the candidates a chance "to present the issues." Republican Leonard Hall said at the time that the debate had "aired the issues," but a later source quoted him as saying he rushed to a meeting afterwards with Nixon, and was astounded to see the difference between the poised and confident Nixon and the haggard, harried man he had seen on the television screen.

All members of the broadcasting community expressed delight. Frank Stanton, for CBS, called it a "basic breakthrough for broadcasting." Robert Sarnoff for NBC predicted the debates would become a "permanent feature of campaigns." John Daly for ABC noted the "complete subordination of everything to the principals," and Robert F. Hurleigh for the Mutual Broadcasting System radio network concluded that the handling of the debate showed that "Broadcasting fully recognizes its responsibilities as a mass communications public service to all our people."

The printed press was more reserved. The *New York Herald Tribune* thought the style was corny, but it left the electorate better prepared. The *New York Times* viewed it as two capable young efficiency experts preparing to oil up the same machine. The *Miami Herald* (independent) called it a "decorous draw," while the *Atlanta Journal* pointed to the "sincerity, honesty, good taste and ability displayed by both men." The *Seattle Times* (independent) called for "more verbal punches, and less of an eye on the stopwatch." The *Wall Street Journal* gave the edge to Kennedy; it noted that Nixon was nervous, hesitant, and tired; and it judged the questions as "incredibly bad." The candidates, if left to themselves, would have gotten themselves quickly to the hard and important questions.

The immediate impact on the party organizations was prompt and decisive. For the first time, a broad surge of confidence swept throughout the Democratic organization. Their man did not look hopelessly outclassed; he might overcome the apparently insuperable odds of Nixon's apparent stature and Eisenhower's blessing; and Nixon looked as if he might do a good bit to defeat himself. The Republicans were incredulous; some were stunned. What had happened to their champion? Why was he so apprehensive and so unsure of himself?

The Second Debate

By the time of the second debate, on October 7, the Nixon forces had regrouped themselves and reconsidered their strategy of an above-the-fray approach for Nixon; their candidate had decided to argue much more vigorously. Kennedy obviously had no reason to depart from his apparently successful tactics of two weeks before. In front of a somewhat smaller audience, then, a Nixon who no longer looked thin or emaciated put his attacking opponent on the defense by reading him a lesson on international proprieties in dealing with such issues as the Cuban problem, and by tempting Kennedy onto the dangerous ground of appearing to sell his country short. The candidates drew a sharp issue on the proper treatment of the U-2 incident, with Kennedy asserting forthrightly that it would have been far better to regret to Mr. Khrushchev than to lie to him, if thereby the Summit Conference could have been saved.

There was still a good deal of agreement on the seriousness of the cold war and on measures necessary to pursue it. In the discussion, Nixon took every opportunity to enhance his stature as the man better able to stand up to the Communists. Edward Morgan injected into the discussion the issue of proper treatment of the Quemoy-Matsu issue; this stayed as a key point of disagreement until the end of the campaign. Nixon read his man a lesson on the principles of international action to foil the Communists and uphold the peace; Kennedy responded with a detailed argument on the "facts" involved, showing intimate familiarity with the political and military testimony of high administration officials. As a result, both scored; Nixon by his palpable determination to hold the line for the free world and to keep the Communists confused and at bay; Kennedy by his palpable demonstration of familiarity with the niceties of issues that must have bewildered an audience previously uninstructed on details, but which nevertheless spoke loudly though implicitly of experience in matters of state.

The questions, by and large, were better on the second debate, but one question came close to the end that posed special difficulties for Nixon. Why did he take off the party label when seeking votes as President? Unwilling to refer to his party as a minority party, Nixon made a lame answer, and Kennedy in rebuttal time dwelt on the strength of his party.

Again partisans for both sides claimed victory, while neither of the candidates did. Kennedy won a victory for his desires in staging of the show, insisting that the temperature be brought up from the cool 65° asked for by Mr. Nixon, and insisting on equality of lighting treatment for both lecterns. The broadcasting newsmen were joined as interlocutors by two representatives of newspapers and of magazines, chosen by lot from those who had been traveling with the candidates. The industry made much of the fact that the questions and answers were unrehearsed. The net of the event was, in the judgment of James Reston, a victory for the Vice President in an "informative show."[7]

[7] *New York Times,* Oct. 8, 1960.

The Third Debate

On the occasion of the third debate, on October 13, the rhetorical temperatures rose as the differences narrowed and sharpened. The questions drove immediately at international issues: Berlin, Quemoy, the role of military strength, and U-2, although there were questions on the role of labor unions and on tax depletion allowances. Humor entered the debates for the first time, as Kennedy suggested that only Mrs. Truman might have some influence on the former President's public profanity. This tempted Nixon to answer unwisely on the Republican celebration of new respect for the Presidency, forgetting that he was the man at issue, not Eisenhower. Both candidates distinguished themselves by the promptness and vigor with which they threw discussion of the religious issue out of the campaign debates. As the debate closed, Kennedy returned to the prestige issue by quoting administration testimony (from George Allen, Director of the United States Information Agency) that American prestige was suffering abroad. Nixon took the extreme position that our prestige was never higher. But he had the last word, warning his hearers not to take Kennedy's advice on how to deal with Quemoy-Matsu.

Both parties took heart. Chicago's Democratic Mayor Daley called the debates the "greatest thing that ever happened," and predicted they would be "compulsory" in the future.

The industry demonstrated its flexibility by presenting the antagonists on a split screen, with Nixon speaking from Los Angeles and Kennedy from New York, thus underlining the technical capability for confrontation without requiring the competitors to be in the same room or the same town. The audience was probably the smallest for the four debates—some 61,000,000, according to one survey.

The Fourth Debate

The fourth debate, on October 21, returned to the format of the first, with broadcaster newsmen asking the questions, and a CBS monitor. Nixon devoted his opening statement to his qualifications to meet the fundamental question of the debate and of the campaign—how to keep the peace. He found the answer in his known record of anti-communism, and the fact that he knew Mr. Khrushchev and had dealt with him personally. Kennedy devoted his opening statement first to counterpropaganda ("let me try to correct the record on Quemoy and Matsu") and then to his position on the "real issue": Are we moving to peace and security? Our relative strength is decreasing, and the people of the world don't identify with us closely enough.

The newsmen's questions kept the debate almost wholly on issues of foreign affairs, and it was not until the closing statements that the candidates each tried for a general balance that obviously had to include their stands on some important domestic issues. The debate as a whole probably did less than others to enlighten its audience—second most numerous for the four at some 70,000,000—on the candidate positions on issues. But it did as much as any to show the contenders in full tilt at one another, and to permit comparisons of personality and debating effectiveness. In general, Nixon held the small margin of debating superiority that he had gained in the second and third debates, but at one point Kennedy was able to show to marked advantage. Midway in the proceedings a newsman asked Nixon whether Quemoy-Matsu should remain as a campaign issue. This gave Nixon an opening he desired, to say that he would talk about the issue as long as his opponent persisted in his errors on it, and tempted Nixon into a debater's tailspin as he tried to instruct his opponent and the audience on what his opponent must do to "win" the debate. As Nixon got more and more involved and heated as he tried to tell Kennedy what he had to say if he were to be "consistent" on the issue, the television camera (probably not by accident) caught Kennedy smiling broadly at his opponent's tactics. This was one of the few instances in which either candidate ever permitted himself to look as if he were taking the debates and himself with anything less than deadly seriousness. For Democratic partisans certainly, and for many of the uncommitted if not of the opposition, the gesture attested Kennedy's poise and confidence as nothing in the debates had done before.

Both candidates ended with force and dignity, as Kennedy, lawyerlike, adjured his audience that "it is incumbent upon us," defenders of the freedom and leadership of the United States, to get America moving again. And Nixon denied the allegation with dignity: America is not standing still. And moving past the momentary humor of a double meaning in asserting—twice—that America cannot stand pat, he committed his cause and his country to the tide of history, predicting that the political leadership of the country would be great as the country was great, in a contest with atheistic communism.

Net Effects and Closing Action

To this point, one might say that Kennedy had scored a win in only one of the debates, the first, but that he had closed the distance between himself and his rival. For whatever it is worth, there is the testimony of the Republican refusal to accept a fifth debate except on terms that would have been disastrous for Kennedy, to indicate that they had had enough. Other forms of campaigning were worth more to them. And they took whatever political losses were involved in their refusal to accept a fifth debate immediately before the election, rather than risk a sharp Kennedy upsurge at a critical point. The Democrats sensed the Republican weakness, and played their unwillingness to accept another round of the battle for all that it was worth.

A thorough assessment of the immediate and subsequent impact of the debates on the voting must await panel studies in depth. But the immediate surveying indicated clearly that Kennedy gained both on the counts of preference as to who would win and the prediction on the victory.[8] Surveys also showed that those who heard the debates on radio were much more favorably impressed by Nixon, and their responses did not agree with that

[8] See Sindlinger survey reported in *Broadcasting,* Nov. 7, 1960, Vol. 59, No. 19, pp. 27-29. The chart reflecting answers given on the day after each debate as to prediction shows that Nixon did not lose, but Kennedy gained, *after the first debate.* As to preference, the chart shows a slightly declining trend line for Nixon, and a more sharply inclining trend line for Kennedy.

of the general sample (hopefully including a proper proportion of televiewers) on either preference or prediction. One other survey finding is of interest: public acceptance of the debates went sharply up, and the proportion of those thinking the debates were a bad idea, went sharply down. Those with no preference or opinion declined only slightly and remained fairly high (about 17 per cent) after all four.[9]

The debates put other campaign speeches in the shade. On being asked what other Republican appearances were of first moment, the Republican officials queried agreed that Nixon's acceptance speech at the convention was probably the most prominent and telling. Democrats thought the television coverage of Kennedy answering the questions of clergymen on his views of religion and the Presidency was probably the most useful. During the later stages of the campaign, both candidates made numerous appearances, and some of these may have been of some special influence. Some of the accompaniments of the speeches may have been as important as the speeches themselves. Despite the general view of political analysts that Kennedy was losing ground in the final stages of the campaign, it seems plausible that the effect of crowd acceptance of his visits and speeches was favorable—surely to energize party machines, if not to swing voter sentiment in the large. The television shots in Chicago, for example, showing Kennedy going to Soldiers' Field for a late rally speech that came close to being a rabble rouser, were in sharp contrast to the kind of popular apathy that dogged Stevenson through so much of his 1956 campaign. Nixon, in contrast, was being far less boisterously welcomed.

As Nixon moved toward the end of his effort, he strove more and more toward the full image of the new Nixon, the heir of the dignity as well as the power and acceptance of the Eisenhower regime. Only his last-day telethon, in which he took on a variety of questions screened through a panel of professors and specialists, smacked of the gimmickry so commonly charged to him by his

[9] *Ibid.*

opponents. On his election-eve appearance, the objective of the arrangement was dignity and self-confidence, with charity for all. Kennedy, in contrast, opened himself up to a full range of productions by his television advisers. The election-eve program for the Democrats plumbed the capabilities of the medium of television for associating the candidate with former greats of his party —not least of whom was Franklin Roosevelt—and with traditional citadels of American freedom. Both sides provided a full panoply of family and home, and devotion to the American way.

The Election Coverage

As the electorate went to the polls, the media were quiet, for a time. But only until time to start reporting the earliest poll results, and to let the modern miracles of electronic prediction start the media off to their estimates of who would win and to provide copy for experts of all sorts to comment on the results as they came in from across the country. Again, the broadcasters and the news media concentrated on being correct prophets first. They interspersed reporting with comment and prediction, as one of the greatest television audiences of all time followed, with unknown degrees of watchfulness, the unfolding of the count. During that evening, both candidates were wiser, more restrained than their supporters. Kennedy refused to claim victory prematurely; Nixon refused to concede. The closeness of the ultimate count testified to the wisdom of both. The electronic media and the reporters hung around hopefully, long after the newspapers had made their judgments, elected their candidate, and gone to the streets with their early editions. Nixon was never more dignified and courageous than in his hour of defeat; the contrast between his demeanor and that of his fellow-partisans at the election-eve events did him great credit. Kennedy stayed behind doors until the time was to come for him to accept a message of concession or a clear indication of victory. That was not to come on election night.

Did the Media Elect Kennedy?

Again in a speculative mood, for the definitive data and analysis are yet to come in, one may ask what role the media had in shaping the Kennedy victory. First, as to television, one can point out that the testimony of party people, if not of the general public, is clear on the point that television made the difference for Kennedy. There is Kennedy's own testimony that he did not think he could have won without it; his campaign manager brother and his media director J. Leonard Reinsch were unequivocal on the point.[10] Most Republican testimony was equally unanimous, although Nixon himself was silent on the point.

As to press performance, the differences in press attention and prominence in 1960 as against 1956 and earlier were compatible with a pro-Kennedy effect, if they were not wholly compatible with the opinion credited to Nixon that the favoritism of the working journalists gave the victory to Kennedy. Press endorsements for Nixon were about as preponderant if not as ringing as earlier proportions of editorial sanction given to Republican candidates in former years.

As to the relative performance of the candidates in dealing with the press, a slight edge must be given to Kennedy. Nixon turned in his usually smooth and thoughtful performance—press releases issued promptly, press arrangements as convenient and adequate as possible, and other technical matters well handled. But Nixon's campaign technique called for "the speech"—a central statement of position that did not vary much from place to place or town to town. For those members of the working press who had to hear it constantly, even protean form did not prevent boredom. And as

[10] Interviewed by *Broadcasting* magazine, Reinsch said: "The first debate was the big one. First, we broke down the Republican charge that Sen. Kennedy was immature. Second, we solidified Democrats who had wondered if Sen. Kennedy was the right choice to defeat the Vice President. That debate convinced campaign workers, governors and others that we had a strong, fighting candidate. It scared and shocked Republicans." *Broadcasting,* Nov. 14, 1960, p. 32.

the campaign neared its end, the candidate separated himself more and more from the journalists, as he had done in previous trips. Kennedy, by contrast, was less tidy but more newsworthy. He too had his core of doctrine, but he took special pains to adjust it to the personalities or the particular conditions of each occasion. His press releases did not always reflect the main emphasis of what he said, but he used press conferences to ratify the differences. And he grew in the esteem of those with whom he traveled. They saw him develop under the stress of the campaign and revised earlier opinions of his lack of qualifications. They responded to his un-deviating attention to his tasks, and to his responsiveness to all sorts of people—and to their increasing acceptance of him. It is believable, then, that informal polls taken among journalists who traveled with both candidates at various points in the campaign showed that the preference of the working journalist was for Ken-nedy. Whatever might be done by editors or managers later on to filed copy, the benevolence of these key communicators was a clear advantage to Kennedy.

What, in sum, can we say of the role and influence of the mass media in 1960? Their effect on the nominations was relatively small—the Nixon choice was a foregone matter, won in the party organizations long before and impervious to whatever attacks Rockefeller or Goldwater might bring up in the last moments. Kennedy was helped more, probably most, by his performance in West Virginia. But his image was to be fashioned more by the performance at the conventions and later than by anything that had gone before. The reasons for our judgment that the effect of television on the election was critical and that of the press benev-olent to Kennedy have already been made clear. Analysis of the places where Kennedy got his biggest critical votes reveals the big cities—prime television territory. Yet the Scottish verdict of "not proven" must prevail, for in 1960 television carried the campaign to the whole country, and it is yet to be demonstrated whether it was in fact critical in rolling up the big city majorities, or whether it was even an important catalyst in getting the most out of or-ganizational efforts, registration drives, labor union activities, and other elements that worked on balance in Kennedy's favor.

Problems of the Future

What of the future? What will, or should, happen to the device of presidential campaign debates? What issues of policy arise out of the treatment of politics by mass media, and vice versa, during 1960?

Should the Debates Continue?

As for the future of the debates, attitudes are easier to measure and to predict than events. The most telling attitude so far on the record is that of the President himself. He has said that if he is the candidate in 1964, he will debate. Yet the immediate partisan interest of an incumbent is usually judged to work against debates. Why should a President confer such an advantage on an opponent, in particular, a dangerous one? Even so doughty a campaigner as Franklin Roosevelt would not do so, preferring to accept a slight embarrassment rather than to risk a major overturn, if not for the instant election, possibly for a later one.

The Republican attitude in 1964 will presumably be determined by their answer to the question: Could we win with it, or at least gain for the future? The assessment of this issue is by no means a foregone conclusion. Any challenger accepts debate with the President at a considerable strategic disadvantage. The President and the Presidency command a sort of respect that makes attack difficult; whenever the issues go to vital aspects of foreign policy or military posture, the challenging candidate must temper his charges. Moreover, the President can tap resources of intelligence information going beyond those commonly made available to challengers and is often in a position to speak from secret information bearing on high policy. Yet any serious and competent challenger is already in the position of questioning the President and his party on issues of deep-reaching import to the country. A clever one could use such debates to force re-thinking of public policy on the basis of information that is commonly shared by the public at large—and to which the President himself would be compelled to contribute in a genuine debating situation.

Most of the political commentators have favored the debates, even though some have felt that the format and execution could be markedly improved. The electronic media are unequivocally for a continuation, especially if arrangements for debates in the future can be coupled with a relaxation of the legal trammels on political broadcasting arising from Section 315 of the Federal Communications Act.

The public policy question whether there should be debates turns on the probable functions of such discussions and their values. If the debates of the future feature the personal characteristics of the candidates to the same extent as did those of 1960, they may not be of utmost moment. A President must be more than a persuader; he must be an executive, a chief of state, a party leader. Skill in debating does not necessarily argue administrative competence, although it can do much to demonstrate what sort of character a candidate would bring to the forensic and chief of state functions of the Presidency. Possibly more important, such debates might tell much about a candidate's ability to generate consensus in the face of criticism.

But even the foregoing questions cannot be effectively answered in the absence of some assumptions about the format of these confrontations. Are they in effect debates or glorified quiz shows? Is it possible to develop a subject in depth when limited to an initial statement of eight minutes and later responses of three minutes or less? Is it necessary to have unrehearsed questions and to depend on the usual preference of the newsman to catch his man in a contradiction or a cover-up than to illuminate fundamental issues facing the country in an election? Will a tradition of debates in future campaigns have serious effects on the choice of candidates, overstressing forensic talents?

Even if these questions—and their implications—cannot be fully answered, it still can be judged that the "debates" were useful in 1960, and that they or some equivalent could perform a weighty and desirable function in the nominations and elections of the future. For if these events did nothing else than bring the major candidates face to face and force them to talk on the same question under conditions in which one could not distort the position of the other without risking an immediate and authoritative reply, they have added immensely to the realism of the campaign process. They may not be adequate evidence of qualifications for all aspects of the Presidency, but they offer important information on aspects of personality that affect most of them. And possibly most important, the debates can assemble an audience of partisans of both major parties and thus overcome the otherwise almost inescapable tendency of partisans to give attention only to their own candidate. The confrontation can take place in full view of the electorate, and electronic campaigning can go beyond the reinforcement and rallying of those who already know their preferences.

The debates could contribute to the objectives of a shorter campaign—an objective that seems at the moment to be nearly universally sought by many critics, if not by party officials. Spread out, the debates would be equally compatible with a longer campaign schedule. If there are ten major issues in a campaign, for example, why cannot there be ten debates, one a week, to deal in some agreed-on order with each of them?

Possible improvements are easy to suggest and come from many quarters. One would be to have genuine debate on predetermined issues—at least on one of the occasions of confrontation, at which each candidate would have ample time to state his position, rebut and counter, and sum up. An hour and a half is not too long for genuine debate or too great a charge on television's prime time, or too great a strain on an audience's attentiveness. Another suggestion would be to have a varying series of questioners, drawing on panels made up not just of newsmen, but of educators, businessmen, labor leaders, farmers, lawyers, men who have achieved eminence and a sense of objectivity and relevance in the service of one of the country's great interest groups, and of the country itself. Such a battery of questioners might help assure that major emphasis would be placed on important issues. Another would be to have a final session between the two contestants on election eve, as a sort of summit confrontation in which each candidate, in the presence of the other, can make his final summation on whatever issue or issues of the campaign he feels are of utmost relevance. The important thing to aim at is a confrontation in which each candidate has the opportunity to discipline the other in a discussion of a topic of relevance to the election, and to the country's concerns.

Public Policy and the Media

Preconditions to such electioneering in the future are more courage among broadcasters and more good sense on the part of the FCC, or a definite relaxation of Section 315 of the Communications Act. Admittedly the broadcasters were on good behavior during 1960 and admittedly their behavior was exemplary. But there is room for improvement, and not only on the part of the broadcasters. Both parties have progress to make in the design and execution of political conventions. The media have yet to move toward the incisive, summarized reporting that is now well within their technical capabilities and their understanding of the nature of political events. In the case of the campaigns, again there is room for improvement, although they do not necessarily have to become shorter and more encapsulated. The candidates and parties are free today to make campaigning easier on themselves— if they want to take the competitive risks of being convicted of lack of respect for political groups and places now accessible through modern transportation. In a world in which the increasingly accepted role of the state favors action and creativity rather than restricted efficiency and prudence, the qualities of physical and mental endurance and a predisposition to carry the political fight to its widest regional ramifications are not irrelevant to rational electoral choice.

The dangers are: first, the ever-present risk of inequities in giving access to a vital medium; and second, the subtle threat to the electoral process itself that could arise from greater success not only in reporting the earliest election results, but also in predicting their significance for the eventual national outcome. Such predictions might improperly influence electoral decision in the West. Of the two dangers, the former is the more enduring and much more serious. But as things stand now, the broadcasting industry operates within a framework of interests that cause it to de-emphasize controversy and to maintain some balance between the political demands of the two major parties—in turn historically and traditionally geared to the seeking of compromise rather than to the searching out of the political fringes.

This conservative and reinforcing tendency clearly does not favor the emergence of third parties, but it does not rule them out either. The broadcasters, and even more the newspapermen, are concerned with news—including news of changes in political preference and structure. New candidates and new beliefs can be, and are being, brought to public attention. Their political potency is not simply determined by the preferences of those who rule the press. Much more depends on the appeal and appropriateness of proposed innovations to the political temper of important groups within the electorate. If these are strong, and the response palpable, the press cannot ignore them.

Meanwhile, the media are well articulated to the party system we have. Both major parties and their candidates were well served in 1960. The electorate was given the best information about the relative capabilities of the candidates that it had available in any election since the introduction of universal suffrage.

5

Financing the Parties and Campaigns

HERBERT E. ALEXANDER[1]

MANY YEARS AGO a British campaign agent adopted a principle that appears to have guided American politicians responsible for financing the parties and candidates in 1960. It went: Win the election; never mind the expense; a defeat is the most expensive of all contests.

Acting on this principle, the various committees operating in politics at the national level spent about $25 million in 1960, as shown in Table 5.1. This figure compares with $17.2 million spent in 1956,[2] and represents a 46 per cent increase. Major party na-

---

[1] Director, Citizens' Research Foundation.

Portions of the data in the present chapter were collected by *Congressional Quarterly, Inc.,* under a cooperative arrangement with the Citizens' Research Foundation and are used here with the permission of both organizations. The present study will be published by the Citizens' Research Foundation in an expanded and revised form, in which additional supporting details and documentation will be provided. The pamphlet will be entitled "Financing the 1960 Election."

There was no major congressional investigation of campaign funds in 1960, as there had been in 1956, hence the reliance of the present study on private investigations. These in turn were very largely limited to national-level sources of information, particularly the reports that are required to be filed with the Clerk of the House of Representatives. Committees and candidates that make expenditures only in a single state are not required to make such reports.

Attempts were made to verify findings through numerous interviews with finance managers and others. The writer wishes to express his appreciation to the many persons—too many to acknowledge individually—who provided information and explanations.

[2] This figure is derived from *1956 General Election Campaigns,* Report to the Senate Committee on Rules and Administration, 85 Cong. 1 sess. (1957), Exhibit 4, p. 41. (Cited hereafter as *Gore Report.*) The figure represents total

TABLE 5.1. *Summary of Political Spending at the National Level, 1960*

(In thousands of dollars)

Committees[a]	Gross Reported Disbursements[b]	Known Debt	Total Campaign Costs	Transfers to Candidates and Committees[c]	Direct Expenditures[d]
17 Republican[e].....	$10,600	$ 700	$11,300	$1,172	$10,128
13 Democratic[f].....	6,767	3,820	10,587	790	9,797
21 Labor..........	2,277	—	2,277	1,434	843
19 Miscellaneous...	850	—	850	144	706
Total..........	$20,494	$4,520	$25,014	$3,540	$21,474

[a] The number of national-level committees increased from 49 in 1956 to 70 in 1960, but the same criteria were used in identifying them. See *1956 General Election Campaigns*, Report to the Senate Committee on Rules and Administration, 85 Cong. 1 Sess. (1957), Exhibit 4, p. 41.

[b] Data derived from reports filed with the Clerk of the United States House of Representatives.

[c] Data in this column may be incomplete due to difficulties in recapitulating data found in the House reports. The same level of transfers at $3.5 million was found in 1960 and 1956, despite general increases in income and outgo in 1960. This may indicate greater stability in transfer patterns, or possibly because of ambiguities in available data, all transfers may not have been counted.

[d] Details on all categories of expenditures were not obtained from the campaign fund reports. Hence direct expenditures were determined by subtracting from total campaign costs all transfers of funds out. If more transfers of funds were made than available data indicate, then direct expenditure totals would decrease. Though the totals in this column may be subject to error, enough evidence is available to indicate that totals represent fair approximations.

[e] For further information, see Table 5.3.

[f] For further information, see Table 5.2.

tional campaign costs in 1960, disregarding spending by labor and miscellaneous committees, were about $21.9 million. This is about 16 cents per voter per party for the 68,832,818 votes cast in the presidential election, a figure 4 cents less than various legislative proposals would have permitted as an expenditure ceiling.

These figures omit state and local expenses on behalf of the national tickets. Campaign costs for congressional candidates are also omitted, except as they benefited by transfers from national level committees. The costs of nominating campaigns in preparation for the presidential and congressional races are omitted, along

Republican, Democratic, labor, and miscellaneous committee disbursements from January 1 to November 30, 1956, plus unpaid bills as of November 30, 1956. Disbursements in December 1956 are not known, hence the 1956 total lacks comparability to this extent with the 1960 figure, which covers the entire twelve months.

with all of the campaign costs for state, county, municipal, and other offices. Finally, there is no cost equivalent inclusion for the free broadcast time provided to the presidential and vice-presidential candidates.

Total political costs at all levels for 1952 and 1956 were estimated respectively at $140 million and $155 million.[3] A comparable figure for 1960 would probably approximate $175 million, bearing in mind such factors as the following: the increase in the national level totals; the large amounts spent on scurrilous literature and the religious issue, and on efforts to overcome their impact; the greater use and cost of private public opinion polls; special efforts in many states to gain control of state legislatures, thereby to control decennial reapportionment; increased travel costs, especially in use of jet aircraft; the general price rise of 8 per cent since 1956.

Offsetting sources of possible reductions in total expenditures are not easily found. There was a considerable increase in the total amount of broadcasting time made available to the parties without charge by the radio and television networks, and this brought a small reduction in expenditures at the national level. But the total expenditures for political broadcasting at all levels combined increased from 1956 to 1960 by about 50 per cent, as will be shown later.

In 1952 and 1956, Republican expenditures considerably exceeded those by the Democrats and labor combined.[4] In 1960, the Republican party had no advantage over combined Democratic and labor spending at the national level. The Republican figure, from Table 5.1, is $10.1 million, while the combined Democratic and labor figure for direct expenditures is $10.6 million, with most labor money going for the support of Democratic candidates.

The main factor in closing the Republican-Democratic gap was the willingness of the Democrats to go into debt to the extent of

---

[3] Alexander Heard, *The Costs of Democracy* (University of North Carolina Press, 1960), pp. 7-8.
[4] *Ibid.*, pp. 19-20.

$3.8 million—probably the largest national party campaign deficit in American history. The net Republican deficit, as shown in Table 5.1, was $700,000. Democrats claim that their 1960 deficit occurred because certain obligations were assumed at the national level whereas in other years such costs had been paid at state and local levels, but no evidence is available to show actual reductions in Democratic expenditures at lower party levels. Whatever the case, spending by both parties increased dramatically in 1960.

The Preconvention Campaigns

There is no federal requirement that the expenses of nominating campaigns be disclosed, and not all states require disclosure of local expenses in presidential nominating campaigns. After Senator John F. Kennedy received the Democratic presidential nomination, he voluntarily permitted a reporter to go through his financial records, something no other candidate did at the time. The resulting article set forth in some detail basic financial data for the Kennedy prenomination campaign.[5] For the present study, some data have been obtained from responsible participants for the campaigns of all other major Democratic candidates. Unfortunately, Vice President Richard M. Nixon's prenomination expenses could not be ascertained.

The Democrats

A strategy conference held in 1957 by an unnamed politician is said to have produced a presidential nomination budget of $2.6 million, of which something over a million was scheduled for expenditure in 1960. Amounts on the order of $2.5 million were spent in both the Eisenhower and Taft campaigns of 1952.[6] By this

[5] Edward F. Woods, "How Much Did Kennedy Spend on His Campaign?" *St. Louis Post-Dispatch,* Aug. 7, 1960.
[6] Paul T. David, Ralph N. Goldman, and Richard C. Bain, *The Politics of National Party Conventions* (The Brookings Institution, 1960), pp. 286-87.

standard, the admitted expenditures of the Kennedy campaign are relatively modest. Known Kennedy campaign expenditures for 1959 and 1960 through the convention, have been reported as totaling $912,500, though, as will be seen, this figure does not include all state and local spending on his behalf.[7]

The national Kennedy prenomination campaign received $543,939 from five state Kennedy-for-President committees; in addition, $90,000 came from members of the Senator's family, and $60,000 from the Senator himself. These contributions aggregated $693,939, leaving a stated deficit of over $217,000, which the postconvention National Citizens for Kennedy-Johnson assumed.

Members of the Kennedy family also formed a Ken-Air Corporation to buy a $385,000 airplane, which was leased to the Senator at the rate of $1.75 a mile. Additional family contributions that cannot be measured in dollars include the services of each member, working without salary and paying his or her own expenses. Of course, Senator Lyndon B. Johnson also campaigned in a privately owned airplane, and the smaller family of Senator Stuart Symington campaigned for several months under conditions similar to the Kennedys. No one can object to family help; someone has asked what family would fail to help. But the matter of wealth in 1960 was highlighted by the size and cohesiveness of the Kennedy family, and by the striking contrasts between the personal resources of Senators Kennedy and Hubert H. Humphrey, and later between Senator Kennedy and Vice President Nixon.

The Kennedy family assiduously avoided any financial arrangement that would have embarrassed the Senator, and this tended to limit excessive spending during the nominating campaign. During the election campaign, the gifts of each member of the family were restricted under federal law, although there was no limitation on spending by the candidate himself, nor was he required to report

[7] Unless otherwise stated, all Kennedy sums are taken from the Woods article. Woods notes that much of Kennedy's 1959 travel was in response to invitations, and that hosts paid the expenses. Stewart Alsop has written that a "Kennedy insider" estimated preconvention expenses at $1,150,000. "Kennedy's Magic Formula," *Saturday Evening Post,* Aug. 13, 1960, p. 60.

his spending. No Kennedy family contributions to national-level committees have been found for the postconvention period.[8]

Kennedy nomination campaign expenditures included $176,500 for maintaining national headquarters, $470,000 spent in the primaries, and $37,500 spent at the Los Angeles convention. The remaining expenditures of $228,500, which approximate the stated deficit of $217,000, have not been publicly accounted for. If the 110,000 miles logged in the family airplane are charged at the $1.75 rate, however, most of the discrepancy is explained. The Kennedy campaigns in state primaries cost about $25,000 in New Hampshire, $100,000 each in Wisconsin and West Virginia, $70,000 in Indiana, $55,000 in Oregon, and the remainder in the other primaries.

Throughout the Kennedy campaign, excessive spending was often charged, but no proof was offered. The West Virginia primary brought on searching inquiries by Democratic opponents, the press, Republicans, and the Department of Justice. Some irregularities were found, but none could be attributed to Kennedy money. The Kennedy reaction was to deny the charges, demand proof, counterattack—and then let the voters decide.

Senator Lyndon B. Johnson's total campaign costs, according to one political associate, were roughly $250,000 for the Texas and Washington, D.C. operations. Several hundred Johnson-for-President clubs operated in these and other areas, and full-page advertisements were run in 18 newspapers in 15 major cities. The rumored deficit following the Los Angeles convention of $100,000 was not assumed by the Citizens for Kennedy-Johnson, as Kennedy's had been.

Senator Stuart Symington's campaign reportedly involved expenditures of around $320,000 for the national effort in 1960, of which $55,000 was contributed by a Century Club for Symington, organized to solicit $100 gifts.[9] In addition, a Midwest Committee

[8] However, Mrs. Hugh D. Auchincloss, the President's mother-in-law, contributed $500 to the Citizens for Kennedy-Johnson.

[9] Ralph G. Martin and Ed Plaut, *Front Runner, Dark Horse* (Doubleday, 1960), p. 470.

for Symington, operating out of Kansas City, spent $30,000. Thus, $350,000 was spent, not including out-of-pocket expenses of the Symington family.

Senator Hubert H. Humphrey's campaign books showed total expenditures of $251,500. Major expenditures were $116,500 in Wisconsin, $23,000 in West Virginia, $9,500 in Oregon, and $102,500 for national headquarters. Senator Humphrey also ran in the District of Columbia, where about $15,000 was spent by local supporters, and in South Dakota, where there was no contest and only local funds were spent.

The "on-again, off-again" campaign on behalf of Adlai Stevenson in 1960 cost about $250,000. A National Draft Stevenson Committee spent about $126,000, mainly in New York, Washington, and Los Angeles. A separate "grass-roots" group in New York raised about $65,000 and another in Washington over $11,000. Similar local funds in Chicago totaled $14,000; in Philadelphia, $8,000; and in St. Louis, probably over $10,000. In addition, about $15,000 was spent by James Doyle, a campaign leader who operated with separate funds, but as an integral part of the national campaign.

Campaigns for other candidates for the Democratic nomination cost over $50,000 in the case of Senator Wayne Morse and at least $25,000 to $50,000 in the case of Governor Robert Meyner. Funds in unknown amounts were spent at the convention on behalf of the candidacies of Senators George Smathers and Frank Lausche and Governor Luther Hodges. A Faubus for President committee, located at Hollywood, California, reported expenditures of $4,500.

The visible and nonoverlapping items in the previous estimates of expenditures add to approximately $2.1 million for the Democratic nominating campaigns in 1960, but this figure does not include amounts spent on behalf of some candidates by state and local groups.

The Republicans

Vice President Richard M. Nixon had no announced opposition and did not openly campaign, but his name or slates supporting him were entered in ten primaries—to stimulate interest, to provide a legal basis for electing committed delegates, and hopefully to attract turnouts that could be compared favorably with Kennedy's. Only fragmentary evidence is available concerning expenditures on behalf of the Nixon candidacy, but according to one report, Nixon supporters spent over $23,000 in the New Hampshire primary.[10] In Oregon, about $48,000 was spent, according to reports filed with the state government. The Indiana primary was probably Nixon's costliest, coming at a time and in circumstances requiring a good showing. Kennedy admitted spending only $70,000 in Indiana, but charged that Nixon supporters had spent at least $150,000.[11] Nixon forces admitted only a fraction of this amount, later estimated at $70,000.[12] The three figures for New Hampshire, Oregon, and Indiana suggest expenditures averaging $35,000 per primary, or a total of perhaps $350,000 for the ten primaries in which Nixon ran. There were undoubtedly expenditures in other states, as well as the obvious costs involved in maintaining a substantial national headquarters and an enlarged staff, culminating in outlays at the Chicago convention; $500,000 would seem a low estimate for the total costs of the Nixon campaign. Much of the money was raised in a centralized national effort under J. Clifford Folger, who became chairman of the Republican national finance committee during the election campaign.

Governor Nelson Rockefeller of New York was not an announced candidate, but engaged in much political activity in both 1959 and 1960, maintaining a large personal staff quartered in a privately owned building. His may have been the most expensive case of "noncandidacy" on record. Little is known about the movement to nominate Senator Barry Goldwater, but it obviously proceeded on a scale involving substantial expenditures by the Senator's supporters. It is impossible to estimate total expenditures on behalf of candidacies—actual or potential—for the Republican nomination, but they were high considering the near-unanimous outcome.

[10] *New York Herald Tribune,* March 20, 1960.
[11] *Washington Post and Times Herald,* May 12, 1960.
[12] *Newsweek,* May 16, 1960, p. 32.

Campaign Finances and Strategy

Financial urgencies are the product of campaign strategy, but also have their own effects, best illustrated in 1960 on the Democratic side. Senator Kennedy had been a strong prospective contender since 1956, but to win the nomination, he needed all possible evidences of popular and party support, including large turnouts and a string of victories in the primaries. It was obvious that a successful Kennedy campaign would be expensive, but costs were held down by three factors: (1) the unusual press coverage and free publicity that Kennedy received because of his religion, his wealth, and his youth; (2) the fact that Senator Humphrey was his only major opposition in the primaries; and (3) the tactical successes in avoiding intensive campaigns in primary states as expensive as Ohio or California.

The threats to enter Ohio and California contained elements of calculated risk; if Kennedy had been required to enter both, it probably would have added a million dollars to his prenomination costs.

As the frontrunner, Kennedy had to anticipate and resist the combined efforts of any "stop-Kennedy" movement that might develop—and this could not be done cheaply. Moreover, much Kennedy spending, during both the prenomination and the postnomination periods, was directed to neutralizing the religious issue or turning it to his advantage. Poorer candidates might not have been able to raise the funds to meet the issue as well; on the other hand, had Senator Kennedy not had to face a religious issue, the impact of his wealth undoubtedly could have been greater. If religion had not been an issue, as much might have been spent, but for other purposes.

In the final stages at the Democratic national convention, Kennedy's wealth gave him no special advantage against Johnson and Symington, who also had all the political resources money could buy. The question of Kennedy's wealth thus reverts to whether he could have won the primaries as well without it. Given his aggressive political approach, the answer must be "yes."

Financing the Conventions

Disclosure is not required with regard to the financing of national party conventions, but the available data indicate that those of 1960 were the costliest ever. The Democratic party spent $749,070 in holding its 1960 convention at Los Angeles—more than double the $318,000 spent at Chicago in 1956—with a convention deficit of $155,000 remaining as late as March 1, 1961. The Republican party collected $642,800 for its 1960 convention at Chicago and spent all of it. Adaptation of the conventions to television requirements added greatly to the expense to the parties, particularly since the conventions were held in different cities, and there was thus no sharing of costs.

The cities of Los Angeles and Chicago each pledged to provide $400,000 for the respective conventions, while also providing fringe benefits that held down costs and facilitated convention operations. Contributions were raised by the respective host city committees, mainly through gifts from businesses that expected to benefit from the presence of the convention. Such contributions are regarded as business-related expenditures, and are therefore tax-deductible.

The Democratic Convention Program for 1960 carried a substantial amount of paid advertising and grossed $240,000, for a net return of $181,500 to the Democratic Arrangements Committee after printing, distribution, and other costs.

The Democrats found their first western convention much more costly than anticipated. Everything about Los Angeles seemed expensive, but doubling the size of the convention by using the half-vote rule would have added to costs anywhere. Travel expenses were high for most delegates; some state delegations were forced to raise funds to cover costs for transportation and subsistence for impecunious delegates and staff assistants.

The General Election Campaigns

A presidential campaign constitutes a vast and arresting spectacle. It also suffers from a special malady, brought on by the immensity of the constituency and the high stakes. In effect, a multimillion dollar operation is run by an amazing assemblage of amateurs and professionals, family and friends, specialists, job seekers, old hands and new faces, party bureaucrats, statesmen, and hangers-on. In 1960, the Democratic campaign was operated from at least seven major staff centers in Washington, not counting the senatorial offices of Kennedy and Johnson or the congressional campaign committees on Capitol Hill. The Republicans managed with fewer but larger offices. The Democratic campaign staff in Washington rose from 80 to 370, while the Republican permanent force of about 100 grew to more than 400 paid and volunteer workers.

The finances of various national committees affiliated with the parties are outlined in Tables 5.2 and 5.3. The principal Democratic organizations in the presidential campaign were the Democratic National Committee (DNC) and the Citizens for Kennedy-Johnson, each of which operated close to the statutory limit of $3 million. The major Republican organizations were the Republican National Committee (RNC), the Republican Congressional Campaign Committee, and the Independent TV Committee, a year-round Republican affiliate that also handles closed circuit television for Republican fund-raising dinners. The National Volunteers for Nixon-Lodge operated independently of the party.

Funds channeled through the various committees were spent for a variety of purposes, some of which are examined in the pages that follow.

Television and Radio Broadcasting

A presidential campaign is essentially a presentation of candidates, parties, and issues, achieved through publicity devices, requiring heavy media expenditures, mainly for television and radio broadcasting. For such purposes, the DNC and the Citizens for Kennedy-Johnson paid at least $2.4 million (including the usual agency commissions) to Guild, Bascom, and Bonfigli, their advertising agency. The Republican party formed a special agency, Campaign Associates, to handle its account in 1960; nine national-level Republican committees made payments to it of at least $2.3 million. Payments to the two agencies amounted to almost 30 per cent of major party direct expenditures at the national level.

Payments to the television and radio networks for presidential and vice-presidential broadcasts were $3 million in 1960, of which the Democratic portion was about $1.1 million and the Republican $1.9. Television charges were almost identical with those of 1956, but radio costs declined somewhat. Increasing amounts of free time made possible a slight reduction in the use and cost of paid time on the television networks, but the fewer paid programs cost more both for production and station charges.

The networks made available much prime viewing time without charge, in view of the statutory changes described in Chapter 4. Some 429 television stations averaged six and a half hours of free time given the presidential and vice-presidential candidates, including the time provided for the debates, as against an average of almost ten hours of paid time per station for these candidates. In 1960, the two major parties received and used approximately equal amounts of free sustaining time; in some instances free time was available that could not be used. The increase in use of free time on three TV and four AM networks from 1956 to 1960 was 131 per cent for the Democrats and 71 per cent for the Republicans; for the minor party candidates, there was a decrease of 85 per cent.[13]

The cost to the networks of the free time provided for the presidential campaign was apparently of the order of $4 million or $5 million, of which the cost of the four Kennedy-Nixon debates was probably over $2 million. NBC has estimated that its "network-produced television programs" would have cost $1.7 million if

[13] These figures are from the Federal Communications Commission's report, *Survey of Political Broadcasting, September 1-November 8, 1960,* Table 10.

TABLE 5.2. *Receipts and Expenditures, Democratic National Campaign Committees, January 1-December 31, 1960*

(In thousands of dollars)

Committee	Gross Reported Receipts	Adjusted Receipts[a]	Gross Reported Disbursements	Total Transfers Out	Direct Expenditures[b]
National...............	$2,992	$2,915	$2,999	$ 75	$2,924
National congressional...	83	83	59	5	54
Congressional campaign..	210	200	210	210	—
Senatorial campaign.....	262	253	250	202	48
Congressional liaison	4	4	4	2	2
Total..............	$3,551	$3,455	$3,522	$494	$3,029
Business and professional men and women for Kennedy-Johnson.....	$ 149	$ 141	$ 140	$ 28	$ 112
Citizens for Kennedy-Johnson..............	2,999	2,903	2,999	244	2,755
Total..............	$3,149	$3,044	$3,139	$272	$2,867
Miscellaneous[c]..........	$ 124	$ 112	$ 105	$ 24	$ 80
Total[d]..............	$6,824	$6,611	$6,766	$790	$5,977

[a] Adjusted for lateral transfers from national-level Democratic, labor, and miscellaneous committee groupings included in the tables.
[b] Direct expenditures were determined by subtracting all transfers of funds from gross disbursements.
[c] Johnson for Vice President Committee; Homebuilders for Kennedy-Johnson; Kennedy Campaign Conference; Kennedy TV Fund Committee; National Committee of Arts, Letters and Sciences; Women for Kennedy. Totals for some of these committees may have been subsumed under those listed in the table.
[d] Minor discrepancies between items and totals are due to rounding.

paid for, while CBS put its costs at $1.4 million on a somewhat less inclusive basis. ABC provided no comparable estimate. For the debates, however, ABC said its total costs would have been about $750,000 if administrative and advertising costs had been included, together with loss of revenue to affiliated stations. CBS estimated $636,700 for the four hours of the debates, for time and production costs only. NBC said the applicable time rates for the

TABLE 5.3. *Receipts and Expenditures, Republican National Campaign Committees, January 1-December 31, 1960*

(In thousands of dollars)

Committee	Gross Reported Receipts	Adjusted Receipts[a]	Gross Reported Disbursements	Total Transfers Out	Direct Expenditures[b]
National..............	$ 2,995	$ 2,992	$ 2,991	$ 57	$2,934
National congressional...	2,413	2,411	2,231	806	1,425
Senatorial campaign.....	673	673	626	270	356
Independent TV Committee.................	1,997	1,997	1,902	—	1,902
Total.............	$ 8,078	$ 8,073	$ 7,750	$1,133	$6,617
Volunteers for Nixon-Lodge...............	$ 2,292	$ 2,288	$ 2,126	$ 14	$2,112
National Nixon-Lodge Clubs...............	437	409	410	9	401
Total.............	$ 2,730	$ 2,697	$ 2,536	$ 23	$2,513
Miscellaneous[c]...........	373	373	315	16	299
Total[d].............	$11,181	$11,143	$10,600	$1,172	$9,429

[a] Adjusted for lateral transfers from national-level Republican, labor, and miscellaneous committee groupings included in the tables.
[b] Direct expenditures were determined by subtracting all transfers of funds from gross disbursements.
[c] Citizens for Eisenhower-Nixon '58; National Federation of Republican Women; National Recount and Fair Elections Committee; Restaurant Voters for Nixon; TV Committee, Republican Campaign Dinners; Vote Getters for Nixon-Lodge; Women's National Republican Campaign Committee; Young Republican National Federation; Committee for the Real Nixon; Nixon-Lodge Unlimited; Builders Committee for Nixon-Lodge. Totals for some of these committees may have been subsumed under those listed in the table.
[d] Minor discrepancies between items and totals are due to rounding.

four debates would have been $444,520, but offered no estimate of other costs.

Free time for the debates and other purposes offered the national parties a substantial amount of financial relief in a situation in which costs otherwise would have risen even more sharply. The audience aspect of the situation, however, was far more important. According to Dr. Frank Stanton, of CBS, paid broadcasts even in prime time periods attracted less than a third of the average audience for the debates, estimated at 71 million persons.

Total expenditures by the parties and candidates for political broadcasting at all levels (TV and AM radio, networks, and stations) amounted to $14.2 million for the period from September 1 to election day, according to the Federal Communications Commission. Of the total, the Democratic portion was $6.2 million, the Republican, $7.6, and for all others, $400,000. In 1956, the comparable total was $9.8 million, according to the *Gore Report*.

The indicated increase from 1956 to 1960 in total charges for political broadcasting was thus at the rate of 45 per cent. All of this increase occurred at lower levels of the political system, since the increased amount of free time for the presidential campaign kept spending for this purpose at the 1956 level. Pressures for making similar amounts of free time available at other than the presidential level will likely become very great by 1964.

The total contribution by the broadcasting industry in 1960 was greater than ever before. Some estimates have put the cost to the industry as high as $15 million to $20 million if allowance is made for convention coverage, election night coverage, newscasts, and special programs, as well as the free time provided the candidates during the presidential campaign. At the same time, the sharp increase in costs for many types of political broadcasting undoubtedly accentuated the problems of campaign finance. A year before he was elected President, Senator John F. Kennedy wrote:

> If all candidates and parties are to have equal access to this essential and decisive campaign media, without becoming deeply obligated to the big financial contributors from the worlds of business, labor or other major lobbies, then the time has come when a solution must be found to this problem of TV costs.[14]

The evidence of 1960 points up the urgency of the Senator's remark.

[14] "The Reporter's Notes," *The Reporter,* Feb. 16, 1960, p. 20.

Campaign Materials

The Democrats established a Materials Distribution Center in Washington that expended over $800,000 in purchasing and distributing goods ranging from buttons to banners to brochures. The total number of buttons and lapel tabs purchased was more than one per Democratic voter.

Private Public Opinion Polls

Private public opinion polls were used extensively by the parties and candidates in 1960 as a means of obtaining information on which to base campaign strategy. Kennedy retained Louis Harris for work continuously throughout the preconvention and election campaign periods; Nixon relied on Claude Robinson and certain state polls. Before 1960, Harris estimated the cost of polling done privately for political purposes at all levels would be $1 million to $1.5 million in 1960.[15]

Coordination and Cutbacks

In both parties, income never seemed to keep pace with outgo, with the result that repeated efforts were made to coordinate activities and cut back expenditures. The Democrats reportedly cut their schedule of paid prime network time from seven to two and a half hours after October 1, later canceling paid telecasts in six states on October 26 and reducing time on election eve.

The Republicans also had their day-to-day shortages, although their totals for the year indicated masterful ability to raise money. On September 14, Chairman Thruston B. Morton reported lack of funds to put on a scheduled Nixon telecast. Again, when the Democrats reported on September 30 that they were skirting bankruptcy, the Republicans announced a cash balance of only a "few thousand dollars." The cry for funds is often part of a strategy to loosen pocketbooks, but in 1960 the needs were real and the cries authentic, as attested by the post-election deficits of both parties.

[15] Louis Harris, "The Uses of Polls in Political Campaigns," in James M. Cannon (ed.), *Politics U.S.A.* (Doubleday, 1960), p. 257.

Labor and Other Committees

Not all campaign spending is done by the major parties, and the Democratic financial picture in particular would be incomplete unless labor spending were taken into account. In 1960, 21 national-level labor committees made gross disbursements of $2.3 million (Table 5.1). This total varied little from that of 1956, but among the disbursements, transfers out, in part consisting of allocations to senatorial and congressional candidates, ran $182,000 less, while direct expenditures by the labor committees were $300,000 more.

The nineteen miscellaneous committees operating nationally in politics in 1960 (Table 5.1) reported receipts of about $190,000 more, and disbursements of about $160,000 more, than such committees in 1956. Four of the committees, Americans for Constitutional Action, Americans for Democratic Action, Christian Nationalist Crusade, and the National Committee for an Effective Congress, accounted for about 80 per cent of gross disbursements.

Scurrilous Literature

According to the Fair Campaign Practices Committee, some 300 pieces of scurrilous literature were circulated in the 1960 campaigns. Many of these items were distributed in massive quantities, with total distribution conservatively estimated at 15 million. At an average of four cents each for production and one cent for mailing—both estimates probably low—the total expenditure for such materials was about $750,000. In a similar type of activity, 24 Texas radio stations carried paid political broadcasts on the religious issue for 15 minutes a day, 5 days a week, for many weeks during the campaign, at an estimated cost of $100,000. These activities required expensive counterattacks and denials by both major candidates.

Sources of Funds in 1960

Fund raising is one of the hardest of campaign tasks, and one that might therefore be thought to require an unusual amount of centralized activity and coordination. The multiplicity of committees listed in Tables 5.2 and 5.3 is in part the result of legal restrictions on the amount of political spending that can be carried on through a single committee, but also reflects efforts to reach or capitalize on different clienteles. The Volunteers for Nixon-Lodge, for example, operated independently because it was thought that it could be more effective on that basis. The finance chairman of the Volunteers, Walter Thayer, accepted the position only on condition that he would not be asked to clear potential contributor lists with other Republican fund-raisers.

Most of the Republican fund raising was centralized in the Republican National Finance Committee, which collects funds and distributes them among the operating committees. The committee had a 1960 campaign goal of $7.8 million, which it more than met.

A Democratic National Finance Committee was organized prior to the 1960 convention in an effort to settle a number of jurisdictional and personality conflicts among top Democratic finance managers. The new committee was largely a paper organization in 1960, but the financial operations of the DNC, the Citizens for Kennedy-Johnson, and the Business and Professional Men and Women for Kennedy-Johnson were partially centralized in the national committee's accounting office.

Broadening the Financial Base

In 1960, the American Heritage Foundation again cooperated with the Advertising Council in urging citizens to contribute money to the party of their choice, and to register and vote. Free advertising valued at $12 million was contributed by the major media. According to a Survey Research Center poll, 11.5 per cent of a national cross section said they had contributed in 1960. The similar figure for 1956 was 10 per cent, and for 1952, only 4 per cent.

Much of the effort devoted to the joint advertising campaign will doubtless be wasted until the parties are better organized to take advantage of any favorable climate the campaign produces. In 1960, all but a few states cooperated in the "Dollars for Democrats" campaign, surpassing previous efforts of this kind. But the shared proceeds reaching the DNC amounted to only $121,060 by the end of 1960. Many states were slow in remitting funds, and others, in desperate need of funds for local campaign purposes, were authorized to retain the national committee's share. The full story is not yet available, but only modest improvement over previous years is evident.

In 1960, the Republicans did not attempt a massive national "neighbor to neighbor" campaign. Efforts were concentrated in marginal congressional districts. One local committee, in Hennepin County, Minnesota, increased its collections from $40,000 in 1958 to $94,000 in 1960, showing the potential when a drive is taken seriously.

Fund-Raising Dinners

Despite efforts to broaden the base, there was a continuing reliance on fund-raising dinners, large contributors, and state quota payments. In 1960, three New York and Washington newspapers reported 213 (142 Republican and 71 Democratic) fund-raising dinners, luncheons, breakfasts, and cocktail parties at all levels. Two events accounted for 119 of the Republican dinners: Dinner with Ike, 83; 1960 Campaign Dinner, 36; with each group of dinners held simultaneously in numerous cities and linked through closed-circuit TV. Estimates of attendance were available for 181 of the 213 affairs and aggregated over 225,000 persons, for an average of more than 1,000 persons each. Gross proceeds of the four national Democratic dinners were about $1.1 million; Republican net proceeds at the national level for the Ike and Campaign dinners were slightly over $3 million.

Large Contributors

As usual, large contributors provided a substantial portion of the available funds. More than 5,300 different individuals contributed $500 or more to committees filing reports with the Clerk of the House of Representatives, Secretary of the Senate, and a few miscellaneous sources, for a total of $8.5 million, 41 per cent of the total reported gross receipts. Ninety-five persons gave $10,000 or more to political campaigns for a total of $1,558,609, as follows:

> 51 individuals gave $10,000 to $14,999
> 26 individuals gave $15,000 to $19,999
> 18 individuals gave $20,000 or more.

Members of 12 family groups, selected for study in 1956 by the Gore Committee, made reported contributions in 1960 of $500 or more as follows:

Republican	$548,510
Democratic	78,850
Miscellaneous	22,000
Total	$649,360

The list of families used in the *Gore Report* was illustrative, did not include all prominent families (although it included all who were most conspicuous in the records of the Gore Committee), and is not intended to suggest that all prominent families made large contributions to political parties.

State Quotas

Quotas are shares assigned to each state for the financial support of the national party; state party organizations are responsible for raising the funds required to meet their quotas, and in turn make levies on local party organizations, hold fund-raising events, make direct or mail solicitations or use a combination of these methods.

The use of quotas is a relatively recent practice in the Democratic party, and full payment of quotas has not become routine. A quota report for the years 1957, 1958, 1959, and 1960 (through May 2) showed total quota assessments of $4.4 million and receipts of $2.8 million. Only six of the 54 states and territories had paid in full or oversubscribed their quotas. The six were Maryland, South Dakota, Virgin Islands, Wyoming, District of Columbia, and New Jersey. Obviously, not all are wealthy states, nor are they all noted for their strong party organizations. Nor were only southern states behind in their payments, as might have been expected from their relations with Chairman Paul Butler. North Carolina ranked ninth in payments and Arkansas thirteenth; well down in the list were New York (38), Minnesota (45), and Illinois (47).

When Butler issued the report, he said that special consideration would be given to the housing and seating requests of the state delegations to the national convention from the states with good records. This apparently was done, although not necessarily with complete consistency. Maryland sat front row center and was housed at the Biltmore Hotel, convention headquarters; Illinois was seated in the rear and housed at a less than deluxe hotel in a run-down neighborhood. In 1961, Illinois was one of the first states to pay its quota.

State quotas have been in use in the Republican party for many years. Quota payments are not revealed, but it is known that some states rarely meet assessments, while some other states, such as Illinois and New York, have excellent payment records.

Labor and Business in Politics

Organized labor and corporate business were both concerned in 1960 with registration, get-out-the-vote, and contributions drives. In each case, party-oriented groups found that their efforts were most effective when devoted selectively to areas where the favored party would get the most benefit. The parties also conducted registration drives: Kennedy started a massive program as soon as he was nominated; the Republicans followed suit with a lesser effort, concentrated in about 500 counties.

The AFL-CIO and COPE

The AFL-CIO Committee on Political Education (COPE) carried on its customary activities to register voters and get them to the polls. Expenditures were not reported, since this was considered a nonpartisan effort. In addition, the AFL-CIO organized a crash program directed by George Meany's special assistant, Carl Mc-Peak, and many affiliated unions carried on their own drives. Mc-Peak's operation was financed by union contributions totaling $535,000; the money was provided by affiliated unions at the rate of five cents per member and came from general union funds.

Liaison was maintained with the official Democratic party drive, which had an announced budget of $500,000 and an announced goal of ten million new registrations. Actual expenditures, however, were less than $200,000, including allocations to states that were matched by local outlays in some cases. The combined Democratic-labor drives increased Democratic party registrations significantly. After the election, COPE asserted that Kennedy would not have been elected without the labor drive, and took steps to put registration work on a year-round basis.

Negro Groups

For the first time, Negro labor and other leaders initiated a Non-Partisan Crusade to Register One Million New Negro Voters. The main efforts were in national publicity, newspaper advertising, spot radio announcements, and direct mail, all geared to the slogan, "Call to Negro Americans." Slightly over $15,000 was spent.

The Teamsters

The Teamsters union, not affiliated with the AFL-CIO but with 1,600,000 members, carried on its own drives. In a bid for greater political power, plans were announced to attempt to secure contributions of 50 cents a month for each member. The only financial report filed with the House of Representatives showed receipts of $56,338. Major efforts were devoted to instructing the members in ballot-splitting, to facilitate votes for Nixon along with votes for Democratic candidates for lesser offices. A special goal was the defeat of 56 House members who had voted for the 1959 Labor Control Act. Teamster money was used against 40 of those seeking re-election; only one was defeated.

St. Louis Teamster Local 688 was responsible for an innovation that may prove significant. Funds for a local union political action committee were derived from the regular dues of members who signed a special authorization. The union officials were prosecuted but acquitted in a directed verdict in which the federal district judge found that the funds had been voluntarily designated and were allocated in amounts not exceeding those volunteered. Should this system be used in future years on a wider scale, it will undoubtedly be tested again and may reach the Supreme Court. The AFL-CIO seems to be assuming that the Teamsters will lose their case in any such test, but if the contrary occurred and the system of "contracting-in" proved legal, all unions would find it much easier to secure political money from their members.[16]

Business Drives

Numerous corporations took special action to urge their employees to register and vote. In some instances, campaigns were directed toward the general public. The Rexall Drug Company, for example, in cooperation with Coca-Cola, provided each of its stores with bulletin boards displaying registration and voting information. In addition, certain corporations undertook political fund-raising drives among their employees.

The Aerojet-General program was the most far-reaching effort of its kind in 1960. First attempted in 1958, some 11,500 of a total of 15,000 employees contributed $24,000 in that year, di-

---

[16] In another case, *I.A.M.* v. *Street,* the U.S. Supreme Court ruled June 19, 1961 that a labor union may not spend a member's dues for political purposes to which the member objects. While the apparent effect of the decision would be to limit labor organizations' political activities, the practical effect will undoubtedly be the subject of further litigation since the court failed to define "political activities" and sent the case back to a lower court for further consideration of remedies.

vided about equally between the parties.[17] In 1960, over 3,000 "new voters" were registered at the plants, and some 19,000 of 25,000 employees contributed about $60,000, of which about $23,000 went to Democratic state party headquarters and about $19,000 to Republican. The remaining $18,000 was designed by the contributors for individual candidates of both parties, including candidates running in the primaries in some instances, and for miscellaneous groups. Aerojet officials attributed the rise in 1960 contributions to the ease of giving under a newly inaugurated voluntary payroll deduction plan that operated from April to mid-October.

The Ford Motor Company began a fund-raising plan in 1960 that provided each employee with a contribution card and two envelopes. An employee inserted a check or cash contribution with the filled-out contribution card in an inner envelope, sealed it, and checked the party on the front of that envelope. Then, placing it in an outer envelope, he sealed it and dropped it in a collection box. Thus the company remains unaware of the party selected, how much or who contributed—unless it takes the time and effort to check official campaign fund reports, which in most states list at least larger contributors. The parties in Michigan reported many contributions from first-time contributors, according to Ford officials, but less success was achieved in other states where Ford facilities were located.

Variations of the Ford plan was undertaken by American Telephone and Telegraph, First National City Bank of New York, Thiokol Chemical, Whirlpool Corporation, and various other major concerns. The Chase Manhattan Bank and some other New York firms provided inner envelopes offering a choice among the finance committees of both parties in three states: New York, Connecticut, and New Jersey.

The economic downturn of 1960 brought on retrenchments that seem to have eliminated at least one company fund-raising program and probably curtailed others. Not all of the company programs were successful; Kimberly-Clark Corporation operated a program

[17] Heard, op. cit., pp. 457-59.

among 2,100 salaried employees in which only 120 contributed, for a total of $2,257. In all cases, the methods used and the degree of top-management encouragement affected the results. Among salaried employees, it may be that contributions of money are easier to secure than contributions of time and effort—an attitude that leaders in the practical politics movement in business have decried as insufficient.

Business efforts in politics in 1960 probably involved even more than the usual ambivalence between the ideals of partisanship and those of nonpartisanship. Speaking before a group of businessmen in February 1961, President Kennedy put the matter of business political support bluntly: " . . . It would be premature to seek your support in the next election, and inaccurate to express thanks for it in the last one."[18] Yet he could have thanked business leaders for the nonpartisan character of many corporate political activities. The range was great, from nonpartisan citizenship programs to much more propagandist efforts to influence employee thinking and create an "improved business climate." Where the background motivations were strongly partisan, businessmen frequently learned in 1960 that nonpartisan corporate efforts in political education failed the selectivity test if measured by management's general Republican leanings.[19]

The Aftermath

In party and campaign finance, the aftermath of an election is seldom the same for the winners and the losers. In 1960, however, there was an unaccustomed equalization of the usual sources of strain. The Republicans ended their losing campaign with a strong financial organization and a relatively small deficit. The Democrats ended their winning campaign in a state of considerable disorganization and with a much larger deficit.

[18] *Congressional Quarterly Weekly Report,* Feb. 17, 1961, p. 291.
[19] *Business Week,* Nov. 26, 1960, p. 34.

The Republicans

The Republican National Finance Committee came out of the campaign with a gross debt of $993,000. This was offset by cash balances and accounts receivable, leaving a net debt of about $700,000 (Table 5.1). By the end of 1960, cash balances in the hands of the national-level Republican operating committees were up to about half a million dollars. A national fund-raising goal of $2.5 million was set for 1961, which was intended to pay off the debt, meet 1961 operating expenses, and prepare for the 1962 campaign. To raise the money, an Associates Program was being emphasized for contributors of $1,000 or more. A fund-raising dinner held in early June in Washington netted about $450,000, for the use of the Republican congressional committees.

The problem of financing election recounts was a special aspect of the Republican aftermath of 1960. Party Chairman Morton and his associates traveled extensively in their investigations, but where actual recounts were undertaken, they seem to have been financed locally. In Illinois, the Nixon Recount Committee received contributions of about $76,000 from over 30,000 persons, much of it in one dollar gifts. Chicago newspapers supported the appeal for several weeks, running a box advising where to send contributions at the beginning of each day's story on the recount effort. The committee spent over $51,000, of which $13,000 was a recount fee required by the Board of Election Commissioners.

The Democrats

The Democratic debt of $3,820,000 demanded a policy of retrenchment that was put in effect as soon as the election was over. As usual every four years, every employee of the Democratic National Committee was sent a dismissal notice. Some were immediately rehired, some joined the staff of the President-elect, and still others went to work for the Inaugural Committee. When these changes had been completed, the DNC staff was stabilized at about eighty persons, with patronage and correspondence divisions increased in size and other divisions cut back. The field service staff of organizers was discontinued. The Democratic Advisory Council, which had cost about $50,000 a year, was disbanded, and the monthly *Democratic Digest* was killed.

For 1961, the Democrats set a national goal of $5,280,000. This contemplated paying off the entire debt of $3.8 million and meeting current operating expenses of $1,460,000. Operating costs were increased by a merger of the financial operations of the DNC, the Democratic Senatorial Committee, and the Democratic Congressional Campaign Committee. In a major change, the DNC agreed to provide $550,000 to the congressional committees from March 1961 through election day, 1962. The agreement was tenuous, being reviewed monthly, but appeared to strengthen as substantial portions of the goal were raised.

A winning party usually finds itself blessed with a special crop of post-election contributions from individuals who had been too "absent minded" to make them sooner.[20] Some of the funds that ordinarily might have been contributed to the winning national committee in 1960 may have been used to purchase tickets to the Inaugural Gala. Held on January 19, 1961 under party auspices, the Gala was an innovation in turning the special circumstances of the inauguration to party fund-raising purposes. The Gala was produced by Frank Sinatra, and tickets were $100 each. Gross receipts were $1.25 million, and net proceeds were about $1 million. The usual Inaugural Ball and related activities were held on January 20 under the auspices of the semiofficial, nonpartisan Inaugural Committee, but did not benefit the Democratic party.

An additional million dollars toward the goal was raised at Washington and Boston fund-raising dinners in late May honoring President Kennedy's 44th birthday. Still another million dollars was pledged when four state committees—New York, Pennsylvania, Illinois, and California—agreed to 1961 quota payments of $250,000 each. The national proceeds from the Boston dinner, the four-state agreement, plus quota assessments to the other 46 states, totaling well over $3 million, indicate a new and greatly increased scale of state quotas, supplemented by special compacts, and sug-

[20] Heard, *op. cit.*, p. 69, note 1.

gest the arrival of new financial relationships between the national
and state party organizations—at least if all state quotas can be
collected. By the end of May 1961, eleven states had paid in full
for a total of $825,000, including $250,000 each by Illinois and
Pennsylvania.[21] North Carolina ($50,000) and Oklahoma
($35,000) were the only southern or border states among those
making early payments.

The program of national sustaining memberships, with annual
dues of $10, continued, and by early June 1961, over $200,000
had been raised by this means.

From all these sources, the Democrats appeared to be well on the
way to meeting their 1961 goal, perhaps leaving a small cash
balance at year's end. By early June, over $2.4 million had been
expended for debt retirement and current operations, leaving a
cash balance of $663,000. This represents great progress from the
spring of 1960, when the Democratic financial outlook was so
black that the congressional committees decided to hold their own
fund-raising dinner; it grossed over $500,000 and was a major
factor in financing national allocations of about $400,000 to the
party's candidates for Congress in 1960.

But clearly, satisfactory financial relationships between the national and congressional committees will depend on the stability of
relationships between the national and state committees. If the
states supply quota monies in ample amounts, as some appear to be
doing, the DNC can supply the congressional committees with adequate funds. The new national-congressional relationships, if but-
tressed by a stable and productive quota system, could have far-
reaching political implications that will bear close watching.

The national party headquarters organization, under new management, seemed less concerned with party stands on matters of
public policy than it had been under the former regime of Paul
Butler—a normal consequence of the change from out-party to
in-party status, with legislative leadership re-established in the
White House. But the problem of generating support for the President's legislative program soon began to engage the attention of

[21] *The Democrat,* June 2, 1961, p. 4.

Chairman John M. Bailey and Vice Chairman Margaret Price. This inspired a new party publication, *The Democrat,* issued bi-weekly as a four-page newsletter.

Transition and New Administration

When a party overturn occurs, the incoming administration has the problem of financing its activities during the period between election and inauguration. So far, no public funds have been made available for these purposes. In 1952-53, the Citizens for Eisenhower-Nixon came out of the campaign with a substantial surplus, part of which was used to foot the bills of the incoming Eisenhower administration. In 1960-61, the bills of the incoming Kennedy administration were paid from reserve balances of the DNC, but constituted an added burden for that debt ridden committee. An estimated $210,000 was provided by the party for transition costs, detailed as follows:[22]

Salaries	$130,000
Hotel	17,500
Space rentals	5,000
Supplies	2,500
Telephone and telegraph	5,000
Air and other travel	50,000
Total	$210,000

Some of the Kennedy staff remained on his Senate payroll until he resigned from that office. Costs incurred by appointees in visiting the President-elect and in preparing for their new duties were in most cases assumed by the individuals concerned. The expenses of the various task forces were often privately assumed, although congressional committees printed the reports in some cases.

The character of a new administration is determined largely by the appointments that are made to the Cabinet and lesser positions. The proportion of large financial contributors among the Kennedy appointees was not great. Of 250 major appointees listed by *Con-*

---

[22] Shortly before going to print, Democratic Chairman John Bailey stated that transition costs were $350,000. The $210,000 estimate was made earlier by a high Democratic finance manager.

gressional Quarterly Weekly Report,[23] 33, or 13 per cent, were found to have contributed at least one sum of $500 or more in the 1960 campaign. Three of these contributors, however—C. Douglas Dillon, John J. McCloy, and James H. Wakelin, Jr.—had given to the Republican cause.

The potential patronage available to the Kennedy administration amounted to about 6,000 federal jobs commanding salaries that average about $9,000 annually for a total payroll of $54 million.[24] Many appointments appeared to be rewards for service during the campaign, but the grosser forms of patronage appeared to be under rather tight control during the early months of the new administration. Campaign contributors were said to have been warned that no commitments for jobs went with their money, and two very large contributions were reported to have been rejected because the intended donors wanted to be assured of diplomatic posts.

President Kennedy set the moral tone of the new administration in speech and action. Two days after his inauguration, he named a special panel to advise him on problems of ethics and conflicts of interest. He sold his personal holdings of nongovernmental securities and converted the proceeds into government bonds. He announced that he would refuse to accept gifts, distributing them instead to the needy or for display in museums. Many of the Kennedy appointees took similar action, and some incurred substantial sacrifices in accepting government salary levels and in divesting themselves of corporate stock holdings in order to meet conflict-of-interest requirements.

Future Issues of Party and Public Policy

The experience of 1960 suggests that a critical point is being reached in which financial necessities may bring on substantial changes in American party organization. Major issues of party and public policy are latent in the situation. These cannot be fully dis-

[23] Feb. 10, 1961, pp. 225-32; March 17, 1961, pp. 429-30; May 12, 1961, p. 830.
[24] *Ibid.,* Jan. 20, 1961, p. 80.

cussed here, but relevant aspects of the recent experience should be noted.[25]

Issues of Party Policy

On the Republican side, the party's fund-raising efforts in 1960 were strongly criticized, despite their relative success. The most overt criticism came from Carlton Ketchum, professional fund-raiser and long-time consultant to the Republican national finance committee. In a post-election letter to the committee, he praised the effort in terms of dollars raised, but argued that there had been too much emphasis on direct national solicitation and on emergency devices, such as dinners and telephone blitzes. For the long haul, he thought the only sound procedure was the operation of unified local drives in every state of the kind recently effective in some states. Specifically, he urged that (1) steps be taken to build more solid organization to raise funds for the 1962 campaign; (2) the necessity for professional help be recognized; (3) fund-raising dinners be omitted in 1961 because they had been used so much in recent years that their efficacy was being impaired; and (4) mail solicitations by national party committees be carefully integrated with and subordinated to personal solicitation through local finance committees.

Similar criticisms were doubtless voiced privately on the Democratic side, and probably with even greater point of view of the size of the deficit and the extent to which Democratic contributors had been subjected to numerous duplicating appeals. Yet both parties continued in 1961 their reliance on fund-raising dinners and large contributors and creditors.

A basic issue for both parties is the extent to which the financial base can be broadened. Essentially, a broad base requires proper organization and a high degree of cooperation at all levels, along with perhaps intensified American Heritage Foundation-Advertising Council campaigns to create a climate favorable to giving. Solicitation of small contributions is most effectively accomplished

[25] For further discussion, see Heard, *op. cit.,* Chap. 16.

through personal confrontation on a house-to-house basis. This requires the recruitment of large numbers of solicitors, preferably by local party organizations. After local committees take their share, the money must filter up to the state and national levels through improved quota systems. But many local politicians ask: Why take the trouble to organize mass solicitations to raise funds for the state and national boys to spend? Especially troublesome is the case of dissident party organizations that reject higher state or national authority while claiming all the rights and privileges that go with the party label. Until national politicians find effective answers or incentives to offer, or agree to apply sanctions, widespread efforts will not be forthcoming. Suggested national sanctions for failure to pay quotas could include the withholding of membership rights on the national committee, or voting rights at the national convention.[26] The effectiveness of such sanctions cannot be gainsaid; but they could be applied only with the concurrence of a majority of state representatives at the national party committees or conventions—a majority not now apparent.

The only apparent alternative to an effective system embracing cooperation, incentives, or sanctions, or a combination thereof, is a more intensive system of direct national solicitation, involving the concept of national party membership. But this would be exceedingly difficult and costly for the national party to operate, would be offensive to local leaders, even so could only skim the cream of potential contributors, and in any case would compete with state and local party units for available funds.

Another issue, explosive at times in the past, is the future relationship between the financing of presidential and congressional election campaigns as national party activities. The logic of the situation, in terms of systematic fund-raising and an avoidance of irritating forms of duplicate solicitation, is mainly in the direction of centralization. But centralization obviously will not continue long in either party unless total monies raised are sufficient to meet the campaign as well as operating requirements of both the congressional committees and national committees. Members of Con-

[26] David, Goldman, and Bain, *op. cit.,* p. 500.

gress seem likely to have ample means for the protection of their own interests in the problems of party finance, in view of their strategic relationship to the issues of public policy that may in the end control the issues of party policy.

Issues of Public Policy

Political parties that are beholden to a small number of large contributors constitute an unhealthy element in the body politic. Debt-ridden parties that exist from hand-to-mouth at the mercy of a few large creditors are in some respects even worse. It is clearly in the public interest to find means by which political parties and campaigns can be routinely and adequately financed in ways that will be free of public suspicion.

There are two major means of reorganizing party finance that offer hope of meeting this test. One would consist of public subsidies to assist the parties and candidates in financing campaigns, perhaps coupled with increasing amounts of broadcast time provided by the radio and television stations that depend on public licenses for their right to operate. Public subsidies have been advocated increasingly by various political leaders in recent years, including members who have introduced legislative proposals in both houses of Congress. President Kennedy spoke out on the subject at his first press conference. He expressed the hope that Congress would consider national government participation in the financing of national campaigns "because the present system is not satisfactory." He later reiterated the position even more strongly, saying that he hoped that "before we get into another presidential campaign . . . we can work out some system by which the major burdens of presidential campaigns on both sides would be sustained by the national government."[27]

Legislation could provide public subsidies in full or in part. The subsidy could be based on an amount, say 5 cents to 20 cents per voter (in a limited number of past elections or according to present registration totals), or on the principle of reimbursement for specified activities, such as broadcast time or travel expenses. The subsidy could provide the franking privilege to candidates for a

[27] *New York Times,* May 6, 1961.

limited number of free mailings to constituents, and perhaps provide the costs for publication of a basic campaign pamphlet for
mailing under the frank. A government grant could be made to
cover transition costs incurred by the President-elect. Along with
the subsidy could go a condition limiting, as one proposal does, the
amount of contributions that can be accepted from any individual,
a restriction designed to reduce reliance on large contributors.

The other line that public policy could take would be to encourage a vast expansion in the numbers of small contributors. This
course does not mutually exclude a policy of partial subsidies. It
would seek to encourage small contributors directly by permitting
tax credits against the federal income tax for half the amount of
political contributions, up to a specified limit of $10 per person
per year.[28] This policy would recognize that political contributions
constitute a reputable form of public service, and would be in
accord with the principle that every public spirited citizen who
has a party preference should contribute financially, in moderate
amounts, to the political party of his choice.

Many other aspects of campaign finance and election law reform
are currently under legislative study. The new Congress meeting in
1961 was faced with an unusually large number of proposals relating to reform of the electoral college, establishment of presidential primaries in additional states, changing the time of the party
conventions or the general election or both to cut down the length
and cost of campaigns, and renewing the legislation under which
the debates were broadcast between the presidential candidates in
1960. All of these proposals are under consideration in one or both
houses. All would affect future requirements for party and campaign finance.

Party and public officials alike have failed to devote enough
attention to the financial problems of the parties and their candidates. Indefinite use of stop-gap measures cannot but affect
adversely the health of the political system. Either government
subsidies or the voluntary broadening of financial constituencies
would herald democratic chances as significant as those brought
about by the broadening of electoral constituencies.

[28] See the author's *Tax Incentives for Political Contributions?* (Citizens' Research
Foundation, 1961).

6

Interpreting the Election Results

V. O. KEY, JR.[1]

EACH PRESIDENTIAL ELECTION has its unique features, but the voting of 1960 manifested an unusual combination of oddities. Only by the thinnest margin did the Democratic candidate, John F. Kennedy, win a majority of the two-party popular vote.[2] His lead over Richard M. Nixon in the electoral college, 303 to 219, was none too comfortable, given the narrowness of his popular margin in several large states.[3] The closeness of the vote caused exceptional delay in the determination of the outcome and brought recollections of the election of 1916. Some Republican leaders encouraged the belief that their candidate had lost in a few states by fraud and fostered hopes that recounts would give him the election. Mr. Nixon did not associate himself with these visionary expectations. The only upset incident to the commotion about the honesty of the

[1] Professor of Government, Harvard University. The assistance of David Mayhew in the statistical analysis is acknowledged with gratitude.

[2] Of the 68,329,540 major-party vote, 50.08 per cent is credited to Democratic electors, a plurality of approximately 100,000. Even this calculation involves a moderate amount of license. It assigns to the Kennedy total the largest vote received by any one of the Alabama electors pledged to him. Six of the 11 Alabama Democratic electors ran unpledged and eventually voted for Byrd. An Alabama voter could vote for each of 11 electors in the Democratic column, 5 of whom were pledged to Kennedy and 6 of whom were unpledged. If only five elevenths of the Alabama vote for "Democratic" electors were to be included in the Democratic national total, the Kennedy vote would be less than a majority of the major-party total.

[3] The remaining 15 of 437 electoral votes were cast for Harry F. Byrd. Six of these were the unpledged Alabama electors, eight were the uninstructed Mississippi electors, and one Oklahoma Republican elector, Henry D. Irwin, earned for himself a footnote in the history books by casting his vote for Byrd.

TABLE 6.1. *Summary of Results of Presidential Election 1960*[a]

State	Popular Vote		Per Cent Democratic	Electoral Vote		
	D	R		D	R	Byrd
Alabama..........	318,303[b]	237,981	57.2	5	—	6
Alaska............	29,809	30,953	49.0	—	3	—
Arizona...........	176,781	221,241	44.4	—	4	—
Arkansas.........	215,049	184,508	53.8	8	—	—
California........	3,224,099	3,259,722	49.7	—	32	—
Colorado	330,629	402,242	45.1	—	6	—
Connecticut.......	657,055	565,813	53.7	8	—	—
Delaware.........	99,590	96,373	50.8	3	—	—
Florida...........	748,700	795,476	48.5	—	10	—
Georgia..........	458,638	274,472	62.6	12	—	—
Hawaii...........	92,410	92,295	50.1	3	—	—
Idaho............	138,853	161,597	46.2	—	4	—
Illinois...........	2,377,846	2,368,988	50.1	27	—	—
Indiana..........	952,358	1,175,120	44.8	—	13	—
Iowa.............	550,565	722,381	43.2	—	10	—
Kansas...........	363,213	561,474	39.3	—	8	—
Kentucky.........	521,855	602,607	46.4	—	10	—
Louisiana.........	407,339	230,980	63.8[c]	10	—	—
Maine............	181,159	240,608	42.9	—	5	—
Maryland.........	565,808	489,538	53.6	9	—	—
Massachusetts.....	1,487,174	976,750	60.4	16	—	—
Michigan.........	1,687,269	1,620,428	51.0	20	—	—
Minnesota........	779,933	757,915	50.7	11	—	—
Mississippi.......	108,362	73,561	—[d]	—	—	8
Missouri..........	972,201	962,221	50.2	13	—	—
Montana.........	134,891	141,841	48.7	—	4	—
Nebraska.........	232,542	380,553	37.9	—	6	—
Nevada..........	54,880	52,387	51.2	3	—	—
New Hampshire....	137,772	157,989	46.6	—	4	—
New Jersey.......	1,385,415	1,363,324	50.4	16	—	—
New Mexico.......	156,027	153,733	50.4	4	—	—
New York........	3,830,085	3,446,419	52.6	45	—	—
North Carolina.....	713,136	655,420	52.1	14	—	—
North Dakota.....	123,963	154,310	44.5	—	4	—
Ohio.............	1,944,248	2,217,611	46.7	—	25	—
Oklahoma........	370,111	533,039	41.0	—	7	1
Oregon...........	367,402	408,060	47.4	—	6	—
Pennsylvania......	2,556,282	2,439,956	51.2	32	—	—
Rhode Island......	258,032	147,502	63.6	4	—	—
South Carolina.....	198,129	188,558	51.2	8	—	—
South Dakota......	128,070	178,417	41.8	—	4	—
Tennessee.........	481,453	556,577	46.4	—	11	—
Texas.............	1,167,932	1,121,699	51.0	24	—	—
Utah.............	169,248	205,361	45.2	—	4	—
Vermont..........	69,186	98,131	41.3	—	3	—
Virginia..........	362,327	404,521	47.2	—	12	—
Washington.......	599,298	629,273	48.8	—	9	—
West Virginia......	441,786	395,995	52.7	8	—	—
Wisconsin........	830,805	895,175	48.1	—	12	—
Wyoming..........	63,331	77,451	44.9	—	3	—
Total..........	34,221,389	34,108,151	50.08	303	219	15

[a] Sources: The basic data of this table were assembled from the final official returns as compiled by *Congressional Quarterly Weekly Report*.
[b] This figure is the total vote for the leading Kennedy-pledged elector on a slate of 11 electors, 6 of whom ran unpledged. The leading unpledged elector received 324,040 votes. The percentage shown is scarcely comparable with the Democratic percentage of the major-party vote for other states.
[c] This is the Democratic percentage of the major-party vote. The Democratic percentage of the total vote, including 169,572 for the Louisiana States' Rights Party, was 50.4.
[d] An unpledged slate of electors won in Mississippi with a popular vote of 116,248. The Democratic percentage of the total vote was 36.3.

count was the transfer of Hawaii's three electoral votes from the Republican to the Democratic column.[4] And in Oklahoma's sixth district, a recount overturned the initial certification and gave the seat to the Democratic congressional candidate.

The suspense created by the closeness of the outcome and the clamor about fraud apparently led all concerned to forget a curiosity that had been persistent before the voting. That was the speculation about what effect Kennedy's religion might have on the voting. Prominent Democratic strategists had predicted that the consequence would be a net advantage to his candidacy, while other observers thought that the religious factor would give the voting pattern of 1960 resemblances to that of 1928.

General Factors in the Interpretation of Voting Returns

The interpretation of election statistics is a black art whose practice requires subtleties of insight (and detailed knowledge of local circumstances) not so widely distributed in the population as are the practitioners of the art. An inspection of election returns tells us how many votes each candidate received and from whence the votes came but not much more. To read meaning into the figures, one must proceed by one or another of the variants of ecological correlation, a technique that establishes relations between aggregate voting behavior within geographical areas and the social characteristics of the inhabitants of the areas. These relations, though, are to be interpreted only with the utmost caution. Survey techniques enable us to connect individual social characteristics far more di-

[4] Republican electors were first declared elected by 92,505 to 92,364 votes. On contest, the official figures became 92,410 Democratic and 92,295 Republican. When the joint convention of the two houses of Congress counted the electoral vote, it had before it a certificate from each set of electors along with a certificate from the Governor of Hawaii of the judgment of the circuit court on the contest. Vice President Nixon, presiding, suggested, "without the intent of establishing a precedent," that the Democratic electors be considered "the lawful electors from the State of Hawaii." See *Congressional Record*, daily ed. (Jan. 6, 1961), pp. 281-84.

rectly with the vote. Yet the analysis of national survey samples, as it portrays the voting of broad categories of persons, also conceals as it averages out local peculiarities in voting behavior that are dimly perceptible from painstaking inspection of election returns.

If we proceed from general propositions about electoral behavior and from 1956 benchmarks established by sample surveys, it may be possible to discover some meaning in the gross statistics of the 1960 presidential election. One relevant proposition is that an individual's vote has a high probability of being the same as it was at the preceding election. Another is that an individual's sense of party identification functions as a powerful determinant of his vote. Still another is that loyalties to nonparty groups may, when such groups are salient in a person's political perceptions, either reinforce the tendencies induced by party identification or offset them.

What benchmarks do the survey data give us about the pattern of the 1956 voting? Or what were its characteristics that might be plausibly supposed to be especially relevant in the determination of the vote in the circumstances of the 1960 campaign? The vote for Eisenhower consisted in critical measure of persons who regarded themselves as Democrats but who, under the conditions of 1952 and 1956, liked Ike enough to repress their normal Democratic predilections. Defectors from the Democratic party, with 1948 as the base point, were especially numerous among workers, farmers, and Roman Catholics.[5] On the other hand, the Stevenson vote of 1956, only 42.2 per cent of the major-party total, probably consisted principally of persons so strongly identified with the Demo-

[5] The data of the Survey Research Center, University of Michigan, indicate the following Democratic percentages of the two-party vote by demographic categories:

	1948	1952	1956	1960
Professional and Business	20	31	32	46
White Collar	50	35	38	44
Skilled and Semiskilled	78	56	45	59
Unskilled	74	69	55	59
Farm Operators	65	37	46	32
Negro	—	80	64	70
Protestant	47	36	35	37
Catholic	65	51	45	81

cratic party that they remained unmoved by the appeals that drew many of their less steadfast fellow partisans into the Republican camp.

Given the pattern of the 1956 vote and the bearing of party identification on voting, what might reasonably be expected to occur in 1960? The absence of General Eisenhower from the ticket deprived the Republican party of its principal attraction to Democratic identifiers and to independents. The motivation of the 1956 vote had been heavily colored by an admiration for the General untinged by policy considerations.[6] Nixon in 1960 presented an image to the electorate of a genuine Republican, a factor of utility in holding Republican identifiers in line but of limited value in retaining the support of those Democrats who had been lured from their normal partisan posture by Eisenhower. Kennedy, on the other hand, presented himself as a certified Democrat and missed few opportunities to activate the loyalties of Democratic identifiers. Had these been the only operative factors, they would have been expected to bring the popular vote more nearly into line than in 1956, with the preponderant Democratic identification within the electorate.[7] Another factor, though, muddied the waters: Kennedy's religion. That element, given the total situation, might have been expected to reinforce a tendency of those Catholic Democrats who defected in 1952 and 1956 to move back to their partisan home. It might also have been expected to offset the same tendency among Protestant Democratic defectors and perhaps even to drive some 1956 Stevenson voters to Nixon.

[6] See Angus Campbell *et al., The American Voter* (Wiley, 1960), Chap. 19.

[7] Of the Survey Research Center's 1958 national sample, 29 per cent regarded themselves as Republicans; 47 per cent, as Democrats. These figures include both "strong" and "weak" identifiers with each party but exclude those "independents" who felt "closer" to one or the other of the parties.

A Gross State-by-State Analysis

A rough check on these expectations about voter movements may be made by a state-by-state comparison of the shifts in the presidential vote from 1956 to 1960. Table 6.2 shows the relationship from state to state between Roman Catholicism and the movement of the popular vote toward the Democratic party from 1956 to 1960. So gross a correlation must be regarded with reserve for technical reasons as well as because of the imperfections of the data on church affiliation.[8] Yet the data of the table support several broad propositions.

The most marked accretions to Democratic strength from 1956 to 1960 occurred in the states with extremely high proportions of Roman Catholics. Among the states with fewest Catholics are to be found some in which Kennedy's vote was only slightly greater than Stevenson's 1956 percentage or even lower as in Georgia, Oklahoma, and Tennessee.[9] And the correlation between Catholicism and Democratic gains, becomes quite ragged among those states not at the high or low extremes of Catholicism. Whether a state was 30 per cent or 1 per cent Catholic might make considerable difference in its electoral behavior, yet, on the average, it made

[8] Church membership, as reported by ecclesiastical authorities, suffers from some of the same shortcomings as the numbers of registrants under systems of permanent registration. The procedures for purging the rolls are defective. Nevertheless, the data probably rank states according to their population proportions Catholic.

[9] Table 6.2 shows the percentage-point difference between the 1956 and 1960 Democratic percentages of the two-party vote. Because that is a simple but treacherous figure, it is supplemented by a Republican defection ratio. Say that the Democratic percentage in a state increased from 20 to 25. That five-point increase would produce a Republican defection ratio of 6.25, that is, 5 as a percentage of 80. The basic difficulty with the percentage-point measure is that an identical movement in different localities may produce different percentage-point differences. Assume three precincts, 90 per cent, 50 per cent, and 20 per cent Republican. If 10 per cent of the Republican voters uniformly moved over to the Democratic side, the percentage-point differences would be 9, 5, and 2. The data of Table 6.2 are such in range, however, that the principal advantage of the ratio is that it inflates differences among the states and makes the figures easier to handle.

TABLE 6.2. *Shifts in Presidential Vote, 1956-1960, in Relation to 1956 Democratic Percentage of Vote, Ranked within Groups by Roman Catholic Percentage of Population*[a]

1956 Democratic Percentage of Vote	State	Republican Defection Ratio[b]	Democratic Percentage Point Gain 1956–1960[c]	Catholic Percentage of Population
25–29	Vermont	18.7	13.5	30
	Maine	18.3	13.0	25
30–34	New Jersey	24.1	15.8	37
	New Hampshire	19.2	12.7	36
	Kansas	7.6	5.0	11
35–39	Connecticut	27.3	17.4	37
	New York	22.7	13.9	30
	Wisconsin	16.1	10.0	30
	Arizona	9.0	5.5	25
	North Dakota	10.2	6.3	22
	Ohio	12.8	7.8	19
	Wyoming	8.3	5.0	17
	Colorado	9.2	5.6	16
	Nebraska	5.2	3.4	15
	Indiana	8.1	4.9	12
	Idaho	12.1	7.4	5
	Utah	15.2	9.8	4
40–44	Rhode Island	37.6	21.9	59
	Massachusetts	33.4	19.9	48
	New Mexico	14.5	8.4	44
	Pennsylvania	13.8	7.8	27
	Illinois	16.3	9.7	27
	Montana	10.1	5.8	24
	California	9.5	5.3	22
	Michigan	12.2	6.8	22
	Maryland	22.7	13.6	19
	Texas	12.0	6.7	18
	Nevada	15.9	9.2	17
	South Dakota	0.3	0.2	17
	Iowa	4.0	2.4	14
	Delaware	11.0	6.1	11
	Oregon	4.7	2.6	7
	Florida	10.1	5.8	5
	Oklahoma	+ 7.1	−3.9	4
	Virginia	10.6	6.3	3
45–49	Minnesota	8.4	4.5	23
	Washington	5.7	3.1	11
	Kentucky	1.8	1.0	9
	West Virginia	12.6	6.8	5
	Tennessee	+ 6.6	−3.3	1
50–54	Missouri	0.2	0.1	15
	Arkansas	0.9	0.4	1
	North Carolina	2.8	1.4	0.7
	Georgia	+12.0	−4.0	0.6

[a] Alabama, Louisiana, and South Carolina are omitted from the analysis because a large third-party vote in one or the other of the election years makes the type of comparison attempted not feasible.
[b] The Republican defection ratio is the Democratic percentage-point gain as a percentage of the 1956 Republican percentage.
[c] The percentage-point difference is the 1960 Democratic percentage minus the 1956 Democratic percentage. All values, except those so indicated, are positive.

little difference for a state's vote whether it was 6 per cent or 24 per cent Catholic.[10]

The moral is that factors in addition to Catholicism had a bearing on the net electoral shift from 1956 to 1960. Not only the averages but the deviant rankings of individual states in Table 6.2 point to that fact. Democratic gains in Arizona, for example, are out of line on the low side.[11] Idaho and Utah show Democratic gains considerably out of line on the high side as does Maryland. An ecclesiastical determinism would have predicted a lesser shift than occurred in West Virginia; and in Missouri, a wider one.

Analysis at the County Level

Correlations between huge aggregates, such as those employed in Table 6.2, are rightly suspect. The relationships that appear in that table might, for example, be accounted for by degree of industrialization, by sectionalism, or by other factors rather than by differences in religious composition among the states. If, however, Catholicism was the determinative factor in abnormally wide Democratic gains, we should expect to find among counties within

[10] This point is established by another arrangement of the data of Table 6.2. This array of the data also represents a means by which statistics can be doctored to suggest to the unwary that a more regular relationship exists between two variables than actually prevails. It follows:

Per Cent Catholic	Number of States	Mean Democratic Percentage Point Gain, 1956-1960	Mean Republican Defection Ratio
35 plus 6		16.0	26.0
30-34 1		13.5	18.7
25-29 5		10.8	17.4
20-24 6		5.7	9.9
15-19 9		5.7	9.6
10-14 5		4.3	7.3
5-9 9		4.2	7.2
0-4 8		1.7	2.5

[11] Arizona's deviant position in the ranking may be in part a data problem. The religious figure is for 1952. The rapid increase in population (74 per cent from 1950 to 1960) may have changed the state's religious complexion and its political coloration as well. Arizona's increase in total presidential vote from 1956 to 1960 (37 per cent) exceeded that of any other state.

individual states a pattern like that shown by Table 6.2 to exist among states.

Counties of high Catholic population, for example, whether they were urban or rural, would show wide movements to the Democratic side. Table 6.3, which conducts a quick survey across the country to check that possibility, indicates the shift that occurred in the three most Catholic counties in each of the states listed. These counties rallied far more impressively to Kennedy than did the states of which they were a part.

While information such as that in Table 6.3, along with other data to be presented, underpins the poll findings that Catholics as a group moved sharply Democratic in 1960, detailed inspection of the county figures also suggests the existence of considerable variety from place to place in the behavior of Catholic voters.[12] Even the limited information of Table 6.3 indicates some of that variety. Note the exceptionally sharp movements in the New York counties listed; their Democratic percentages exceeded even those of 1936. It may be a fair inference that those Catholic Republicans who deserted their party in 1960 were especially numerous in upstate New York. As one inspects the table, though, it becomes apparent that the electoral shift associated with the agglomeration of Catholic population varied from place to place. Some of the variation doubtless develops from the defects of the measures employed.[13] Even so the magnitude of the differences points probably to a varied response among Catholics to campaign issues. Generally, the data from states west of the Mississippi show a less marked electoral shift associated with Catholicism. In New Mex-

---

[12] Dr. Gallup's American Institute of Public Opinion estimated the Democratic percentage of the presidential vote among Roman Catholics in 1960 at 78 per cent; 1956, 51 per cent; 1952, 56 per cent. The comparable figures for union members are instructive: 1960, 61 per cent; 1956, 57 per cent; 1952, 65 per cent.

[13] In the comparison of two elections the analyst is plagued by the peculiarities of two elections. Some of the oddities of 1960 may really be the oddities of 1956. Thus, in eastern industrial centers the 1956 defection of Catholics from the Democratic party was especially high in comparison with that in the Far West. Another is the untrustworthiness of the data on the religious composition of the population. The chances are that the county data rank the counties according to population composition less reliably than the state data rank the states.

TABLE 6.3. *Democratic Gains, 1956-1960, in Counties of Highest Catholic Proportions in Selected States*[a]

State	Counties	Per Cent Catholic	Per Cent Democratic 1956	Democratic Percentage Point Gain	Republican Defection Ratio
New York	Clinton...............	59	29.5	25.2	35.7
	Franklin..............	59	28.7	23.8	33.3
	Erie..................	56	36.3	20.4	32.1
New Jersey	Hudson...............	61	36.8	23.7	37.5
	Middlesex.............	45	39.2	19.1	31.4
	Mercer...............	41	48.5	12.7	24.6
Pennsylvania	Lackawanna...........	50	46.4	15.3	28.5
	Elk...................	48	38.1	15.9	25.7
	Luzerne..............	46	41.3	18.3	31.1
Ohio	Mercer...............	49	31.1	18.9	27.4
	Putnam...............	48	29.6	17.3	24.6
	Cuyahoga.............	33	46.3	13.5	25.1
Michigan	Delta.................	43	45.5	9.6	17.6
	Bay...................	43	39.4	13.0	21.4
	Leelanau..............	42	30.1	9.8	14.0
Indiana	Dubois................	59	42.7	18.9	33.0
	Perry.................	36	44.9	8.0	14.5
	Franklin..............	33	36.7	9.5	15.0
Illinois	Clinton...............	52	36.5	15.5	24.4
	Cook.................	39	43.1	13.4	23.5
	LaSalle...............	39	35.4	14.6	22.6
Kentucky	Marion...............	41	49.8	16.3	32.5
	Nelson...............	40	44.1	16.8	30.0
	Kenton...............	31	41.7	5.4	9.3
Wisconsin	Portage...............	64	45.7	16.3	30.0
	Kewaunee.............	61	31.6	20.3	29.7
	Brown................	61	29.3	20.9	29.6
Minnesota	Stearns...............	68	36.1	22.3	34.9
	Benton...............	58	42.1	13.6	23.5
	Scott.................	57	45.3	17.0	31.1
Missouri	Ste. Genevieve.........	69	47.3	14.8	28.1
	Osage.................	57	44.3	8.0	14.4
	Perry.................	45	34.8	8.6	13.2
North Dakota	Stark.................	60	29.5	27.1	38.4
	Emmons..............	51	22.8	30.6	39.6
	Rollette...............	52	54.5	9.1	20.0
New Mexico	Taos..................	81	46.9	11.6	21.8
	Santa Fe..............	79	42.8	15.2	26.6
	Mora.................	74	41.5	10.4	17.8
California	San Benito............	43	40.4	8.1	13.6
	Merced...............	40	53.9	2.5	5.4
	Sacramento............	38	54.8	1.7	3.8
Oregon	Marion...............	17	35.8	4.9	7.6
	Gilliam...............	12	40.4	5.5	9.2
	Sherman..............	12	38.5	4.9	8.0
Washington	Yakima...............	17	39.6	1.3	2.1
	Spokane..............	15	48.3	3.6	7.0
	Kittitas...............	15	48.1	5.9	11.4

[a] The county data used as the basis for the computations of this table, as well as those used elsewhere in the chapter, rest in part on unofficial sources. That dependence may produce a degree of error in some individual cases, but does not vitiate the general argument.

ico, for example, the traditional Republican attachments of many Hispanic Catholics probably provided an anchorage resistant to the religious appeal. In California voter shift also appeared far less marked in the strong Catholic counties than might have been expected.

The county data of Table 6.3 make clear that factors in addition to Catholicism had a hand in the 1956-1960 gains in Democratic strength. Some of these factors are well known, such as the Democratic recapture of Negro support, which had sagged sharply in some localities in 1956.[14] Others, not readily identifiable by ecological correlation, were also contributory. Their existence is made manifest in correlations between Roman Catholic population percentages and county Republican defection ratios. In New Jersey, for example, a fairly regular relationship prevails between these variables. In Maryland, on the other hand, the correlation is low which suggests the existence of additional factors in the 1956-1960 voting shift in that state. Sketchy analyses of upstate New York votes also show considerable irregularity in the relation of religion and voting shifts.[15]

The possibility was suggested that the 1956-1960 shift to the Democratic column by Roman Catholics may have been in large measure a return of Democratic identifiers to their traditional voting posture. While correlation analysis does not permit much of a check on the hypothesis, scraps of evidence support it. In Minnesota, for example, the seven counties highest in Catholic population percentage tended to approximate in their 1960 presidential vote their 1948 Democratic presidential percentage. In these counties Senator Humphrey's vote also closely resembled the 1948 vote.

[14] The American Institute of Public Opinion estimated the Democratic percentage among Negro voters in 1952 at 79; 1956, 61; 1960, 68.

[15] For example, in those upstate counties 20-24 per cent Democratic in 1956 the increase in the percentage-point Democratic gain 1956-1960 did not vary as closely with Catholic population as might have been expected. The mean Democratic percentage-point gain in relation to Catholic population percentage in these counties was as follows:

Per Cent Roman Catholic	5-9	10-14	15-19	20-24	25-29
Mean Democratic Percentage-Point Gain	10.2	12.1	12.3	15.4	14.4

The means, incidentally, conceal rather wide dispersions among the counties within the groups averaged.

Another condition prevailed in counties under 10 per cent Catholic and with more than twice as many Lutherans as Catholics. In these counties, Humphrey's vote resembled the 1948 presidential vote, but Kennedy failed by far to match Truman's showing.[16] A similar result flows from the application of a different technique in Wisconsin, that is, a comparison of the 1948 and 1960 vote in the six counties with the highest Democratic percentage-point gain in the presidential vote from 1956 to 1960 and in the six counties with the least such gain. In the volatile counties, both the presidential and gubernatorial vote closely resembled that of 1948. In the stable counties, the Democratic gubernatorial vote approximated the 1948 presidential level, but Kennedy's vote fell far below that point.[17] The projection of these findings to the national population would be scarcely justified, but the data strongly suggest that the electorate contains a substantial sector of persons disposed generally to vote Democratic who remained unmoved by Kennedy's candidacy.[18]

The Other End of the Spectrum

If we transfer our attention to the predominantly non-Catholic areas, evidence may be assembled indicative of the voting behavior of Protestants. The data yield a mixed picture. In some Protestant areas, Kennedy polled a higher percentage of the vote than Stevenson drew in 1956; in others, the Democratic percentage of the

[16] The mean Democratic percentage in these groups of counties was as follows:

	President 1948	President 1960	Senator 1960
High Catholic	62.3	60.4	61.7
Low Catholic	57.1	46.5	55.3

[17] The mean Democratic percentage in these groups of counties was as follows:

	President 1948	President 1960	Governor 1960
High Gain Counties	50.0	49.3	49.5
Low Gain Counties	54.0	40.9	51.0

[18] These observations find re-inforcement in the fact that in the Midwest and in the West the Democratic gubernatorial or senatorial candidate who polled a smaller percentage of the vote than Kennedy attracted was exceptional.

vote declined. These county shifts, measured in percentage points, tended to be considerably narrower than the marked movements in heavily Catholic counties such as those listed in Table 6.3. Nevertheless, the figures suggest that a considerable number of 1956 Stevenson voters turned up in the Nixon ranks in 1960. That desertion from the Democratic ranks was counterbalanced by an opposite movement of 1956 Eisenhower voters among non-Catholics to Kennedy.

A rough and ready way to determine whether an election tends to split the electorate along some line of potential cleavage is to ascertain the direction of the shift in the vote among counties. If there has been no such effect, that is, if the impact of the campaign moves all sorts of people in the same direction, the odds are that the vote in most counties will shift, in comparison with the preceding election, in the same direction. Thus, in 1932 about 99 per cent of the counties showed Democratic gains over 1928. In 1952 about the same proportion of counties moved, in comparison with 1948, toward the Republican party.[19] On the other hand, when the issues of the campaign have a differential impact that widens the cleavage between classes of citizens (provided they are at least to some extent geographically segregated), contradictory shifts in voting occur among counties or other small electoral units.

Application of this technique to scattered states across the country provides some indication of the degree to which a scissors effect characterized the movement of the vote from 1956 to 1960. The broad picture is one of a movement toward the Democrats in most counties accompanied by a countermovement that differed markedly in its geographical extent within individual states. In the northeastern states of Maryland, New Jersey, and New York, 100 per cent of the counties registered Democratic gains over 1956. While the size of those gains varied among counties, the uniformity of the direction of movement makes plausible the hunch that in the northeastern part of the country factors were operative that moved

[19] For this analysis, see V. O. Key, Jr., *Politics, Parties, and Pressure Groups* (Crowell, 4th ed., 1958), p. 569.

most sectors of the population toward higher support of the Democratic ticket than in 1956.

In the interior of the country, however, contrasting movements appear. While in most of the counties in the states examined, Kennedy increased the Democratic vote over that of Stevenson, in some counties Nixon ran ahead of Eisenhower's 1956 percentage. The differences among states in the geographical spread of the growth in Democratic support provide clues to the peculiarities of the behavior of some states. The percentages of the counties in selected states in which the Democratic proportion of the vote increased from 1956 to 1960 were as follows:

Pennsylvania	76	Wisconsin	93
Ohio	96	Minnesota	83
Michigan	97	Iowa	69
Indiana	76	Nebraska	68
Illinois	87	Missouri	24

While the geographical generality of the movement to Kennedy in the counties of these states makes it clear that his gains were spread widely through the population, the data are also indicative of a special weakness in several states. In about a fourth of the Pennsylvania counties, Kennedy did not do so well as Stevenson, a circumstance that made his strong showing in Philadelphia of crucial importance in winning the state's electoral vote.[20] The Ohio figure and the ranking of that state in Table 6.2 create skepticism about estimates of the prodigious feat of the Republican organization in carrying the state for Nixon; these limited data make it appear that Democrats gained in Ohio to about the same extent as they did in other states of similar demographic characteristics.

Among the states just listed, Missouri departs most markedly from the general pattern; as seen in Table 6.2, Missouri's Democratic gain fell considerably below what might have been expected in the light of the size of its Catholic population. The deviation appears to rest in the exceptional weakness of Kennedy in the rural counties. While the easy, and doubtless partially correct, explana-

[20] Philadelphia was one of the five major cities in which the Democratic percentage approached or exceeded that at the high tide of Democratic fortunes in 1936. The others were Boston, Baltimore, Detroit, and St. Louis.

tion would be that Missouri Protestants found Catholicism especially uncongenial, the data intimate that another factor may also
have had some weight. That is, in some areas Republican identifiers
who had defected to the Democrats may have been re-inforced by
the events of the 1960 campaign in a tendency to revert to their
traditional partisan position.

In the states just west of the Mississippi, Republicans had shown
signs of conversion to the Democrats on a fairly large scale in
1948. These Republican defections continued in varying degrees in
1954, 1956, and 1958, depending somewhat on the status of farm
prices. Kennedy's candidacy may have supplemented, or at least
offered no resistance to, the disposition of these defectors, in the
absence of countervailing considerations, to vote their party. To
illustrate the point: Missouri's southwestern congressional district, the seventh, probably deserves to be regarded as Republican;
at least a district that sent Dewey Short to Congress for many
terms seems to merit that characterization. In this district, the
presidential vote in 1960 almost exactly matched, county by county,
the 1944 presidential vote.[21] Many voters in this district may have
merely returned to their normal voting pattern. If this was indeed
the case, the same phenomenon may have been operative to some
extent throughout the trans-Mississippi area. That is, non-Catholic
Republican identifiers may have moved within a pattern of motivation similar to that of Catholic Democratic identifiers.

In another group of states, the oddities apparent in the state
analysis in Table 6.2 also manifest themselves in the vote movements within counties. Here are the percentages of counties in
which Kennedy gained over Stevenson in these states:

Idaho	100	Oregon	91
Utah	100	California	90
North Dakota	93	Washington	85
New Mexico	81		

In Idaho and Utah county figures parallel the position of these
states in the state-by-state comparison in which they demonstrated
far wider Democratic gains than might have been expected. Evi-

[21] The mean Democratic presidential percentage in the counties of this district
was 32.7 in 1944; 37.9 in 1948; 30.9 in 1952; 36.7 in 1956; and 32.1 in 1960.

dently some pro-Democratic tendency of special strength was in operation in these states, though it did not suffice to place them in the Democratic column. In Utah, Democrats won a Republican seat in the House of Representatives as well as a majority in the state senate. In Idaho the voters retired a Republican representative.

The foregoing inspection of counties in selected states indicates that contrary movements existed in the electorate from 1956 to 1960. When attention is focused on counties at the lower end of the distribution according to their Catholic population percentage, a more precise notion may be had of the response of Protestants to the issues of the campaign. The broad conclusion that emerges is that predominantly Protestant areas did not uniformly turn in a decreased Democratic vote. In some such counties Kennedy gained over Stevenson; in others he failed to maintain Stevenson's 1956 vote. Yet in neither type of area was the difference between the Democratic percentage of the vote in 1956 and 1960 ordinarily large.

In the tabulation that follows, those counties reporting less than 5 per cent Catholic population are classified according to whether the 1960 Democratic percentage was smaller or larger than that of 1956. (The Wisconsin and Minnesota counties are those less than 10 per cent Catholic; the Texas counties are those reporting no Catholic population.) The numbers of these types of counties for a few states are as follows:

State	With Democratic Gains	With Democratic Losses
Pennsylvania	5	9
Ohio	24	3
Indiana	24	21
Michigan	13	1
Illinois	23	6
Wisconsin	3	5
Minnesota	9	9
Missouri	3	72
New Mexico	1	1
Texas	32	2
California	3	0
Oregon	15	3
Washington	3	3

If Protestantism had been uniformly associated with a movement away from the Democratic party, the counties tabulated above would have all shown Republican gains. That they do not manifest such a pattern indicates that Protestants of different areas (and perhaps of different denominations) responded to the campaign differently and that the religious factor was at times outweighed by other influences. The above data also supplement earlier observations about the peculiarities of individual states. Whatever the measure employed, Missouri appears as an area marked by exceptional coolness toward Kennedy. On the other hand, the Pacific Coast states turn up as areas in which the relation between religion and voting shifts seemed to be relatively muted.[22]

In this quick reconnaissance, it has not been possible to search out the peculiarities of those Protestant counties that increased and those that decreased their Democratic percentage from 1956 to 1960. Both the increases and the decreases were usually relatively small, often small enough to be accounted for by variations in organizational endeavor, either ecclesiastical or partisan. Broadly, though, they point to the inability of Kennedy to build Democratic strength appreciably in these areas. The probabilities are that in those counties of this type in which Democratic strength increased, the normal pull of party was supplemented by other considerations. Thus, Jewell finds: "Every Kentucky county where the Democrats ran at least 4% above their 1956 percentage of the vote fell into one or more of these categories: it was urban, above average in Catholic population, a major coal-producing county, or in the depressed area of southeastern Kentucky."[23]

[22] The American Institute of Public Opinion estimated the Democratic percentage of the vote of Protestants at 38 per cent in 1960; 37 per cent in 1956. The election returns make it evident that these national figures conceal 1956-1960 movements by Protestants from Republican to Democratic and from Democratic to Republican.

[23] Malcolm E. Jewell, "The Presidential Election in Kentucky," *Review of Government* (Bureau of Government Research, University of Kentucky, January 1961).

The Special Case of the South

Memories of the campaign of 1928 generated a good deal of interest about how the South would respond to the issues of the 1960 campaign. Probably the most noteworthy features of the 1960 voting were happenings that did not take place. Significant for the long run was the demonstration that the 1952 and 1956 Republican vote in the South had by no means depended entirely on the personal popularity of General Eisenhower. In no state of the erstwhile solid South did the Republican vote decline substantially. As was plain even in 1952, the South has come to be territory in which Republican presidential candidates have at least a fighting chance.

On the other hand, no movement away from the Democratic ticket comparable to that of 1928 occurred. Doubtless a major reason for this was that those southerners most susceptible to Republican appeals had become presidential Republicans in 1952 and 1956; many of those who remained in that status in 1960 were re-inforced in their predilections by the religious issue. Moreover, some additional defections from the Democratic party occurred through shifts of 1956 Stevenson supporters and through the attraction to the polls of 1956 nonvoters.[24] In Tennessee, Georgia, and Oklahoma, Kennedy polled a smaller percentage of the vote than Stevenson had. On the other hand, Kennedy did better than Stevenson in North Carolina, Texas, South Carolina, and Louisiana. The net figures conceal, of course, contrary movements within states.[25] On the whole, the Kennedy candidacy in the South did

[24] The South was well represented among the states ranking high in the percentage increase of their presidential vote from 1956 to 1960. The top eleven states, in the order of rate of increase, were: Arizona, Louisiana, South Carolina, Florida, New Mexico, Mississippi, Maine, California, Texas, North Carolina, Minnesota.

[25] Illustrative of these contrary movements are percentages of the counties in selected states in which Kennedy's proportion of the vote was greater than Stevenson's in 1956: West Virginia, 98; Texas, 71; North Carolina, 59; Tennessee, 28; Oklahoma, 12.

not so much push Democrats into the Nixon camp as fail to activate the loyalties of Democratic defectors of 1956. To all this West Virginia was a notable exception, if that state is regarded as southern. Kennedy's gains over Stevenson there were striking and were accompanied by the displacement of the Republican state administration.

Elections to Other Offices

To some extent the simultaneous elections of representatives, senators, and state officers may be fitted into the pattern of movement of the presidential vote.

The House of Representatives

A shift of party control of the Presidency is accompanied normally by the capture of a goodly number of House seats by the new President's party from the opposition. On the other hand, those House candidates of the President's party who are incumbents rarely suffer defeat, even if they come from marginal districts. Their own strength is supplemented by the impetus of the swing in the popular vote to the head of their ticket. At least these relations tend to prevail when the popular strength of the new President is congruent with that of his party generally.[26]

The distribution of Kennedy support was such that his party, on balance, lost seats in the House of Representatives, yet the location of Democratic losses and gains by and large accorded with the tendency of House results to follow the presidential voting. The great accessions to the Democratic presidential vote came mainly in areas already represented by Democrats; the position of these representatives was so secure that they needed no help to get reelected. On the other hand, Democratic candidates from districts marginally Democratic in 1958 often had no help from the na-

[26] For a comprehensive analysis of the question, see Milton C. Cummings, Jr., "Congressmen and the Electorate," Ph.D. dissertation, Harvard University, 1960.

TABLE 6.4. *Results of 1960 House Elections in Relation to 1958 Party Division of Popular Vote by Districts*

Per Cent Democratic 1958	Number of Districts	Held by Democrats	Changed R to D	Changed D to R	Held by Republicans
0–34	12	—	—	—	12
35–39	31	—	1	—	30
40–44	49	—	4	—	45
45–47.4	36	—	3	—	33
47.5–49.9	25	—	—	—	25
50–52.4	32	12	—	20[a]	—
52.5–54.9	12	8	—	4	—
55–59	20	18	—	2	—
60–64	40	37	—	3	—
65–100	180	180	—	—	—
Total	437	255	8	29	145

[a] Includes Iowa 4, which switched to Republican in 1959 special election.

tional ticket; their districts were in areas in which there was no surge to Kennedy. A goodly proportion of these Democratic candidates lost. Similarly, the local strength of those Republicans who held marginal districts enabled them to withstand the Democratic tide, which often ran at a low level in their localities if it ran at all. The net outcome of these forces was that Democrats picked up only eight districts that had been won by Republicans in 1958; Republican candidates carried 29 districts that had returned Democrats in 1958. The Democratic party came out of the election with 262 seats in contrast with the 282 it held after the election of 1958.

Those House seats that Republicans took from Democrats were principally in Nixon territory, although some Democrats in such areas were well enough entrenched to survive despite Nixon's strength. Republican successes in 1960 depended in part on the special circumstances of 1958 that had given Democrats victories in districts usually regarded as Republican or as only marginally Democratic. The mobilization of Republican identifiers by the Nixon candidacy aided in the displacement of the fortunate Demo-

cratic candidates of 1958. Of the 32 districts won by Democrats
by 50 to 52.4 per cent of the vote in 1958, Republicans carried
20 in 1960. (See Table 6.4 for the detailed data.) Nixon led Kennedy in 18 of these 20 districts, often by a substantial margin.[27]
In most of the districts that Republicans won from Democrats,
Nixon's activation of Republican loyalties and the straight-ticket
tendencies of presidential years doubtless contributed to Democratic woes.[28]

In general, those Democratic representatives who managed to
hold on to marginal districts did so on their own power and without much help from the head of the ticket. Of the 19 marginal
districts (50-54.9 per cent Democratic in 1958) in which Democrats turned back Republican challenges in 1960, Kennedy carried 7.[29] Moreover, the odds are that local circumstances rather
than the trend of the presidential vote were principally controlling
in the eight districts that moved from Republican to Democratic.
In 5 of them Nixon ran ahead of Kennedy; the rather wide Nixon
leads in Idaho 2 and Utah 1 suggest that the Democratic winners
in those districts must have had exceptional campaigning skills or
benefited from some other favorable factor.

[27] The two districts in which Democratic incumbents lost, despite Kennedy's
local plurality, were Pennsylvania 10 and Minnesota 3. In Pennsylvania 10,
William W. Scranton, described as a folksy, millionaire candidate, bested the
Democratic incumbent despite the fact that the district gave about 54 per cent of
its presidential vote to Kennedy.

For data on the presidential vote within congressional districts, I am obliged
to Richard Scammon, then Director of Elections Research, Governmental Affairs
Institute.

[28] Mention of some of the districts that shifted to Republican control will
suggest something of the geography of Republican gains: Colorado 2; Indiana
5, 6, 9, 10, 11; Kansas 2, 3; Iowa 2, 4; Nebraska 3, 4; Ohio 6, 17; Oregon 4;
North Dakota 1 at large; Maine 1, 2; Vermont 1 at large. In all the districts
listed Nixon drew a majority of the popular vote. In two additional districts the
Nixon plurality was spectacular. In Missouri 7, the Ozark district, he polled 63
per cent of the vote. In Pennsylvania 19, the York district, the Democratic
incumbent Quigley was handicapped by his own Roman Catholicism as well as
by the fact that Nixon won 62.4 per cent of the district vote, a shade better than
Eisenhower's 1956 performance.

[29] It ought to be added that in the marginal districts (50-54.9 per cent Democratic in 1958) retained by Democrats the mean Kennedy percentage of the
vote, 48.7, was higher than the mean Kennedy vote, 43.6, in those marginal
districts lost.

TABLE 6.5. *Senatorial Election Results in Relation to Popular Presidential Vote, 1960*

Percentage Democratic Presidential	Seats Retained by		Changed	Total Won by	
	D's	R's	D to R	D's	R's
35–39	1[a]	2	—	1	2
40–44	1[b]	3	1[c]	1	4
45–49	5	4	—	5	4
50–54	10	1	1[d]	10	2
55–59	1	—	—	1	—
60–64	3	1[e]	—	3	1
Total	21	11	2	21	13

[a] Eastland of Mississippi.
[b] Kerr of Oklahoma.
[c] Wyoming.
[d] Delaware.
[e] Saltonstall of Massachusetts.

The Senate

An examination of the results of the senatorial voting shows that incumbent senators have an excellent chance for re-election, no matter how the presidential race may go in their state. Yet the Republican party was fortunate that it had few incumbent senators standing for re-election in those states in which Kennedy's candidacy produced a marked upsurge in Democratic strength. Two incumbent Republicans held their places as Kennedy carried their states. Senator Clifford P. Case, of New Jersey, it is probably not unfair to say, did so in part because he had differentiated himself in the mind of his constituents from the Republican party. Moreover, the Kennedy margin in New Jersey was narrow. Senator Saltonstall's re-election in Massachusetts, in the face of a heavy Democratic presidential plurality, gave a striking indication of his hold on the Massachusetts electorate.

The only shifts in party control of Senate seats occurred in Wyoming and Delaware. In Wyoming, the Democratic incumbent was not a candidate for re-election, a fact that made it more probable that the outcome of the senatorial voting would coincide with that of the presidential voting, as it did.[30] In Delaware J. Allen Frear, the Democratic incumbent, lost to the Republican, J. Caleb Boggs, as Kennedy carried the state. Yet in this partisan divergence there was a certain ideological consistency: Mr. Frear had a conservative voting record; the labor unions of the state supported Mr. Boggs.

The Governors

The elections of governors showed only a slight net change in the partisan division. Fifteen Democrats and twelve Republicans won, a net gain of one for the Republicans, but the figures concealed a good deal of turnover. Democrats captured six governorships from Republicans; Republicans took seven from Democrats. Of these thirteen changes, eight were moves in line with the state's presidential vote. The remaining five were contrary to the trend of the presidential vote. The deviant results probably measure the popular impact of exceptional circumstances. North Dakota and Indiana elected Democratic governors as they gave their electoral vote to Nixon. In both states the results probably reflected in part the existence of a goodly number of Democrats not disposed to support the national ticket. That interpretation is re-inforced for North Dakota by the Democratic capture of a senatorial seat at a special election in June 1960. The Indiana Democratic victory, however, doubtless hinged in considerable measure on what might be called the exceptional record of the Republican state administration. In Minnesota, New Mexico, and Massachusetts, Republicans replaced Democratic governors despite Kennedy pluralities. The changes in Minnesota and New Mexico were accomplished by extremely narrow pluralities, but the Massachusetts Republican victory against a Kennedy landslide undoubtedly expressed an adverse electoral judgment of the outgoing Democratic state administration. Of the four governorships kept in Democratic hands

[30] The Republican winner of the Wyoming Senate seat, Keith Thomson, died before taking office. The Democratic governor filled the vacancy with a Democrat.

TABLE 6.6. *Results of Gubernatorial Elections in Relation to Popular Presidential Vote by States, 1960*

Democratic Presidential Percentage	Governorships Retained by		Changed		Total Won by	
	D's	R's	R to D	D to R	D's	R's
35–39	1[a]	—	—	1	1	1
40–44	—	2	2	3[b]	2	5
45–49	3	3	—	—	3	3
50–54	5	—	3	2	8	2
60–64	—	—	1	1	1	1
Total	9	5	6	7	15	12

[a] Nebraska.

[b] Includes Maine in which the governorship was held by the former lieutenant governor, a Republican, who had succeeded after the death of the Democrat.

against the pull of a Nixon presidential plurality, two—Wisconsin and Washington—were instances in which incumbent governors sought re-election, a circumstance that often provides the margin necessary to resist the pull of an opposition presidential ticket. The third, Florida, occasions no astonishment, but Democratic success in Nebraska, given the Nixon vote in the state, must have indicated the presence of exceptionally powerful factors operating to favor the Democratic candidate.

Summary

Only a limited range of interpretations of voting may be derived from ecological correlations. Even more limited are those that may be drawn from the necessarily crude and incomplete analysis on which this discussion has had to rest. Yet several broad findings appear to fit the data at least provisionally.

1. The presidential voting in 1960 may be interpreted broadly in terms of the pull of partisanship and of the disturbances of the

basic pattern of partisanship by the events and appeals peculiar to the campaign. The absence of Eisenhower as a candidate removed from the scene a person who had in 1952 and 1956 drawn many Democratic identifiers from their normal partisan posture. The candidates adapted their strategies to this new situation. Senator Kennedy sought to arouse the partisan spirit of Democrats to capitalize on the Democratic advantage in the balance of party attachments. Vice President Nixon attempted to project an image of himself as something more than a Republican, an endeavor not simple of execution in the circumstances. Probably the net effect of the appeals of the campaign was to make individual electoral choice more nearly congruent with party identification in the electorate as a whole than it had been in 1956.

2. Of the appeals peculiar to the campaign, the religious issue evidently by far outweighed all others. For some people, it reinforced the pull of partisanship; for others, it ran counter to the tugs of party loyalty. In Catholic counties, both urban and rural, Kennedy's gains over Stevenson's 1956 vote were usually wide. Catholic Democratic defectors of 1956 were doubly moved to return to the fold in 1960. Kennedy cut into the normal Republican vote among Catholics, but as the polls made clear, he by no means wiped out that source of GOP support.

3. Protestants were subjected to conflicting pushes by the campaign. Their religion tended to prompt Protestant Democratic defectors of 1956 to remain in the Republican ranks; their partisanship tended to draw them to Kennedy. Protestants who supported Stevenson in 1956 had some motivation to vote Republican in 1960. These forces netted varying results in different localities. In some Protestant areas Kennedy made a better showing than Stevenson had; in others, notably in the South but not limited to that region, the Kennedy percentage did not match that of Stevenson. In the country as a whole the proportion of Protestants voting Democratic was approximately the same in 1960 as in 1956. Dr. Gallup estimated the percentages Democratic at 37 in 1956; 38 in 1960.

4. The estimation of the relation of religion to voting is affected by the choice of a benchmark against which to compare the 1960 vote. The use of 1956 as a base produces a result with a different

appearance from that which would come from the use of 1958. In comparison with 1958, the 1960 vote would show a massive shift by Protestants away from the Democratic party and a far less marked movement to the Democratic party by Catholics.[31] Comparisons between 1956 and 1960 lead to marked underestimates of the effect of the Kennedy candidacy in depressing the Democratic vote among Protestants. Even the 1960 returns alone make it obvious that a goodly number of Democrats could not bring themselves to vote for a Catholic for President.

5. Inspection of the county data suggests that the national survey data on the voting behavior of Protestants and Catholics (and other categories of persons as well) conceal variations from place to place in their political response. This appearance of variation may flow in part from the limitations inherent in aggregate data, though the differences from place to place among Protestants certainly are not attributable solely to the nature of the data. The detailed elections data dimly suggest the existence of some type of sectional differential which becomes most apparent in the contrast between the Far West and the Northeast. It seems probable that northeastern Catholics behaved differently from those of the Far West and that western non-Catholics probably responded differently, in degree, from their northeastern counterparts.

6. Probably the best guess is that Kennedy won in spite of rather than because of the fact that he was a Catholic. It is thus premature to conclude that the election overruled once and for all the custom that excluded Catholics from eligibility to the Presidency. If the performance of the Kennedy administration brings in the minds of substantial numbers of people an acceptance of the new rule, that fact will, in the absence of disturbing factors, be reflected in the pattern of the 1964 popular vote.

[31] The American Institute of Public Opinion estimated the Democratic percentage of the Protestant vote in the 1958 congressional elections at 51. In several states Kennedy's percentage of the 1960 vote was more than 5 points less than that of both the Democratic gubernatorial and senatorial candidates in 1958 or less by the same margin in those instances in which only one of these offices was filled. These states (excluding southern states) were: California, Colorado, Indiana, Iowa, Kansas, Maine, Missouri, Montana, Nebraska, Nevada, Ohio, South Dakota, Utah, Vermont, Washington, West Virginia, Wisconsin, and Wyoming.

7

The Impact on Foreign Relations

JOHN M. HIGHTOWER[1]

SINCE WORLD WAR II each national election in the United States has aroused interest throughout the world. But the 1960 presidential contest, after a slow start, excited extraordinary attention. There were several reasons for this. At the outset it became evident that, whether a Republican or a Democrat gained the victory, the enormous power concentration in Washington was destined to pass into the hands of a new and more vigorous generation. The religious issue gave the contest, in foreign eyes, an extra dimension of moral significance; for foreigners, this controversy grew into a test of America's idealism and its worthiness to lead the Free World. The foreign policy debate also caught and held foreign interest, with a curious consequence. Positions taken by Senator Kennedy and Vice President Nixon in the heat of debate were not dismissed abroad as empty campaign oratory; they were seized upon as forecasts of future action. Foreigners, seeing their interests directly involved, were drawn emotionally into the campaign. When Kennedy won the Presidency, it was obvious that people all over the world were ready and waiting for him to turn his campaign promises into the dollars and deeds of an action program on the new frontiers abroad.

---

[1] State Department Correspondent, Associated Press.

This chapter was prepared as a lecture given at the Brookings Institution in January 1961, and revised for publication in April 1961.

Kennedy's election and inauguration opened a new era in international relations by elevating to power youthful officials who had matured in public affairs after World War II. The era of men who gained high responsibility during the war—men like Eisenhower, Macmillan, and de Gaulle—began its final transition into history. The change to a new generation enlarged the prospect for creating new patterns of policy and new styles of diplomacy. But in the months following his inauguration, Kennedy made it evident that whatever foreign policy he built in the future would not start with the destruction of the past. In his first official declarations, he reaffirmed the fundamental policy positions of his predecessors, with all their obligations abroad, as valid foundations for his own administration to build on.

This onward rush of internationalism in Washington carried logically into the new administration one of the significant but generally ignored aspects of the 1960 campaign. No major candidate during the long months of debate invoked isolationism. No voter was told he had to choose between his own interests and those of foreigners. The political argument turned not on whether this country should play the fateful game of international power politics but whether it was winning. The election debate thus made it clear, by omission as well as assertion, that during the decade of the 1950's the United States had decided to accept as permanent its position of leadership, power, and responsibility in world affairs.

The Vanishing Shoreline

While the world position of the United States is now firmly established, the rules and techniques by which it should conduct its business with allies, neutrals, and foes are still in a formative stage. This is very apparent during a national election when a matter of vital concern, especially to allied peoples, is decided by the citizens of the United States. Strict nonintervention is the rule for foreigners, but not the invariable practice. It sometimes seems that the premier of the Soviet Union, being a competitor, has more opportunity to try to influence American politics than the allied prime minister of Great Britain. Even so, there are ways in which the British can make their feelings known; the only limitation is one of diplomatic propriety.

Seventy-two years ago the British envoy here was sent home for intervening in the Harrison-Cleveland contest of 1888. No other minister has had to be taught the same lesson as Lionel Sackville-West. Yet there is an interaction of internal and external events among today's interdependent nations that goes on continuously, even in an election year. The failure of commentators in many foreign countries to generate an even stronger enthusiasm for Senator Kennedy resulted less from respect for nonintervention than from a lack of real differences between the candidates in the field of foreign policy.

Bipartisanship

The relationship between politics and foreign policy, of course, has two sides. The effort to lessen the impact of partisan politics in the United States on this country's external relations began during the Roosevelt-Dewey campaign of 1944. The rivals reached an understanding that put the United Nations project beyond major political controversy. Other nations were thus given a cause for confidence in the main direction of United States foreign policy regardless of the vote.

The late Senator Arthur H. Vandenberg, a pioneer in the bipartisanship movement, used to say that "Politics stops at the water's edge." As with many a sound maxim, the truth of this grows thin if it is spread too far. The fact is that the interplay of foreign and domestic forces has become a constant condition of political life in all nations of consequence. For the United States, the water's edge is a boundary, but it is not a barrier.

Said the London Sunday *Dispatch*[2] shortly before November 8:

[2] Newspaper quotations and references in this chapter were taken from various

"If we appear to take almost too keen an interest in the outcome of [the American] election, it is because we know that what happens will be our business. For whoever succeeds next week to the leadership of the United States must also be the leader of the West."

Among peoples accustomed to democratic rule, the practice of having their leader selected by the voters in another country would surely be difficult to accept were it not that the nation-state system affords no other arrangement. The allies are cast perforce in the role of kibitzers, looking over the shoulders of the American electorate.

A Weakness of Coalition

To define the problem this way is not to suggest that the allies should vote in American elections. Merely to state the proposition is to show its absurdity. My intention rather is to isolate a weak point in the coalition arrangements through which the Democratic powers seek to assure their survival. The practical question raised is this: What would happen if the American people in some future election chose a president unacceptable to the allies—one whose record and policies could not command their confidence?

Early in 1960, Candidate Kennedy declared that the times demanded for the Presidency "a man capable of acting as commander-in-chief of the Grand Alliance."[3] Obviously, he felt some months later that his victory in November met that demand. With some exceptions government leaders, editorial writers, commentators, and other opinion makers abroad seemed to agree with him.

That settled the matter for 1960. But it will continue to arise every four years so long as the United States seeks to secure its safety and well-being through interlocking systems of allies.

---

sources, including American press accounts and U.S. Government summaries. Since much of this secondary source material is not available to reference, exact footnote references are not given.

[3] Speech to National Press Club, January 14, 1960. *Washington Post and Times Herald*, Nov. 13, 1960.

The Problem of Campaign Duration

The active presidential campaign extends over a period of approximately one year, and each time it is held, foreign voices are heard asking, "Why does it take so long?" The question became more insistent in 1960 as jet planes and TV sped the contest over the nation at a pace undreamed by our forefathers. The British press made clear that it regarded the whole operation as excessively prolonged. European diplomats expressed similar views in private conversation. They feared the creeping paralysis of politics over national action, the build-up of anxiety abroad, the danger that debate might open an allied flank to the Communists. The issue raised by many sympathetic foreign observers of the 1960 election scene thus was whether the duration of such disabilities could not be substantially reduced.

Growth of Interest Abroad

Foreign awareness of the campaign began to develop slowly in the fall of 1959. It was stimulated by Governor Nelson Rockefeller's drive to establish himself as a challenger for the Republican nomination. Rockefeller's announcement in December 1959 that he would not run served—in terms of foreign relations—to focus attention on Vice President Nixon. And by settling Republican uncertainties, it raised the level of interest abroad in the Democratic party contestants.

On the Democratic side, Stevenson was well-known and generally admired. Kennedy, in a popular sense, was unknown. If foreigners had had a vote in those very early months, Stevenson would undoubtedly have won out over Kennedy. Another popular figure in many foreign countries was Senator Humphrey with his reputation for liberal views on disarmament, negotiations with Russia, and foreign aid. When Stevenson faded from the competition, active foreign interest began to develop in the Humphrey-Kennedy primary races, and it centered around the religious issue.

Religion: A Focal Point

The Soviet Union was indifferent to the dispute over religion. But Kennedy's Catholicism aroused the most intense excitement in Western Europe and South America with their high ratio of Roman Catholics. It also created great interest in the non-Christian countries of Asia and the Middle East because of the question of tolerance. Underlying this surface question was the more fundamental concern of foreign peoples: Would the United States live up to its own political ideals? Would it prove itself worthy to lead the free world?

Foreign correspondents in Washington reported their editors wanted reports on every detail of the religious dispute when no other campaign subject interested them. The *Guardian* of Manchester, England, sharply defined the basic foreign feeling:

> Religious toleration is one of the principles on which the United States is based. To allow the shadow of intolerance to decide the result of the presidential election would be to deny a fundamental part of . . . "the American dream." The president who is elected next November will not be able to assert his country's leadership if he owes his election to religious bigotry. His most precious asset would have been thrown away.

That was an almost universal point of view a year ago, and it carried throughout the campaign. In this respect the way was prepared for a very favorable reaction to a Kennedy victory at the polls in November. Rome's influential newspaper *Il Tempo* stated after the election that the United States had "demonstrated its maturity on the religious plane." The *Journal de Brazil* declared a majority of the voters had "swept aside racial and religious preconceptions" to elect Kennedy. At Karachi the *Pakistan Observer* remarked hopefully that "America may very well have grown up completely."

With the religious issue sharply drawn in the primaries, the midsummer conventions established another point of overriding importance to foreign relations: Neither the Republicans nor the Democrats favored any fundamental alterations in American for-

eign policy. Both parties and both candidates committed themselves to preserve and strengthen this nation's alliances, to oppose
Sino-Soviet expansion, to assist the development of nations in need.

Politics vs. Foreign Policy

The foreign relations problems peculiar to an election year do
not arise because the President and the Secretary of State abandon
policy for politics. In our recent experiences quite the contrary has
been true. They arise, primarily, because the President in office
is running out of power. There is a deadline on the commitments
he can carry out and therefore on the commitments he can make.
They arise, in the second place, because other governments worry
about the actions they may be called on to take when the new
President comes to power; until he takes over, they tend to act with
caution. And third, there is the danger that the antagonist in the
Kremlin may sense weakness on the allied side and seek to profit
from it.

Speculations about these problems in the American and foreign
press prompted Secretary of State Christian A. Herter to issue a reassurance to the allies in August and a warning to the Sino-Soviet
bloc.[4]

> . . . A presidential election period is no bar to national action,
> [he said]. Our allies and other nations of the free world can rest
> assured that when action is necessary it will be taken. Our opponents
> should take warning that the American government and people can
> move with speed, force and unity during this period just as at any
> other time.

In support of his declaration, Herter cited the 1948 airlift that
overcame the Red blockade of Berlin and several other examples.
The words were strong and the record cited was good. But Herter
spoke essentially in a defensive sense. On the whole, the actions
he mentioned were protective necessities. Even as he spoke, it was
apparent that no new initiatives would be forthcoming until a new
government took over. Dynamism like time was running out for
the administration in power.

[4] Department of State Press Release No. 438, Aug. 9, 1960.

That, one can be sure, was not the way President Eisenhower had planned it. But a series of events, some shaped by his own decisions, had denied him all real initiative during his last eight months in the White House. This result necessarily had a profound effect on the attitude of foreign peoples and governments toward a change of leaders in Washington.

Pre-Election Diplomacy

These fateful events began in the spring of 1959 when the reins of foreign policy control fell from the experienced hand of John Foster Dulles. As Secretary of State, Dulles had dominated United States relations with the rest of the world for the first six Eisenhower years. The President called on Under Secretary Christian A. Herter to take over. But it was known that Eisenhower intended to play a far more active part in foreign affairs.

When Foreign Ministers' negotiations failed to resolve the Berlin crisis in the summer of 1959, Eisenhower struck out boldly on his own. Being under British pressure for a summit conference and hoping, himself, to move the world away from nuclear destruction, the President invited Khrushchev to the United States. He promised a return visit to Russia. This new course in American diplomacy not only produced the Camp David talks between Eisenhower and Khrushchev in September 1959 but also led to the President's travels to European, Asian, and African countries preliminary to the summit gathering at Paris in May 1960.

Whether Eisenhower's strategy was offensive or defensive—it seems actually to have contained both elements—he had committed his foreign policy for the rest of his term to his "Crusade for Peace." On that he pinned his hopes for staving off a Berlin showdown with Khrushchev. On that he based his plans for an active diplomacy up to the day he left office. One may speculate that the President even saw certain political advantages for Mr. Nixon in such a course.

The President's strategy was not successful. One reason was the way he handled the U-2 affair. But another was the decline in power available during his last year in office. Khrushchev, certainly, had some choice of his own course of action. Beginning in May he chose to do everything in his very considerable power to embarrass and humiliate Eisenhower and the United States government. But it seemed highly significant at the time that Khrushchev indicated his anti-American campaign would be limited to Eisenhower's remaining months in office. The implication was clear that he felt he would not have to pay too high a price for a diplomatic offensive against the United States provided it stopped short of the next President. The carryover danger was that he would receive from his swashbuckling behavior exaggerated views of Soviet power and United States patience.

End of the Eisenhower Era

The collapse of the Paris summit conference left President Eisenhower without a positive, dynamic policy line. This was realized far more quickly in Europe and Asia than in the United States. In this country, the popular magic of the President's personality faded very little and very slowly. But after communist-led agitators forced the Japanese government to ask the President to stay away from Tokyo, it became clear overseas if not at home that the President's powers were declining. As the political campaigns picked up momentum in the United States, the administration lost momentum abroad.

The summit conference was not the only casualty. Cancellation of a proposed Eisenhower visit to Russia was an expensive forfeit. The humiliation of Tokyo was worse than that of Paris. Khrushchev pulled his five communist delegations out of the ten-power disarmament talks at Geneva. Talks on a nuclear weapons test treaty began to drag.

A few short weeks after the summit explosion in Paris, the Eisenhower administration, seen from abroad, had the look of a caretaker government preserving the nation's security and fulfilling its minimum obligations but offering the world no new inspiration. Inevitably, that became the governing fact in foreign reaction up to the election of Senator Kennedy. Editorial writers proclaimed what government leaders whispered more guardedly from Tokyo to

Delhi to London: That a new young leader in Washington surely would mean a new and more vigorous American leadership in world affairs. The winds of change that blew across America on November 8, though fitful and faint, scattered seeds of hope around the world. The greatest hope was that Kennedy would make good on his proclaimed intention to "get America moving again."

The Campaign Drama in Foreign Eyes

The hope for vigorous leadership flourished partly because the campaign was so thoroughly reported abroad. The coverage exceeded any that had gone before, due to the exportation of the television debates. These were shown full length in many countries—among them Britain, West Germany, Argentina, and Japan. Millions of words were sent overseas by radio and cable. Foreign diplomats visited American polling places at the invitation of Eisenhower and Herter. Two hundred and twenty leaders from 65 countries were brought here by the State Department for a first-hand look at political democracy in action. The Voice of America mounted a global propaganda operation on the campaign and the election.

The use of all these techniques showed the world once more how the United States chooses and changes governments as compared with the Soviet Union. Austria's independent *Salzburger Nachrichten* struck this theme in an editorial November 10: "We, who all too easily criticize the Americans, ought to stop for one moment and ponder where the cause of freedom, democracy, and the state of law are better safeguarded—in Moscow and Peking or in Washington."

But the detailed and highly personalized presentation of the campaign debates had another effect also. For domestic political purposes Kennedy assailed Eisenhower administration programs—or lack of programs—in every part of the world. He declared he would do better and do more. His words reached not only the

Americans he aimed at but also millions of eagerly receptive foreigners who were led to expect virtual miracles of achievement from Washington after the inauguration. The importance of this result cannot be too heavily emphasized.

Self-interest is the common denominator of foreign reaction to American politics. Every foreign comment on the election, every reaction to it, disclosed something about the hopes and fears of the country from which the response came, whether the country was allied, neutral, or communist. Let us now examine the response of each of the major groupings of states, beginning with the allies.

Allied Response

As soon as news of Kennedy's victory flashed around the world messages began pouring in from allied leaders. These contained not only the usual congratulations but also promises of cooperation. Notes and statements either forthrightly or implicitly assured Kennedy of recognition as leader of the allied world. Nor was Khrushchev a laggard in opening his campaign for renewed Soviet-American contacts; but that is another matter.

The message from Chancellor Konrad Adenauer contained these words, more significant in fact than may appear on the surface:

> The trust of the American people has summoned you not only to the highest office of your land but also to the most important and responsible position in the gift of free people. The German people and its government share the trust of the American voters and offer you every success and happiness in your task.

Thus the old Chancellor put himself and his government in position to cooperate with the new American leader. The necessity for this act of statesmanship clashed with his personal wishes for what might have been. He was a fervent admirer of the late Secretary Dulles and had worked closely with President Eisenhower. He considered Nixon the man to carry on their German and Berlin policies. He was disappointed by Nixon's failure to win. But he accepted the American vote verdict promptly.

German reactions were naturally colored by this year's German elections. Apart from the needs of his foreign policy, Adenauer found it essential to demonstrate close ties with the President-elect. So did Socialist Leader Willy Brandt. The Berlin Mayor undertook during the campaign here to show that if he were to be the next Chancellor he could work with either Nixon or Kennedy.

Brandt made his point in identical letters to the American candidates in October:

> As the candidate of my party for the post of Federal Chancellor, [he wrote], I have advocated that our place must be in the western community and that friendship with the United States must remain a cornerstone of our policy. . . . I pledge myself in favor of joint action as far as that is possible on questions of foreign policy.

Apart from his message to Kennedy—which drew a brief, friendly reply—Adenauer engaged in another maneuver. He let it be known through publication of an interview November 12 that he "expects to exercise determining influence upon the course of western policy after the assumption of office by the new American president." (The interview was published in *Neue Ruhr Zeitung* and *Neue Rhein Zeitung*.)

Then word came out of Bonn that Adenauer would visit the United States in February and talk with Kennedy. This bid for a conference at the very outset of the administration was quietly discouraged by some of Kennedy's associates in Washington. When the old Chancellor shortly afterward became ill, his aides used the occasion to begin backing away from the February project. But negotiations for a meeting were later renewed, and Adenauer finally visited Washington in April, following Kennedy's talks with Prime Minister Macmillan of Britain.

French Reaction Cool

Elsewhere in allied Europe Kennedy's victory was widely welcomed. France showed less enthusiasm than other countries. But the French were preoccupied with the Algerian tragedy. Their chief reaction, in fact, was conditioned by this. They remembered that three years before Senator Kennedy had made a speech that they interpreted as a call for Algerian independence. During the 1960 campaign Kennedy modified his position. He asked for an Algerian solution worked out in association with France. That was more acceptable in Paris, and the French subsequently considered Kennedy to be, on the Algerian problem, less of an enemy and more of an unpredictable friend.

De Gaulle hailed his election in the following message: "Welcome, Dear Partner. With my friendly congratulations I send you, in the name of France, all my wishes for the United States. General de Gaulle."

To which Kennedy replied in a warm, perceptive note: "Both France and you have played a historic role in the life of my country and in the defense of the cause of freedom. I look forward to working with you for the strengthening of our common purpose."

Britain Favored Kennedy

Like other allied governments, that of Prime Minister Harold Macmillan had held itself in readiness to work with either Kennedy or Nixon. Britain's basic interests could not tolerate the danger of pre-election partisanship in any official sense. But every available piece of evidence gathered as the campaign progressed showed a strong British trend in favor of Kennedy.

The reasons for this were numerous, as explained in news dispatches from London. The British never really liked Dulles as Secretary of State though they respected his strength and ability. They liked Herter with genuine warmth, but they deplored a progressive decline in American leadership—what some openly called a bumbling diplomacy. As with other nations and governments over the world, they were strongly impressed by the campaign debate about prestige. The British like most other European allies remembered Adlai Stevenson with admiration, and their press looked to Kennedy as the heir of Stevenson. The press also acclaimed him as the heir to the tradition of Franklin D. Roosevelt, a point that Khrushchev also played on.

On election night American correspondents gave a huge party in London. It attracted almost every political leader except the Prime Minister. The *Baltimore Sun* reported that "big cheers in the Anglo-American crowd came when the Voice of America reported Kennedy gains, and most of the moans followed the news that Vice-President Nixon made headway."

The *New York Times* said Britons found the campaign boring. They certainly were, in fact, somewhat less excited than many peoples over possible American policy changes. Toward the end of the campaign the London *Times* told its readers in a dispatch from New York: "There is little to suggest that the nation has been roused to a militant mood in which it would deliberately cast off (Eisenhower's) middle-of-the-road policies." Cassandra, the *Daily Mirror's* public scold, wrote that Nixon was a "hollow" man and Kennedy a "prefabricated man" who "wants to please too much." In a word, Cassandra was skeptical.

But after the election of Kennedy the dominant mood became optimistic. The Laborite *Daily Mail* declared that "after Ike's pathetic doddering America desperately needs a man of vigor at the helm. So do America's allies." The *Daily Express,* a conservative journal, said exuberantly that Kennedy should "blow like a fresh wind through Washington . . . and quickly make his presence felt in the wider world."

British Hopes and Reservations

The British then waited to be shown by Kennedy's actions whether he has the abilities of leadership. They were perhaps skeptical, knowing the vast need, but in their own interest they were eager for him to prove himself. They feared the difficulties of new personal adjustments between Pennsylvania Avenue and Downing Street; yet they longed for more dynamism in Washington. They worried about the impulsiveness of youth; but from their vulnerable island they looked to Kennedy for all those qualities—wisdom, generosity, firmness, flexibility, boldness, and restraint—which would be necessary to preserve freedom and assure survival.

Into this situation Prime Minister Macmillan moved with extreme caution. Conscious of his long association with Eisenhower, he behaved like an elderly colleague who hoped to guide yet feared to offend Eisenhower's young successor. He wanted to visit Kennedy but not as an intruder. London journalists wrote at length on the problem of transition as it involves Downing Street and the White House. Dispatches from London in mid-November produced a confusing succession of reports that Macmillan would come and would not come to Washington, a trip he finally made in April.

Macmillan's message to Kennedy reflected his strong concern for maintaining his special relationship with the White House in the new circumstances. It also showed his restraint in approaching the problem. Delivered personally to Hyannis Port by the British Consul-General in Boston, the note was hand-addressed to "My Dear Senator."

> I send you with this short message, [it said] all my good wishes and those of the British government and people. You have been elected to be President of the United States. Since my mother was American, I know what that has always meant to all your citizens, but today it means that you will be taking the most powerful position in the world with responsibility matched by equal opportunity. I look forward to working in the causes which the people of this country and the United States both hold so dear.

In reply, Kennedy recalled that his father had served as Ambassador in London and said he, himself, had formed a "warm affection" for the British people. He added: "I know that our two great countries will work together in the future as they have in the past to further the cause of freedom throughout the world."

Allies Reassured

In late November Senator Lyndon B. Johnson, the Vice-President-elect, and Senator J. W. Fulbright, then a potential appointee as Secretary of State, stopped in London after attending a meeting of NATO parliamentarians in Paris. The press reported that Macmillan and his foreign secretary, the Earl of Home, were reassured by what they heard from Kennedy's associates. They felt they could look forward confidently to close cooperation and a revival of strong leadership in Washington.

The British public, and perhaps the British government, would have been highly pleased by the appointment of Adlai Stevenson as Secretary of State. For them Dean Rusk, like Kennedy a few months earlier, was almost an unknown man when he was named to the post. The London press promptly concluded that Kennedy meant to be his own Foreign Minister and would employ Rusk as a glorified technician. Kennedy's foreign policy combination of Rusk, Stevenson, and Chester Bowles drew much favorable comment abroad, comment that consistently underestimated Rusk.

Reaction Follows National Interests

In other parts of the world, as in Europe, allied reaction, so to speak, followed the flag.

At Tokyo the government of Prime Minister Hayato Ikeda described Kennedy as a "new and vigorous personality" but said he would not change American policy toward Japan. The opposition socialists, nonetheless, predicted that Kennedy would go along with their advocacy of Japanese neutralism.

The Japanese press reflected fears of some industrialists that because of his Massachusetts background Kennedy would impose restrictions on Japanese textile imports. Other industrialists thought the need to maintain United States prosperity at a high level would mean a large volume of imports during Kennedy's rule, with resulting benefit to Japan.

The newspaper *Yomiuri,* considering the broader problem of the Soviet-American power conflict, predicted "the world will soon find itself at a serious crossroads."

"There are many countries," *Yomiuri* said, "which will feel some uneasiness about Mr. Kennedy's victory, much as they might welcome his fresh approach."

At Seoul, Korea, government officials declared they expected the United States under Kennedy to continue to press for Korean unification. One cabinet member said the government was concerned about whether American public opinion would favor the neutralization of Korea on the Austrian pattern. While formal comment on the election was generally favorable, there was evident worry among Korean leaders concerning the chance of policy changes toward Red China, mainly growing out of Kennedy's talk about withdrawal from Quemoy and Matsu.

During the campaign, nationalist China had objected strenuously to the very thought of withdrawing from the off-shore islands under any conceivable conditions. When Kennedy won the election, the general reaction at Taipei was one of regret.

The press of two other Far Eastern allies, Philippines and Thailand, was also preoccupied with the off-shore islands problem and the related possibility of changes in American-Chinese relations. Thailand's leading newspaper, *Siam Rath,* expressed confidence that regardless of his campaign position Kennedy would not turn Quemoy and Matsu over to Red China. Other journals were not so certain.

In Latin America, apart from Cuba, the most common comment was that the advent of the Kennedy administration would open a new era in relations with the United States. The retiring President of Brazil, Juscelino Kubitschek, in a message to Kennedy November 12 stressed this theme. He said Kennedy had "repeatedly demonstrated a real interest in the problems relating to the Latin American countries," and added: "This warrants great expectations on our part as to Your Excellency's future action."

At Buenos Aires, Argentina, the newspaper *La Prensa* on November 17 acclaimed the post-election consultation between Kennedy and Nixon as an example of "political maturity." The demonstrated willingness of the two candidates to put aside campaign rivalries and work for national unity drew editorial applause in many countries.

The Prestige Issue

Several types of reaction cut across so many allied countries that they may be better dealt with as general responses unlimited by geography.

The prestige problem, as the great bone of contention in the campaign, got through to people all over the world and probably evoked more editorial comment than any other issue. Sometimes this subject was combined with comment on Kennedy's youth and vigor in contrast to the age and fading energies of Eisenhower.

The Vatican newspaper, *L'Osservatore Romano,* said Kennedy represented "a new political generation which started its career after the war and which is in perfect accord with its own era."

In one pre-election editorial the *Daily Telegraph* of London deplored the prestige issue as a ridiculous point over which to contest the Presidency.

> It is tantamount to giving foreigners the right to choose the next American president [the *Telegraph* fumed]. . . . While this is flattering to us, it cannot be said to reflect very well on the political maturity or good sense of the candidates who have found this new way of making the electors' task even more confusing than it was already.

Perhaps with tongue in cheek, the *Telegraph* then confused the question of popularity with the question of prestige as if they were the same thing. More vigorous leadership would not make Americans more popular, the newspaper said, and anyway they ought to be thinking about the kind of impression they really wanted to make on the world.

"President Eisenhower," the newspaper declared, "has successfully created an image of America as a blundering but a basically well-meaning giant, as against Mr. Khrushchev's successful promotion of Russia as a basically ill-meaning and non-blundering giant. Which is the most prestigious image?"

Thus was added another warning to those voiced abroad even as Kennedy's campaign gathered momentum—a warning to the new leaders against becoming too efficient and too zealous. At the same time, Europeans began preparing themselves for a clearer, stronger lead from Washington. Said the *Süddeutsche Zeitung* of Munich: "We Europeans . . . should get used to the idea that the (United States) under new leadership will speak a firmer language with us than previously. This may *not* be comfortable at all times, but it has its advantages, too."

The United States Information Agency's prestige polls, which became public during the campaign, were widely reported abroad. They recorded what the foreigners already knew—that since the first Soviet Sputnik, Moscow's prestige as a scientific and military power had increased while that of the United States had declined. That knowledge whetted allied interest in change in Washington. But when the change presented itself in the personality of a youthful and dynamic President-elect, apprehension tempered the satisfaction of the major allies. The *Yorkshire Post* summarized this double-edged reaction with the emphasis on optimism:

> If Senator Kennedy fulfills all his promises, the United States will in all probability recapture [its] sense of mission, [its] leadership of the western world, in a time at once dangerous and bright with opportunity. . . . No man in our time faces a greater, more splendid chance or challenge.

Neutral Response

The European allies feared President-elect Kennedy would shift the main focus of United States interest from allied Europe to neutral Afro-Asia. His pre-election use of former Ambassador Bowles as a foreign policy adviser strengthened that impression. The European concern was similar to that of American allies in the Far East. They feared Kennedy would modify American opposition to any contact with Red China. Yet, precisely that modification was desired by many neutral nations, including the biggest and most influential—India.

Senators Johnson and Fulbright tried to set the Europeans straight on Kennedy's aims when they visited Paris and London in November. They offered assurance that Kennedy wanted the United States and its allies to work together in assisting the African and Asian nations. Press dispatches reported western leaders were pleased with that word.

The Red China Question

No such reassurance was given to the Far Eastern allies regarding Red China. Indeed, that would hardly have been possible. For Kennedy was pledged to try to work out some new approach to China policy though he did not contemplate radical change. Bowles had advocated movement toward a two-China position. A degree of maneuver and instability in the Far East seemed sure to result from this talk of changing relationships until Kennedy's course became clear.

On both these major cold war questions, one essentially economic and the other intensely political, the neutrals considered their positions strengthened. Some suggested it was about time they were heeded. A few days before the election, the *Times* of India explored the subject during a discussion of the prestige issue. After citing the known progress of Russia in science and technology, in military power, and in economic resources, the *Times* said:

> Its influence especially in Asia and Africa has increased a hundredfold; while American failure is writ large everywhere—in Korea, in Iraq, in Japan, in Turkey.
>
> Election controversies apart, the next President must become more realistic and grapple with this sorry state of affairs if his country is to retain world leadership; otherwise, rather too early in the day, some Gibbon may be tempted to write the Decline and Fall of the American Empire.

Nehru Hopeful

An item from New Delhi in the *New York Times* of November 9 recorded evidence of pleasure at Kennedy's victory on the part of Prime Minister Nehru. He was reported to have told a closed meeting of Indian state governors that he hoped Kennedy's election would bring a change for the better in United States foreign policy. Precisely what he meant was not explained. Publicly, Nehru said he would cooperate with Kennedy as he had with Eisenhower. N. Sanjiva Reddy, the President of Nehru's governing Congress party, said he was pleased that "a young man has come to the helm of affairs," bringing "a new outlook for a solution to world problems."

The themes of youthful vigor and of Kennedy's outspoken interest in helping India were common to the press throughout that country. Other subjects were also widely developed. Kennedy, Indian newspapers told their readers, would give the world new hope for a summit conference, would improve relations with Russia, would tackle the Red China problem boldly, would strengthen United States support of freedom of Algeria and other African areas, and would promote Negro civil rights, social legislation, and American economic growth.

Pakistan Apprehensive

The good will felt toward Kennedy in India was offset somewhat by worry in neighboring Pakistan. The Moslem country is an ally of the United States, but its attitude toward the new administration appeared most significant in comparison with the attitude displayed in neutralist India.

Two newspapers, *Dawn* and the *Morning News,* both said, "Misgivings . . . exist" about the future development of United States policies. The *Morning News* added, however, that President Mohammed Ayub Khan had said the United Sates supplied military aid to other countries in its own interest. The newspaper concluded that aid to Pakistan, therefore, was likely to continue.

The *Evening Star* declared America's allies were nervous about statements made by associates of Kennedy. "It is only to be hoped," the *Star* said, "that such controversial figures as Chester Bowles will be kept away from important appointments like that of Secretary of State."

Africa and the Middle East

In Africa, news coverage of the election campaign was extensive with interest centered on Kennedy's statements that the United States must do more for the newly independent nations. One point of special interest emerged with respect to North Africa. The press there reported Tunisian authorities had urged Algerian leaders to await the advent of the new administration before involving themselves too deeply with the Sino-Soviet bloc. Tunisian leaders evidently hoped that in view of Kennedy's interest in the Algerian crisis, they would win a more favorable reception for their views in Washington.

Another area of the world that has produced more than its share of crises and knows the importance of American power is the

Middle East. Perhaps no area better reflects the conflicts of national interest and the limitations of opportunity that serve to restrict the range of action available to the new administration.

Editorials in the Israeli press throughout the campaign showed confidence that whether the Presidency went to Nixon or Kennedy, American interest in the welfare and security of Israel would continue. The consensus was that, while the United States approach to the Soviet Union might change greatly, the United States approach to the Middle East would remain about what it had been.

By contrast Arab commentators denounced what they called the practice of "appealing to the Zionist-Jewish vote." They took it for granted that from their point of view the new administration would favor Israel.

In summary, nothing that was said respecting the advent of a new government in Washington suggests optimism or receptivity for a fresh start toward stability in the Middle East. The prospect facing the new administration there is no less complex and no less explosive than that which has sporadically shaken Washington—and the world—for more than a decade.

Communist Response

In diplomacy as in society it takes two to tango. The *Times* of Pakistan covered this principle in a cogent comment on the election. "Whoever rules in Washington," the *Times* said, "America cannot hope to bring about an improvement in great power relations unless Russian rulers . . . make a positive move toward détente."

Initial Sino-Soviet Moves

Premier Khrushchev was not slow to make a move. Nor for that matter was Premier Chou En-lai of Red China. But, as had become so common, these allies in communism seemed to be moving in different directions. Chou laid down impossible terms for a rapprochement with the United States; he demanded the United States abandon Taiwan. Khrushchev said he was ready and anxious to get back to the conference table. Chou's statement was certainly not a positive move toward a détente. Khrushchev's statement was intended to appear positive, and over the world many people considered it so. Therein, of course, lay the danger for President Kennedy, the danger of attractive illusions fostered by Khrushchev as weapons of diplomacy. Yet there was always a hope that Khrushchev might be willing to strike an acceptable bargain on some issue, and no American President could afford to ignore any constructive Soviet offer for improvement in Soviet-American relations.

The Communist split reflected in the actions of Moscow and Peiping was subsequently patched over by a Moscow agreement in early December on the strategy and tactics of Communist party operations. The belligerent Chinese agreed to soften their tone; the Khrushchev Soviets, to harden theirs. The basic differences between the two red giants remained under the patchwork of words. Nevertheless, they had achieved an understanding, and it may have been due in part to the prospect of a new government in Washington. Khrushchev and the leaders of Red China could not readily afford to face a period of predicted Western dynamism in a condition of open discord.

Khrushchev and the Campaign

Khrushchev's whole election year performance showed some awareness of American political sensibilities. In retrospect his course suggests that first he wanted to intervene in the United States election against Nixon. Then he realized that might hurt his own purpose. And finally when Kennedy defeated Nixon, he jumped fast for the bandwagon. In all of this his purposes seem reasonably apparent.

Khrushchev was happy enough to wage cold war on the United States and its President after the summit breakup at Paris. He identified Nixon with Eisenhower and Dulles. He identified Kennedy with Franklin D. Roosevelt. Perhaps he believed his propaganda on these points. He said at Paris in May 1960 that he hoped for a new American President in the Roosevelt tradition. Then and on one or two other occasions he made remarks that were interpreted as being anti-Nixon.

Perhaps, too, Khrushchev reads the news reports. Many commentators in the United States pointed out the obvious; if he strongly attacked one candidate, it would surely help strengthen the other. Suddenly in the summer Khrushchev became neutral as between the candidates.

"They are a pair of boots," he said in Moscow. "Which is better, the right or the left boot? It would be difficult to distinguish between them." The Soviet press and radio took up Khrushchev's cue. Nixon and Kennedy, they said, were "Tweedledum and Tweedledee."

A Moscow literary newspaper (*Liturna I Zhizn*) used the weekend before the voting to argue for the Soviet as against the American system:

"Our elections are genuinely free. They show that there is only a miserable hundredth of one per cent opposed to socialism—this is, only one idler for every 10,000 people."

The Soviet press and radio in both domestic and foreign output also sought to ridicule the American political campaign. Trivial matters of United States press discussion over the clothing styles of the candidates' wives were picked up and magnified. Above all the communist press generally seized with glee on Kennedy's charge of a decline in American prestige. It trumpeted claims of expanding Soviet power and influence.

During this period, the Soviet, Red Chinese, and Cuban progagandists were all playing more or less in harmony. Castro's men were most consistent in their denunciations of the American candidates, accusing both of "imperialistic" designs. When Kennedy won, the newspapers *Revolución* and *El Mundo,* both ran headlines saying, "The same dog with a different collar." An editorial in *Revolución* said an American could win the Presidency only with "the backing of millions of dollars and the support of those powerful monopolies with their oligarchy connections."

The Break With Cuba

Premier Fidel Castro finally changed his line slightly after forcing his anti-United States campaign to the point of a diplomatic rupture. Perhaps Castro had not expected decisive action from President Eisenhower in the closing days of his administration. At any rate, Castro ordered the United States Embassy staff in Havana cut from about 125 persons to 11 persons. Within 24 hours, on the night of January 3, Eisenhower broke off relations. The Castro cabinet then announced that it hoped for better relations with the incoming Kennedy administration. It may have entertained such a hope. But the announcement could also be explained as a device to make it appear that the break was the fault of Eisenhower, not Castro.

In the end the Soviet Union was not so persistent as Cuba or Red China in pressing its attacks on the United States. Its national, political, and propaganda interests appear to have been construed differently. When Kennedy won, Khrushchev and his drumbeaters instantly changed their tune. In black headlines *Izvestia* proclaimed "Return to Roosevelt." Radio commentators told the world that in defeating Nixon "the American people voted against the cold war and the arms race." The press ran a brief biography of Kennedy reporting his service in the Navy during the war and his father's service to Roosevelt—both "good" items in the Soviet view.

In Peiping there was no echo of Moscow's jubilation. The Communist New China News Agency said November 9 that Kennedy is "no different from Nixon in pushing the aims of the aggressive and reactionary policies of the United States ruling circles." The article predicted he would use tax boosts and inflation "to greatly increase military spending and extend war preparations."

Soviet Bid for Talks

Meanwhile from Moscow that same day came the announcement that Khrushchev had sent Kennedy a message. In it he expressed hope that American-Soviet relations would "again follow the line along which they were developing in Franklin Roosevelt's time."

The message was friendly in tone. It made abundantly clear that Khrushchev did not wish to carry over to Kennedy his feud with Eisenhower. Instead he was opening a new campaign for a summit conference.

"We are convinced that there are no insurmountable obstacles to the preservation and consolidation of peace," Khrushchev said. He called for negotiations on disarmament, the German problem, and other critical issues, declaring, "Any steps in this direction will always meet with the full understanding and support of the Soviet government."

Cold War Prospects

The Soviet leader played out his role as he had predicted when he turned so violently on Eisenhower. This did not mean he actually envisioned a process of negotiation and compromise leading to settlement. His propagandists could attempt to persuade the world that was his aim. The prospect before President Kennedy was much grimmer.

Khrushchev seemed to believe there had been a significant change in the power relationship between the United States and Russia. He regarded negotiation with Western leaders as the way to capitalize on the advantages. His words were friendly, but every available piece of evidence indicated his actions would be aggressive and often hostile. His support for the rapid communization of Cuba was a case in point. So was the crisis in Laos. Any who hoped a new and easier era in East-West relations was at hand were well advised to study the Moscow Manifesto on December 6, 1960.

"Peaceful co-existence of states with different social systems," said this blueprint for militant communism, "does not mean reconciliation between the socialist and bourgeois ideologies. On the contrary it implies an intensification of the struggle of the working class and of all communist parties for the triumph of socialist ideas."

Analysis and Conclusions

The aggressive hostility of the Sino-Soviet bloc is the force that gives urgency to all foreign enterprises of the United States. Without this external pressure many of the great problems would remain, but they could be dealt with in a more relaxed and deliberate manner. In the face of this challenge, the United States, its allies, and indeed the world must live constantly in the presence of danger. American political processes are not exempt from this circumstance. The presidential election of 1960 with its preceding campaigns and its aftermath of interregnum created special problems for American leadership in the world. These problems are no less real because in some instances they are insoluble.

It is quite evident that under any political system the transfer of power from one government to another involves painful readjustments. These are extreme in the case of a dictatorship, as witness the tensions and fears in Moscow on the death of Josef Stalin. They are far less unsettling under democratic rule. Democracy anticipates and plans for change in orderly and peaceful ways. But the procedures of democracy, like those of any social institution, fall short of perfection. It is the imperfections as they bear on foreign relations that we are primarily concerned with here.

Politics Ascendant

The first and most obvious of the election year difficulties is that throughout the upper levels of government the growing preoccupation with politics tends to distract attention from other matters. This means a reduction in creative energies devoted to policy making. It also means that pending policy decisions must be considered for their domestic political impact. During the years of the Cold War the progressive isolation of the State Department from the political arena has minimized the effect of campaign activities on the conduct of foreign relations. But some disability remains and must be considered inescapable.

Diminishing Power

As the waning administration moves toward a caretaker position, it suffers another handicap. Its ability to make its will felt on friend or foe diminishes steadily. Its threats and its promises have only a short time to run. Even the President himself may become vulnerable if in the employment of personal diplomacy he is exposed to attack. Khrushchev exploited this condition when he wrecked the summit conference in the spring of 1960 and helped to block Eisenhower's path to Tokyo that summer.

Transition Time

Foreign governments and foreign observers were sensitive to these problems last year as the campaign developed. Western Europeans, especially the British, questioned why the business of picking and installing a new chief executive should take a full year or more.

Though the territory of the United States is far greater than that of its European allies, airplanes, the press, television, and radio now make possible speedup techniques that were unavailable when the founding fathers worked out the present political system. One point certainly is true: to the extent that the handicaps of a campaign period are magnified by its duration, they can be modified by shortening the time.

Points of Advantage

The 1960 campaign had certain advantages from a foreign viewpoint that worked to offset the disadvantages cited here. One was the lack of any great dispute over basic United States foreign policy. Another was the fact that both candidates had the appeal of youth and the prospect of providing a more dynamic leadership. The election of either one promised a break with the past in style and energy. Each man, with some reservations, was acceptable to the allies as a leader. This complex of favorable factors may not, of course, hold true in future election campaigns.

Essentials of Foreign Reaction

The election of Senator Kennedy was acclaimed abroad for two principal reasons. He was judged in foreign countries to have won out over the religious issue, and this was interpreted as encouraging evidence of political maturity in the United States. Furthermore, foreign observers believed that Kennedy, operating along established foreign policy lines, would bring a bold, resolute spirit and a new sense of purpose to the leadership of the Free World.

Apart from his conduct during the campaign, Kennedy was, nevertheless, a largely unknown personality to other world leaders. His vigor was a source of concern as well as reassurance. His election meant a break in the generation of rule by men who first made their marks in World War II. His every move after the election received the closest scrutiny overseas. His meeting with President Eisenhower to arrange for the orderly transfer of power was well received, as was his earlier meeting with Vice President Nixon. His appointment of Rusk, Stevenson, and Bowles to key positions was taken as evidence that he wanted competent and experienced men on his foreign policy "team," with minimum regard for political considerations.

But the most striking fact about the foreign response to Kennedy's election lay not in its concern with issues and men but in the vast scope of its expectations. In Africa, Asia, and Latin America, in Western Europe and perhaps even in the Soviet bloc, his political campaign statements were accepted as promissory notes payable in his future policies. Possibly no other President ever carried into office the burden of so many hopes from so many parts of the world. This gave the measure both of the danger and of the opportunity before him.

8

The Transition: Transfer of Presidential Responsibility

LAURIN L. HENRY [1]

IN HIS INFLUENTIAL BOOK *Presidential Power,* Richard E. Neustadt says: "A striking feature of our recent past has been the transformation into routine practice of the actions we once treated as exceptional. A President may retain liberty, in Woodrow Wilson's phrase, 'to be as big a man as he can.' But nowadays he cannot be as small as he might like." Neustadt cites several responsibilities that originally were assumed by individual Presidents as matters of personal initiative but are now assigned all Presidents by law—intervention in labor disputes, maintenance of full employment, and active leadership in world affairs. He adds: "And what has escaped statutory recognition has mostly been accreted into presidential common law, confirmed by custom, no less binding: the 'fireside chat' and the press conference, for example, or the personally presented legislative program, or personal campaigning in congressional elections."[2]

Recent times have brought a rapid growth of "presidential common law, confirmed by custom" in a field that Neustadt did not mention, although he knows it well—the arrangements for

---

[1] Senior Staff Member, The Brookings Institution.

Portions of this chapter and the one following were given in an earlier form as a lecture in February 1961. They were completed for publication at the end of June 1961.

[2] Richard E. Neustadt, *Presidential Power: The Politics of Leadership* (Wiley, 1960), pp. 5-6.

205

transitions between administrations. Prior to 1960, Presidents Hoover, Roosevelt, Truman, and Eisenhower—each in his own time as he entered or left the White House—took important steps to guard the public interest against the dangers inherent in a rigid timetable for elections and inaugurations.[3] In the transition of 1960-61, past experience and precedents exerted a powerful influence. Neustadt's phrase became especially apt: neither Eisenhower nor Kennedy was free to "be as small as he might like." And because they not only fulfilled expectations but produced significant innovations of their own, their successors will be even more firmly guided. Indeed, it is quite possible that before the next turnover occurs some of this "presidential common law" experience will give rise to statute.

Before Election

The 1960-1961 transition was strongly conditioned by the fact that key governmental circles had been alerted well in advance of a change of leadership that might possibly have to be carried out under difficult and dangerous circumstances. From 1956 on, there had been frequent reminders that President Eisenhower was a lame duck, the first President barred from succeeding himself by the Twenty-second Amendment. There had to be a new President, of one party or another, in 1961.

Some of the earliest comment on problems ahead came from veterans of the 1952-1953 transition. For example, Roger W. Jones, Chairman of the Civil Service Commission, warned an audience of federal personnel officers in January 1960 of changes certain to

[3] For detailed accounts of the four party transitions in the Presidency most recently preceding 1960-61, see Laurin L. Henry, *Presidential Transitions* (The Brookings Institution, 1960). For a short treatment, see Laurin L. Henry, "Transferring the Presidency: Variations, Trends, and Patterns," *Public Administration Review*, Vol. 20, Autumn 1960, pp. 187-95; also available as Brookings Reprint 49. For comment on past transitions and anticipations of problems of the Kennedy-Eisenhower transfer, see Stephen G. Benedict, "Changing the Watch in Washington," *Virginia Quarterly Review*, Vol. 37, Winter 1961, pp. 15-33.

come. By stressing the inevitability of change and the need for flexibility, he apparently hoped to give the civil service both internal attitudes and a "corporate image" that might spare it from a repetition of its vicissitudes in 1953, when it had been perceived by the incoming administration as rigid, monolithic, and hostile.[4]

Discreet preparations for a change of administrations could be detected in the Budget Bureau and other units of the Executive Office of the President in the spring of 1960. Through the "executive officers group," an assembly of administrative assistant secretaries and other high-ranking managerial officials, the Budget Bureau suggested to career staffs throughout the government that they begin thinking about steps to ease the transfer. Also about this time, various nongovernmental individuals and groups, including the Brookings Institution, launched projects intended to facilitate the transition.

During the spring maneuvers for the presidential and vice-presidential nominations, there was deepening concern inside the government over Berlin, Cuba, and other trouble spots. However, the aftermath of Camp David, President Eisenhower's successful trip to India, and the initial prospects of the summit conference gave rise to a certain amount of optimism about the international situation. This ended with the U-2 incident and break-up of the Paris conference. Khrushchev's outspoken intention to deal no more with Eisenhower but to await the arrival of his successor underscored the rapidly waning ability of the administration to influence events abroad. Leaders of friendly nations were more polite than Khrushchev but were reluctant to discuss major new ventures and commitments.

In the domestic political arena, the lame duck administration, although clearly not in control of events, proved surprisingly strong on the defense against the Democratically controlled Congress. But there was a growing public sense of an era coming inevitably to an end, and an anticipation of new leadership and new de-

---

[4] "Preparing for Transition to a New Administration," Address before Conference of Directors of Personnel, Williamsburg, Va., Jan. 21, 1960. See also, Roger W. Jones, "1961 Top Team Must 'Hit the Ground Running,'" *Civil Service Journal,* Vol. 1, July-September 1960, p. 2.

partures. Inside the government, the bureaucracy began to temper its service to the Eisenhower administration with a touch of concern for continuity and self-preservation.

The Administration's Attitude

Administration leaders seemed to find distasteful the increasing public discussion of the fact that the President's term was nearly over. With some justification, they feared an impression that the administration was worn out, giving up. Such an impression might weaken the President's ability to resist the "spenders" in the Democratic Congress, or his influence with friends and foes abroad. The humiliation of the President's aborted trip to Japan seemed to increase the sensitivity at the White House to "premature" talk about the end of the administration.

An exception to the rule of silence occurred on March 31, 1960. In response to a press conference question, President Eisenhower said that intelligence briefings on current foreign and security topics would be available, as usual, to the presidential candidates of both major parties. The custom of giving such briefings had been started only during World War II and had not become publicly known until 1952, but Eisenhower made the commitment as a matter of course and seemed a little surprised that anyone had felt it necessary to raise the question. So quickly had a useful innovation become a part of the "presidential common law"!

On July 7, the President said in answer to another press inquiry that after election the winner, whoever he might be, would be given every opportunity to familiarize himself with what the administration had been doing. But apparently the key words were "after election." During the campaign, the White House did permit the Budget Bureau to prepare quietly a number of staff papers on matters a new administration should know about. In August, after assurances of minimal publicity, the White House and the Republican candidate, Vice President Nixon, joined the Democratic candidate, Senator Kennedy, in appointing liaison officers to a Brookings Institution study of the problems of the imminent presidential transfer. But the administration tried to keep these preparations as quiet as possible until after election.

President Eisenhower's approach to a change of administrations differed considerably from the one taken by President Truman in 1952. Truman not only talked a great deal about transition problems but, in an effort to tell his potential successors what he thought they should know and to demonstrate national solidarity on the Korean war and other foreign policy matters, invited both nominees to confer with him personally at the White House. Governor Stevenson accepted his invitation, but General Eisenhower, whose invitation was handled clumsily, declined.

The national situation was almost as serious in 1960 as in 1952, but the political situation was somewhat different. Eisenhower saw the Republican problem in 1960 as one of transferring his own popularity to the Vice President, or at least of conveying the impression that Nixon was a fully trained successor who could step into the Presidency with no strain. Too much recognition that Senator Kennedy might win, or that there would be problems of transition if Nixon won, might weaken the cause. In any case, Eisenhower made no attempt at personal contact with the opposition candidate during the campaign.

The presumed beneficiary of this strategy, Mr. Nixon, seemed in practice to be less rigid in adhering to it than Eisenhower and his staff. While Nixon presented himself as a man who could take over without a hitch, he did not mind occasionally suggesting that things would be a little different. His failure to win left unsettled the question of what problems would have arisen in a transition to a new President of the same party. Probably there would have been a substantial turnover of top-level personnel and a widespread effort to re-examine policy; by inauguration day, Nixon might have regretted not having done more advanced planning. But this must remain in the realm of speculation until there is a modern-day demonstration of an in-party transition by election—an event that has not occurred since Hoover took over from Coolidge in 1929.

The Briefing Arrangements

Kennedy, as the out-party candidate and on the attack, felt no inhibitions on pre-election planning. He made one misstep at the beginning, however. As the Democratic convention was ending, White House Press Secretary Hagerty announced that the administration was preparing to give Kennedy and his running mate, Senator Lyndon Johnson, briefings on the national security situation. Kennedy promptly announced that he was designating Adlai Stevenson and Chester Bowles to receive these briefings and be his liaison men with the White House and the State Department during the campaign. The next day, however, Hagerty announced that the President intended to give intelligence information only to the nominees. Kennedy adjusted his position and his plans for using Bowles and Stevenson. When the President sent him a message offering intelligence information "exclusively for your personal knowledge," he accepted on those terms.

Kennedy was visited by CIA representatives three times during the campaign, according to newspaper reports. The nature of the briefings he received was not revealed, nor was there any indication whether their relative infrequency reflected a low level of interest on Kennedy's part or the number of offerings by the agency.

Kennedy Preparation

As the campaign developed, there was a rapid proliferation of advisers and study groups charged with laying post-election plans. On August 30 Kennedy announced the formation of a special committee, headed by Paul H. Nitze, to study the defense and foreign policy situation. The group's purpose, it was stated, was not to gather campaign ammunition but to consider seriously the security problems a new administration would inherit and what might be done about them promptly after inauguration day. Another committee, headed by Senator Stuart Symington, was authorized to study the organization of the Department of Defense, while Adlai Stevenson was authorized to study the Department of State and certain foreign policy problems. There were additional advisory groups for natural resources, civil rights, and other fields.

An especially important adviser was Clark M. Clifford, a former special counsel to President Truman. Kennedy asked Clifford privately in August to begin considering what a successful candidate would have to do after election. A few days later, he also designated Clifford as his liaison man for the study being carried on at Brookings. Clifford's assignment concerned priority decisions required of a President-elect, organization of a White House staff, jobs that would need to be filled immediately, and relations with the outgoing administration. He drew his material from his own prior experience, from the Brookings project, and from informal consultations with others in and out of the government.

Another adviser was Richard E. Neustadt, a Columbia professor, veteran of the Budget Bureau and Truman White House staff. Neustadt was brought to Washington in September by Democratic National Committee Chairman Henry M. Jackson, whose Senate Subcommittee on National Policy Machinery had for some time been sponsoring staff studies and holding hearings on organizational problems in the national security field. After preparing some material on transition, Neustadt was introduced to Kennedy by Jackson. Encouraged by the candidate to continue working along this line, Neustadt emerged after the election as an influential adviser to Kennedy on White House operations, government organization, and that intangible thing called presidential style.

Pre-election preparations by and for Kennedy omitted one central task in organizing an administration—the recruitment of personnel. There was considerable thought about the sequence in which key jobs ought to be filled, and some speculation about types of people who might fill them, but no effort to canvass prospects— or even to set up a system for doing so later. When asked during the campaign whether he had chosen men for his cabinet, Kennedy dodged the question by citing the fate of Governor Dewey, who had taken up this problem prematurely in 1948.

By about the first of November, the press and the public alike seemed to have had their fill of the campaign. Interest shifted to what the winner would do and what impact the new administration would have. Columnists urged both Kennedy and Nixon to be prepared to name their cabinets and key staff members promptly after election. There were news stories about Clark Clifford's activities on Kennedy's behalf and about some of the preparations for transition going on in government agencies. The Brookings study of transition problems, which had attracted little attention until then, became an object of intense attention by the press, which sought to learn the contents of the confidential memoranda being prepared for the still undesignated President-elect.

A Framework of Post-Election Cooperation

On the day after election, another useful precedent was solidified by repetition. As Truman had done in 1952, President Eisenhower sent a telegram to congratulate Senator Kennedy and to alert him for a more comprehensive message suggesting "certain measures that may commend themselves to you as you prepare to take over next January the responsibilities of the Presidency." Kennedy immediately responded cordially.

Later that morning Eisenhower met with his cabinet for a previously scheduled discussion of the problems of transfer to the new President. Still later that day in a second telegram to Kennedy, Eisenhower offered to meet with him at a mutually convenient time. He suggested that in the meantime, Kennedy designate a representative to meet with the assistant to the President, Major General Wilton B. Persons, to discuss liaison arrangements and to set up meetings between other Kennedy representatives and heads of executive departments and agencies, particularly the Director of the Budget and the Secretary of State. Kennedy responded by affirming his desire to see the President personally and designating Clark Clifford to meet with General Persons.

Three points about these exchanges might be noted.

First, there was an evident determination on both sides to keep the relationship free of personal and partisan rancor. There were no such barbs as President Truman's 1952 offer of the use of the presidential plane "if you still wish to go to Korea." The friendly tone of the Eisenhower-Kennedy exchange was echoed by a Kennedy-Nixon exchange. Kennedy's personal visit to Nixon was further evidence of his desire for friendly relations. Historically, gracious winners have been much scarcer in presidential politics than good losers. Kennedy's rise above the norm seems to have reflected his instinctive feelings about the courtesies due in such a situation. But he was doubtless encouraged by the tenuous hold he had on victory. Even if his majority held up through the lagging returns and demands for recounts in several states, he would need all the good will he could muster if he wanted to be an effective President.

Second, Eisenhower, although willing to assist his successor, was determined to remain President, in fact as well as in law, to the end of his term. His second telegram to Kennedy contained some words that take on added significance in light of what has since been learned about the President's frame of mind. He offered to meet Kennedy to discuss problems of continuity of government and "orderly transfer of Executive responsibility on January 20 from my Administration to yours." But the words "transfer" and "on January 20" were important. In cabinet discussions, Eisenhower expressed a strong preference for the word "transfer" rather than the increasingly prevalent "transition." The latter implied a gradual change from one thing to another, which was inappropriate in any reference to the locus of authority. His administration would run until January 20, and then Kennedy's would begin. In the meantime, he would be prepared to make any necessary decisions. The discipline of the Executive Branch would be maintained. Members of the administration were to confine their relations with the Kennedy people to the authorized representatives cleared through General Persons.

Third, Kennedy arranged to announce the Clifford appointment and to release his second exchange of messages with Eisenhower at a news conference in which, both by his demeanor and the announcements he made, he signified a brisk beginning of the next administration. He also announced the future White House assignments of several members of his personal staff, stated that Allen W. Dulles and J. Edgar Hoover had been asked to remain in office, and said that James M. Landis would make a study of federal regulatory agencies. He also released the text of his conciliatory but noncommittal reply to a congratulatory message from Khrushchev; dodged questions about roles that might be played in his administration by Adlai Stevenson, various members of the Kennedy family, and Richard M. Nixon; and announced that he would have early conferences with Vice President-elect Johnson, Senator Symington, Paul Nitze, and Richard Neustadt.

During the following week, Clark Clifford and General Persons began their series of liaison meetings. Clifford, together with Kennedy's principal policy aide, Theodore Sorensen, also conferred with the Director of the Bureau of the Budget and received a stack of briefing memoranda prepared by that agency. Kennedy soon began receiving daily intelligence summaries, and on November 18 Allen Dulles journeyed to Palm Beach to give him a personal report on the international situation.

There was some speculation that Kennedy might fly almost immediately to Augusta, where Eisenhower was vacationing, to confer with the President. However, neither principal was anxious for the encounter until the seconds had had time to do their work thoroughly; the meeting did not occur until almost a month after election. The election recounts were the subject of much discussion in the interval, but the possibility of an upset had largely disappeared by the time the meeting took place.

On the appointed day, December 6, at the White House, Eisenhower turned out the Marine Band and a military guard in Kennedy's honor. The two conferred privately in the President's office for an hour and 45 minutes, then joined another conference with several aides. The course of Kennedy's conversation with the President has not been revealed, but from all indications it went smoothly, partly because of the preliminary work by Clifford and Persons. A joint statement reported that Eisenhower and Kennedy had discussed "major problems of peace, security and freedom throughout the world," the American balance of payments problem, certain national security operations, and matters involving the Executive Branch and White House staff machinery. As reporters gathered around him afterward, Kennedy again expressed his appreciation of the President's helpfulness. He reaffirmed his belief that until January 20 presidential responsibility was Eisenhower's and could not be shared. President Eisenhower was also pleased and reported to friends that he had been impressed by Kennedy's evident sense of responsibility, grasp of the issues, and demonstrations of personal consideration.

The President-Elect's Preparations

Public discussion of transition problems attached great importance to early designation of the new cabinet and other principal officers, thus giving these persons maximum time to prepare themselves before assuming responsibility. In 1952, it was remembered, Eisenhower had announced the entire cabinet by the first of December.

But, as already mentioned, Kennedy had given little consideration to the problem of appointments prior to election. He and his closest advisers were also well aware that preoccupation with appointments at the expense of other kinds of preparation might in the end defeat the President-elect's broader purposes. Therefore, Kennedy moved first on steps to create the public image of himself that he wanted, to establish suitable relationships with the Eisenhower administration, and to set up the personal staff he would need during the transition period. When he and his staff turned in mid-November from the preliminaries to larger tasks, preparations in the realm of policy and program received attention equal to personnel and organization.

Preparing the Kennedy Program

On policy matters, Kennedy did not start with a completely clean slate. In the background were legislative proposals carried over from the previous Congress, platform and campaign commitments, the earlier pronouncements of the Democratic Advisory Council, and staff work done for Kennedy as Senator. Fresher ingredients included the reports commissioned during the campaign, staff memoranda available from the Budget Bureau, and the advice pouring in from all sides on many subjects. The job now was to fill the gaps, relate this information to the existing situation and the political imperatives as Kennedy saw them, and reach decisions on specific measures to be proposed to Congress or put into effect by executive action after January 20. The requirement for an inaugural address and an intended State of the Union message set deadlines for policy decisions and offered opportunities for explaining them to the public.

The device used to assemble advice and marshal alternatives was the "task force." One tabulation identified twenty-nine such groups established by inauguration day, and a half-dozen more in the succeeding weeks.[5] Some of the topics assigned these groups were extremely broad in scope—disarmament, foreign economic policy, space programs, education, health and social security, agriculture, and so forth. Other task forces were on specific policy problems, particular countries, or particular executive agencies—the balance of payments problem, the United States Information Agency, India, the current threat of economic recession.

Next to Kennedy himself, the key role in establishing the task forces and sifting their results was played by Sorensen, who had responsibility for developing the basic framework of the State of the Union message and a sequence of specific legislative proposals to follow it. Several of the studies were organized and supervised by George W. Ball and John Sharon, Washington lawyers who had assisted Adlai Stevenson in preparing his general report on foreign policy. For the most part, the post-election task forces were not

[5] "Pre-Inaugural Task Forces Unprecedented in History," *Congressional Quarterly Weekly Report,* Vol. 19, April 7, 1961, pp. 620-23. The figure 29 included seven studies authorized before election. Some were large, unwieldy groups, such as the twenty-three man task force to study problems of the depressed areas, headed by Senator Paul H. Douglas of Illinois; for working purposes this group divided into panels for particular subtopics. Other "task forces" were essentially one-man operations, such as the study of the regulatory commissions directed by James M. Landis. Some surveys and reports by miscellaneous individuals were not included in the *Congressional Quarterly* tabulation. A typical task force had a core group of five to ten members, who might call in other consultants on special subjects.

headed by political celebrities; they consisted of academic experts and Kennedy supporters with previous experience as government executives. Some of the groups, such as the one on depressed areas, were publicized in order to demonstrate Kennedy's concern with their problems; most of them were appointed quietly and worked in relative anonymity. Most of the task forces were going concerns by the time the relevant department heads were designated. The future department heads in some cases participated in the later stages of task force work, or drew on task force personnel to fill appointive positions, but it was emphasized to the task forces that their primary responsibility was to the President-elect.

The large number of these groups and their apparently overlapping jurisdictions strongly suggested a deliberate effort to maintain the President-elect's freedom of choice among alternatives in a way that contrasted with Eisenhower's staff methods. This was underscored by an episode reported by Richard Rovere. One person, receiving an assignment from Kennedy, commented that it seemed to overlap a previously announced project and that perhaps some coordination would be in order. The President-elect reacted adversely to the idea of coordination, saying very seriously, "I simply cannot afford to have just one set of advisers."[6]

Most of the task forces reported to Kennedy in late December and early January. About half of the reports were released, either in whole or in part. In addition to their influence on Kennedy, they served to draw public attention to issues and to test reaction to specific ideas for dealing with them. The reports on depressed areas and the general state of the American economy dramatized the recession issue and established a basis for several of the new administration's early proposals. Task force recommendations on education, on health and social security, and on housing and urban redevelopment, likewise foreshadowed post-inaugural legislative proposals. On the other hand, the generally cool public and legislative reaction to the Symington committee's proposals for a drastic reorganization of the military establishment may have had some-

---

[6] Richard M. Rovere, "Letter from Washington," *New Yorker*, Dec. 24, 1960, p. 52.

thing to do with the administration's subsequent caution in this area.

Choosing the Kennedy Team

Paralleling the policy preparations, an intense effort to staff the top posts in the new administration began soon after election and continued until inauguration day. This went on at several levels. The President-elect was searching for a group that would combine ability, reputation, and congeniality, and was apparently aware that his own wide acquaintance among legislators and working politicians around the country did not constitute an adequate field from which to fill high executive posts. He therefore spent long hours consulting "wise men," discussing prospects with his staff, and interviewing potential appointees. He was aided in this by members of his family and close political associates. His brother, Robert, was in touch with the nationwide network of political connections developed during the campaign. His brother-in-law, R. Sargent Shriver, appeared to concentrate more on "outside sources" of talent, seeking out promising leads to men in business, universities, and other more or less nonpolitical circles.

These activities at the Kennedy summit were backed by the work of several staff members who manned a temporary personnel office at the Democratic National Committee. This group bore the burden of receiving and soliciting suggestions, assembling dossiers on prospects, checking them where possible, making preliminary contacts to ascertain interests and availabilities, and forwarding recommendations to the top decision makers. The key "talent scouts" included Lawrence O'Brien, Ralph Dungan, and Richard Donohue, long-time Kennedy aides on Capitol Hill and generally considered the more "political" members of the group, and Harris Wofford and Adam Yarmolinski, young lawyers who had participated in the campaign but had their main lines of communication out to law firms, universities, foundations, minority groups, and the liberal wing of the party. The inner circle was supplemented by a half-dozen volunteer consultants assigned to identifying and sifting prospects for particular departments or functional areas.

The recruiters set out with great enthusiasm and determination to find the most competent people in the nation, wherever they might be, and to raise the practice of political office-filling to an unprecedented level of rationality. There was much talk in public about the so-called "talent search," and a proclaimed intention to get beyond the traditional criteria of service to party or the Kennedy candidacy and to find men of real intellectual and professional distinction. The basic personnel form called for not only the ordinary vocational and political information about a prospect, but also sought ratings by his references on such criteria as "judgment," "toughness," "integrity," "ability to work with others," "industry," and "devotion to the principles of the President-elect."

As inauguration day approached, the original high standards suffered some erosion under the pressures of time, the number of jobs to be filled, the number of applications or recommendations to be "processed," and the number of political obligations requiring recognition. The wide-open setting in which the recruiters worked made it difficult for them to fend off premature discussion of the more strictly patronage jobs lower down, and to concentrate on the top policy jobs that were their prime targets. For many jobs below the cabinet level, neither the canvass for prospects nor the checking of presumptive choices was as thorough as it should have been. Inevitably, there were some embarrassing last-minute changes of mind and minor eruptions because political clearances had not been obtained. Some important positions were long left unfilled. Despite its imperfections, however, the recruiting seems to have been carried on with more sophistication than is usual in such operations.[7]

The President-elect's cautious approach to the delicate business of cabinet-making delayed the top selections considerably longer than the "transition experts" at the Brookings Institution and elsewhere thought desirable. This sentiment was shared, although for different reasons, by the press corps, which huddled about the steps of Kennedy's home in Georgetown in numbing cold weather,

[7] For an "inside view," see Adam Yarmolinski, "The Kennedy Talent Hunt," *The Reporter*, June 8, 1961, pp. 22-25.

waiting for him to announce his choices. Kennedy ran well behind Eisenhower's 1952 timetable, announcing his first cabinet choice on the same date that Eisenhower had announced his final one. The first designation, on December 1, was of Governor Abraham A. Ribicoff of Connecticut to be Secretary of Health, Education, and Welfare. A careful search for a Director of the Budget ended the next day with the choice of David E. Bell of Harvard University. The following day it was Governor Luther H. Hodges of North Carolina for Secretary of Commerce. And on December 7, Representative Stewart L. Udall of Arizona was designated for Secretary of the Interior. Except for the budget job, which Kennedy had been advised by many to fill within a matter of hours after election, these hardly appeared to be the most essential posts to be filled first.

On December 12, the President-elect completed what was probably his most complex staffing problem when he announced his Secretary of State. With several prominent men under consideration, all with significant experience and political backing, he had gone outside the ranks of the politically active to choose Dean Rusk, president of the Rockefeller Foundation, persuading Chester Bowles and Adlai Stevenson to settle for Under Secretary and Ambassador to the United Nations, respectively. On the 13th, Kennedy announced that Robert S. McNamara, president of the Ford Motor Company, would be Secretary of Defense. Then, on the 15th, came Governor Orville L. Freeman of Minnesota for Secretary of Agriculture, and Arthur J. Goldberg, special counsel of the AFL-CIO, for Secretary of Labor. On the 16th, Kennedy announced that Douglas Dillon, Under Secretary of State in the Eisenhower administration, would be his Secretary of the Treasury, and that he had prevailed on his brother, Robert F. Kennedy, to accept the post of Attorney General. The dark horse who seems to turn up in every cabinet arrived on the 17th in the person of J. Edward Day, a California insurance company executive, to be Postmaster General.

By the time the department heads had been chosen, the operations of the Kennedy recruiting staff were far enough along to provide them and the President-elect with suggestions for most of the subcabinet posts, so that the choice of under secretaries, assistant secretaries, and special assistants went along fairly rapidly. There were serious delays, however, in choosing the heads of a few of the noncabinet agencies, which may be of equal or greater importance than some positions traditionally of cabinet rank. These delays created considerable uncertainty in handling problems that were becoming acute. The Federal Aviation Administrator and the Chairman of the Atomic Energy Commission were not chosen until the eve of inauguration day, and the heads of the International Cooperation Administration, the National Aeronautics and Space Agency, and the United States Information Agency were not designated until about the first of February. Nevertheless, Kennedy had his administration about as well organized by inauguration day as Eisenhower's had been.

The nominees were screened and advised with sufficient skill to avoid serious difficulties in the process of senatorial confirmation. There were no such snags over conflict of interest as had been struck by some of Eisenhower's early nominees. Although reluctant committees "sat on" some nominations for an undue time, and subjected a few nominees to severe quizzing, they confirmed them all in the end. The principal difficulty at this stage was that the FBI apparently got seriously behind in the investigatory work that Kennedy required to be done before any name was formally submitted to the Senate. As a consequence, a number of high appointees were publicly designated and on the job in Washington for several weeks after inauguration before being officially nominated and confirmed—a situation that had its financial as well as other kinds of embarrassments.

In strictly political terms, the initial Kennedy cabinet and subcabinet group conformed to most of the traditional rules of cabinet-making, with variations reflecting the specific composition of the Kennedy nominating and electing coalition. In the top ten there were two Jews, one Catholic, and seven assorted Protestants including one Mormon. Just below the top level there was a sprinkling of women (perhaps less than usual), of Negroes (somewhat more and higher than usual), and miscellaneous representatives of ethnic groups. The cabinet itself had appropriate geographical balance; the subcabinet had somewhat less of this quality despite strenuous efforts to avoid the traditional reliance on Eastern metropolitan centers for staffing at that level. Businessmen were dominant in the Commerce Department, Westerners in the Interior Department, and Midwesterners and Southerners in the Agriculture Department. There were rewards both for Northern liberals and for conservative Southerners who loyally supported the Kennedy ticket.

Like most cabinets in recent years, this one included at least nominal members of the opposition party. These, in fact, were some of the most interesting of Kennedy's appointments. Mr. McNamara was from the automobile industry but bore little resemblance to Charles E. Wilson; of the new generation of manufacturing executives, he might have come from the Ford Foundation as easily as from the Ford Motor Company. Republicans, businessmen, and conservatives generally were reassured by the appointment of Douglas Dillon as Secretary of the Treasury—a man of Wall Street origins plucked out of the Eisenhower administration, to the obvious discomfiture of Republican leaders.

The sharpest break with tradition was in the choice of the President's brother as Attorney General. The appointment was politically feasible, despite its dangers, because Robert Kennedy's experience in congressional staff work and his record of opposition to communism and labor racketeering had made him acceptable to members of Congress, including partisan Republicans.

But a traditional analysis, showing that there is something for everyone, does less than justice to the Kennedy cabinet and subcabinet selections. The public sensed that Kennedy made a serious effort not only to fulfill the requirements of political necessity and personal compatibility but to go beyond the minimum standard and assemble a group that would be broadly representative of American excellence. His initial appointments undoubtedly did add greatly to the public support shown in his narrow electoral margin. Regardless of how individual appointees may eventually turn out, it should be recorded that they started off on an unusually high wave of public approbation.

Briefings and Consultations

From early December on, the "Kennedy administration" rapidly took shape in Washington as designees arrived and began conferring with their predecessors, going through briefing sessions, consulting with top career men, and sifting the policy issues in conjunction with the Kennedy personal staff and task forces. Previously most of the communication between the Kennedy group and the administration had been through the relatively restricted channel provided by Persons and Clifford. Contact at the cabinet and subcabinet and staff level was organized as soon as the individuals were chosen on the Kennedy side. Clifford and Persons served as general overseers of the process, dealing with the special problems that seemed to arise at the rate of a dozen a day.

All this was a substantial improvement over 1952, when most of the Eisenhower designees were relatively indifferent to the aid offered by the Truman administration and suspicious of any information they might receive from the bureaucracy. There were some exceptions, but this time most of the incoming group seized on the information available and, in many cases, came back with requests for additional data and staff analysis. As a result of this activity, the Kennedy administration leaders seemed to have a better grasp of the problems facing them and clearer ideas about the courses they wished to pursue than any recent previous set of new appointees.

The unprecedented scale of the Kennedy staff preparation and pre-inaugural occupation of Washington, while contributing to a smoother transition, did raise some problems that had been perceived but dimly, if at all, in previous transitions. How were all these people working in one way or another for the "next administration" to be housed, serviced, and paid? Kennedy's personal staff was supported in the same way it had been supported during the campaign—by a combination of Kennedy's personal and senatorial resources and funds from the Democratic National Committee, mainly the latter. But although the National Committee spent substantial sums to cover the expenses of Kennedy and his aides between election and inauguration,[8] it could not begin to assume the burden of support for all the cabinet and subcabinet designees, task force members, and miscellaneous other consultants who came to Washington, traveled about the country, and spent hour after hour in long-distance telephoning on Kennedy business.

As a matter of courtesy, the Eisenhower department heads offered their successors, as soon as they were designated, limited amounts of office space, secretarial service, and other aid that could be provided without significant additional government expense. But little could be done for designees of lower rank, task force members, and others whose places in the next administration had not been determined. Such persons worked in hotel rooms or borrowed quarters, paid their own travel and hotel expenses, and continued—if they could—to draw salaries from their previous employers. Many of those who knew that they would be entering the new administration found it necessary to sever their previous connections and were without salaries for several weeks. Some, but not all, had sufficient personal resources to do this without difficulty.

Early in January, this problem was eased a little when the Eisenhower administration offered to put on the payroll as temporary employees and consultants a limited number of staff personnel designated by the future department and agency heads. The State and Defense departments, where the need for consultation and continuity presumably was greatest, would each employ ten such persons; the other departments would employ two each. This belated arrangement took care of the personal secretaries and assistants of some of the high-ranking designees but left a great many others, including the principals, uncared for. After January 20, some of the prospective assistant secretaries and others were put on the

[8] According to one statement by the National Chairman the total was $300,000. See Washington *Sunday Star,* March 12, 1961. Cf. Chap. 5, p. 144, in which Herbert Alexander shows a detailed breakdown of $210,000.

rolls as consultants until they could be officially nominated and confirmed, but the allowable per diem rate for consultants is well below the salary level for most positions at that level.

The Eisenhower administration meant to give away none of its own authority or responsibility in offering pre-inaugural consultation, office space, and other services to the Kennedy men. This was clearly understood in the Persons-Clifford consultations. But the presence in the departments of a considerable number of future officials, especially when they dug into the business with as much zeal as most of the Kennedy men did, inevitably created some tensions. No instances have been found in which Kennedy designees seriously transgressed on the hospitality and authority of their hosts, or in which the Eisenhower people declined to fulfill any reasonable request for information or service. In many cases, once the initial contacts were made, the Eisenhower top officials stood aside and let the Kennedy men deal directly with the bureau chiefs and other top career men. Some of these senior career officials, however, had their agility severely tested in satisfying the demands on their time and knowledge made by their future bosses without slighting the duty they owed their existing bosses.

It is one thing for a future department head to ask a civil servant for information. It is another thing to ask him to criticize, or offer alternatives to, a controversial policy of the administration still in power. On the whole, these pre-inaugural relationships worked out reasonably well for everyone concerned, but in the future some attention to ground rules may be required if such arrangements are to be completely fair and beneficial to all.

Eisenhower to the End

While the President-elect prepared himself and his subordinates took up advance positions in Washington, the Eisenhower administration played its hand out to the end. At the President's direction, officials of his administration cleared up as much pending business as possible. Many major matters could not be decided by an outgoing administration, but other pieces of business, particularly items in the form of "cases" requiring executive decision, were pushed to a conclusion.

In such situations there are no clear rules about what kinds of matters should be handled by the outgoing administration and what should be carried over. Most of the Eisenhower department heads seem to have followed the policy of deciding everything that could reasonably be got ready for decision, without worrying too much about whether the Kennedy people would prefer to have the matter left to them, or would be likely to decide differently if it were. In one or two departments there was some post-inaugural grumbling by Kennedy appointees about last-minute decisions made by the Eisenhower people, but no clear cases have been reported of irresponsible conduct or decisions made solely to embarrass the new administration.

The Presidential Messages

Under the anomalous schedule created by the Twentieth Amendment, it was Mr. Eisenhower's duty to present to the Eighty-seventh Congress, when it convened in January, the three major messages that normally start the annual legislative cycle: the State of the Union message, the Economic Report, and the Budget for the fiscal year beginning July 1. This he did in a way that fulfilled the requirements and left his views on record but did not unduly bind his successor.

The State of the Union message on January 12 was a *pro forma* affair, containing no specific legislative recommendations, and deemphasized by being transmitted to Congress in writing rather than delivered personally. Following a well-worn pattern, Eisenhower touched on the major "fields" of governmental activity, reviewing the accomplishments of his administration. Responding indirectly to a main campaign theme of the Democrats, he warned —as he had so many times before—of a "crash-program" approach to military and other affairs and counseled a "steady level of effort, designed for the long pull." But the tone of the message was prosaic and impersonal.

More significant in terms of the transition was the budget Eisenhower sent to Congress on January 15. There had been much advance speculation that this would be a rock-bottom budget, proposing taxes and spending at minimal levels so as to serve as a monument to Eisenhower's fiscal principles and a challenge to the supposedly free-spending Democrats. The budget did have some of these characteristics, calling for a surplus in fiscal 1961-1962 of $1.5 billion, but it was not as low as some had anticipated. Expenditures of $80.8 billion were proposed, up almost $2 billion from the previous year. Most of the increase was in defense, with commitments proposed that would be likely to require even greater increases the following year. A rumored sharp cut in foreign aid failed to materialize. There were a few cautious increases for domestic programs. Thus, while Kennedy might see a need for increasing expenditures in many areas, it would be difficult to charge that the Republicans had left the government grossly underfinanced.

The budget was more controversial on the revenue side. Eisenhower's anticipated $1.5 billion surplus was based on two debatable assumptions. One was that the economic recession would be mild and short-lived, and would not seriously affect revenues in fiscal 1962. The other was that Congress would raise $1.8 billion in additional revenue through higher postal rates and new taxes— a doubtful assumption in view of Congress's rejection of similar recommendations in the past. Thus there was at least some basis for the immediate charges of partisan Democrats that it was a "phoney" surplus. But taking the budget as a whole, it could hardly be called irresponsible. In its weaknesses, if such they were, it was at least consistent: optimistic revenue estimates had been characteristic of the last several Eisenhower budgets.

Eisenhower followed another Truman precedent of 1953 when he made a televised farewell address to the nation on the evening of January 17. Here he showed the personal touch that had been absent from the State of the Union message. He began with appropriate references to his successor, to Congress, and to those who had worked with him during the past eight years. Looking to the future, he saw danger of "indefinite duration" which should be met not with the "emotional and transitory sacrifices of crisis," but with steadiness, moderation, and balance. Introducing some new themes, he noted the necessity for a "permanent armaments industry of vast proportions," but warned against the "acquisition of unwarranted influence" by this "military-industrial complex." Similarly, he expressed concern about the increasing role of the federal government in science and "the prospect of domination of the nation's scholars by Federal employment," or the "equal and opposite danger that public policy could itself become the captive of a scientific-technological elite." He closed, as he had begun in his inaugural address eight years before, with a prayer for peace.

Eisenhower's final Economic Report, submitted in writing on January 18, was a low-key document that took cognizance of the current business downturn and the balance of payments problem but stressed the underlying strength of the economy. The report included a thoughtful review of experience under the Employment Act, some general observations on desirable policies for economic stability and growth, and some fifteen specific legislative recommendations (of which most were reiterations of previous administration recommendations).

Consultations and Decisions

Eisenhower asserted in his initial public statements and communications to Kennedy, as already noted, that he would be prepared to make any necessary decisions right up to inauguration day. The application of this principle in connection with two important matters—the balance of payments problem and relations with Cuba— illustrates some of the difficulties of presidential leadership between election and inauguration when there is a change of party control.

Shortly after election, administration officials began to speak in somber tones of the United States balance of payments deficit and the consequent rate at which gold was being transferred abroad.

To protect the value of the dollar, the administration took two major steps. First was Eisenhower's mid-November order calling for sharp reductions in the number of dependents of military personnel abroad. This was received with great dismay by the military; the Secretary of the Army was openly critical, and there were signs of foot-dragging throughout the military establishment, which obviously hoped that the new administration could be persuaded to see the problem differently. Second was the hasty mission of Secretary of the Treasury Anderson and Under Secretary of State Dillon to Bonn in an effort to persuade Germany to assume some of the cost of maintaining American troops in Europe. Before leaving, Anderson sought out representatives of the President-elect. There were rumors that he was trying to reach Kennedy himself. In any event, he finally saw Paul Nitze, who remained noncommittal. Not surprisingly, Anderson returned from Germany empty-handed. An administration representing a party defeated at the polls and about to leave office was hardly in position to persuade a German government, which itself was beginning to be concerned about elections the following year, to adopt on short notice a policy bound to be extremely unpopular in Germany. Anderson conferred again with Nitze after his trip. The Kennedy side explained to the press that they regarded the Anderson-Nitze talks as "information" or "briefing" rather than "consultation."[9]

Several observations can be made on this effort of the Eisenhower administration to bolster the dollar. First, it demonstrates how hard it is for an outgoing administration to maintain either internal discipline or external effectiveness in delicate international negotiations. Second, it demonstrates the difficulty of holding strictly to a line of not asking the President-elect for any commitments in advance. In retrospect, Anderson appears to have had small chance of success unless he could have somehow represented himself as having the backing of the incoming administration. Realization of this presumably lay at the root of his desire to confer with Kennedy or some authoritative representative, whether or not the Kennedy blessing was ever explicitly sought. Third, Eisen-

---

[9] *Washington Post and Times Herald,* Dec. 1, 1960.

hower's actions raise interesting questions about what is responsible presidential conduct in such a situation. Assuming that he
realized how slight were the chances of accomplishing anything
in relation to the balance of payments difficulty before inauguration, was it irresponsible of him to tackle this issue in his last
weeks in office? Some commentators thought that it was, charging
that the administration had created an unnecessary atmosphere of
crisis about the gold flow. But it should be noted that nothing
done by Eisenhower tightly bound his successor. Was not Kennedy
placed in a stronger position because his predecessor had dramatized and taken a strong position on this issue? If continuation of
a strong policy line was judged necessary, Eisenhower already had
taken the political onus. If softening or modification were possible,
Kennedy could win political dividends—as indeed he later did.

Then there was Eisenhower's decision on January 3 to break
diplomatic relations with Cuba, a grave and unusual step for an
outgoing President to take. As we have since learned, there was
more to our Cuban policy than appeared on the surface. There was
no lack of provocation by Castro's government to justify a severing
of diplomatic ties. After a gradual deterioration of relations, Castro
had suddenly demanded a crippling reduction in the United States
embassy personnel in Havana. Even so, it was not clear why the
break had to be made before inauguration. Eisenhower's action
committed the United States to a policy that the next administration could not have abandoned in the short run without considerable embarrassment, although subsequent events have made this a
moot point.

Eisenhower's Cuba decision at least demonstrated to the world
that the United States could and would make major foreign policy
decisions if they were deemed necessary. Presumably, the total security of the United States was strengthened by having this clearly
understood abroad. But the crisp decision on Cuba made an interesting contrast with the administration's inability to stop the deterioration in Laos during the same period. An outgoing regime
can respond to a clear and immediate threat, or to a threat that is
less than clear and immediate if the power of decision is entirely

in its own hands and the choice is among a limited number of alternatives, perhaps a simple yes or no. But an administration on the verge of leaving office finds it difficult to deal, as in Laos, with a complex situation requiring formulation of new alternatives or extensive consultation with other governments.

According to press reports, the Eisenhower administration did not "consult" the President-elect or the future Secretary of State prior to making the decision to break diplomatic relations with Cuba. Secretary Herter did, however, inform Secretary-designate Rusk after the decision was made but prior to its announcement. At that time, it was reported, Herter asked if the Kennedy administration wished to "associate itself" with the decision. The answer was negative.

It has long been settled doctrine that an outgoing President cannot require his successor to assume any responsibility for decisions prior to inauguration day and, indeed, is foolish even to try to involve him in them. Nevertheless, events and pressures on an outgoing administration tend to push it beyond the act of merely providing information into a middle position of inviting "support," "concurrence," or "association" with a decision that has been or is about to be made. Thus it was with the Truman administration and the Korean armistice negotiations; so it was with the Eisenhower administration on the balance of payments problem and relations with Cuba.

The theory of indivisible presidential responsibility may be more complex than is generally realized. To be sure, the President in office must be prepared to make ultimate decisions in all circumstances. On most matters, he must make decisions in accordance with *his* view of the national interest, regardless of what his successor may think. But there may well be situations of extreme gravity in which an outgoing President cannot decide intelligently what is in the national interest without considering what his successor will prefer or is likely to do. If this is the case, is it not irresponsible for him to proceed without giving the President-elect a chance to state his views? What, then, is the position of the President-elect? Knowing that the President will decide something, and that he as the successor will have to live with the result, is it responsible conduct for the President-elect to shun all involvement? Stating his views or declining to state his views; supporting the decision or declining to support the decision; each of these positions may have unique consequences that the President-elect as a moral man must take into account. The fact is that from election day onward the effective presidential power to influence the future has been divided, and neither President nor President-elect can escape the consequences.

The Transfer

By mid-January, preparations for the transfer of authority were far advanced on both sides. Eisenhower forwarded his series of messages to Congress, presided over his final cabinet meeting, received the Prime Minister of Canada for a ceremonial signing of a Columbia River treaty that had been long in negotiation, traded compliments with high figures of his administration in letters of resignation and acceptance, and supervised the removal of the White House files—some to Abilene and some to Gettysburg.[10]

On the Kennedy side the activity was of greater intensity. During January the President-elect dashed from Palm Beach, to New York, to Washington, to New York, to Boston, to New York, to Washington, to Palm Beach, to New York, and finally back to Washington on the day before inauguration. From wherever he happened to be, announcements of personnel choices for subcabi-

[10] In connection with the latter, modern developments challenged the ancient tradition that all the White House files are the personal files of the President and are taken away when he leaves. In the Eisenhower regime, "the White House" had been extended to include numerous special assistants and interdepartmental coordinating units which had relatively little personal connection with the President and thought of themselves as having functions that would need to be continued in some way. Orders to pack all the papers connected with these operations came as a shock. Nevertheless, in most instances the rule of removal was enforced, although in one or two cases Eisenhower aides secured permission to leave "technical libraries" that might be found useful to the next administration.

net, independent agency, regulatory commission, and additional White House or Executive Office staff positions were emitted at the rate of several a day. Kennedy received the reports of most of his policy task forces and discussed them with the authors. He found time to seek wisdom and broaden his public support by well-publicized consultations with such diverse personages as Herbert Hoover, Governor Luis Muñoz Marin of Puerto Rico, the head of the NAACP, and evangelist Billy Graham.

In Washington, the future cabinet members appeared without incident before Senate committees holding hearings in anticipation of their formal nominations. Practically all of them had, by now, moved into their future departments and were in consultation with outgoing Eisenhower and career officials. Where the Kennedy staffing was relatively far advanced, the consultations extended several levels downward in the hierarchy. There also was some consultation at the White House between Eisenhower and Kennedy aides during the last few days before inauguration, but relatively less than at the departmental level. This was due partly to the fact that Kennedy was organizing his staff along rather different lines from Eisenhower, so that "opposite numbers" could not always be found, and partly because the immersion of the Kennedy staff in personnel recruiting and policy planning activities seemed to leave them less time for briefing. Just as the Truman staff had felt eight years before, many of the Eisenhower people felt a little frustrated because no one was taking advantage of their willingness to pass on hard-earned knowledge.

On January 19, Kennedy visited the White House for his second pre-inaugural conference with President Eisenhower. They talked privately for a time, then with the incoming and outgoing secretaries of State, Defense, and Treasury and various other aides in the Cabinet Room. The discussion was reported to have ranged over the world's trouble spots, the United States economy and balance of payments, and the security emergency procedures with which Kennedy would have to be familiar from then on. Just to show his successor how it was done, Eisenhower used the procedure to summon a helicopter to the White House lawn, as if for an evacuation. Leaving the White House after more than two hours, Kennedy told reporters that the session had been cordial and expressed his appreciation to Eisenhower and other members of the administration for their assistance in easing the transition. A joint press statement described the discussions in general terms, asserted that the President-elect had neither sought nor been asked to assume any decision-making responsibility, and proclaimed American unity.

Later in the day, Kennedy had a long conference with the Chairman of the Joint Chiefs of Staff, which was described as covering "procedural matters" pertaining to the responsibilities as Commander-in-Chief that Kennedy would assume the following day. In connection with the Commander-in-Chief function, it had been announced previously that Brigadier General Andrew J. Goodpaster, Eisenhower's Staff Secretary and the official principally responsible for instantaneous communication with the military-intelligence community, would remain for several weeks to serve the new President and break in a successor.

That evening a snowstorm that will be long remembered in Washington blocked all traffic, stranded commuters, and put a moist blanket over pre-inaugural celebrations. By the next morning, however, the downtown streets were cleared and the inauguration proceeded on schedule. The cordial relations between Kennedy and Eisenhower continued as the President-elect called at the White House and joined the President on the traditional ride to the Capitol. The inaugural ceremony had more than the usual share of color and human interest, and Kennedy's relatively brief inaugural address was an unusually powerful and effective one. Before leaving the Capitol, Kennedy signed the nominations of his cabinet members, which were duly transmitted to the Senate. Eisenhower slipped away to a luncheon with members of his cabinet and then off to Gettysburg. Kennedy reviewed an inaugural parade that ran only normally behind schedule. Later the President and his wife, numerous others of the Kennedy clan, and thousands of Democrats celebrated in traditional festivities at three official inaugural ball locations and many private parties.

9

The Transition: The New Administration

LAURIN L. HENRY

IN A SENSE, it is misleading to speak, as we sometimes carelessly do, of "transferring the Presidency." *Presidential responsibility* is essentially transferred on inauguration day, although even this may not be as simple as it appears. But the *Presidency,* except in its most formal aspects, is not a tangible thing that can be passed along intact from one man to another. Each new President must re-create the Presidency in unique form—starting with the materials at hand, but guided by his own concepts and limited by what events and his own skills permit him to make of the formal office. In the same sense, he may inherit a bureaucracy, but he cannot inherit an administration. He must build his own.

The *presidential transition,* then, consists of those critical decisions, acts, or events by which the new Presidency and new administration are given their characteristic shape, style, and content. Presidencies and administrations are, of course, ever-evolving, and it is impossible to say—at least not until they are over—at precisely what moment the outlines began to be stable. Usually, different aspects stabilize at different times. But certainly the first three months, or the first 100 days, to use the period of measure favored by journalists, are the most critical; by the end of the first six months the essential characteristics of style and approach, if not of continuing substantive policies, are likely to be apparent.

The New President and the New Presidency

During the campaign, Senator Kennedy had so evoked the memory of Franklin Roosevelt and spoken in such terms of what the next President would have to do in his first 90 or 100 days that he had created, at least in some circles, a vague expectation of a "new 100 days" of spectacular action to match the exciting events that followed FDR's arrival in the White House. It was therefore both realistic and prudent of him to qualify his statement of goals in his inaugural address with the assertion: "All this will not be finished in the first 100 days. Nor will it be finished in the first 1,000 days, nor in the lifetime of this Administration, nor perhaps even in our lifetime on this planet. But let us begin."

If Kennedy could not hope to match the early legislative triumphs of the New Deal, there was a more limited sense in which the "100 days" notion was relevant. He could move swiftly on matters clearly within his discretion, taking full advantage of the post-inaugural "honeymoon" to seize the political initiative and bring the Executive Branch to a state of alert responsiveness. His conduct from election to inauguration day had done much to overcome the disadvantage of his thin electoral majority. Arrived in the White House, he moved with energy, skill, and unmistakable personal flair to dramatize his presence, broaden his public support, and take the preliminary steps to convert his public support into effective influence.

The Early Spectaculars

Almost everything Kennedy and his associates did in the first two or three weeks conveyed an image of competence, youthful energy, and attention to important things. Before Kennedy had been in the White House 24 hours, he signed an order making increased amounts of surplus food available for distribution to the needy, and in the following days he announced several other steps to relieve suffering and to stimulate the economy. He dispatched the

Secretary of Health, Education, and Welfare to Florida to see about the Cuban refugees. He sent the Secretary of Labor to New York to help settle a port and railroad strike, and then on a tour of West Virginia and other depressed areas. He announced a softening of Eisenhower's unpopular order about military dependents abroad.

The most spectacular event of Kennedy's first week in the White House was an announcement on January 25 at his first press conference: he had arranged with Khrushchev for the release of the two survivors from the Air Force RB-47, which had been shot down by the Soviet Union several months previously over what the United States claimed were international waters. Kennedy asserted that he had not made specific concessions to win the release of the men, but he did say in response to a question that he was continuing Eisenhower's ban on further U-2 reconnaissance flights over the Soviet Union. In any case, this development—essentially a gesture by Khrushchev—removed one of the most immediate irritants in relations with the Soviets and launched the new administration with a glow of success in international affairs.

The climax of Kennedy's settling-in period was his State of the Union address to Congress on January 30. The speech consisted of a stark assessment of the national situation, a call for action and support, and a partial specification of steps to be taken. Reviewing the statistics and asserting that "the American economy is in trouble," Kennedy listed several kinds of measures to relieve the effects of unemployment and revive economic growth. Surveying the world, he concluded that in such critical areas as Asia, Africa, and Latin America "the tide of events has been running out and time has not been our friend," and warned of "the harsh enormities of the trials through which we must pass in the next four years." Kennedy announced an acceleration of the military missile program, a reassessment of the condition and balance of military forces, and an unprecedented effort to strengthen the non-Communist world through economic and social programs. Well written and presented, the address was applauded for its candor in all but the most partisan Republican circles. Kennedy had secured the public attention that was a prerequisite to the assertion of leadership.

Administrative Theory and Practice

The events and announcements of Kennedy's early weeks in the White House signified that he was establishing a different concept of the Presidency itself—a concept reflecting the Democratic party tradition of "strong" Presidents, the analyses of political scientists such as Neustadt, and Kennedy's own experience, personality, and theories. In contrast to his predecessor, Kennedy sought to make the Presidency the center of policy initiative, to make full use of all the formal and informal powers of the office, and to maximize the President's personal influence not only within the Executive Branch but throughout the political system.

The Kennedy approach was manifested in his White House staff arrangements. Eisenhower, reflecting his military training, had emphasized hierarchy, order, precise assignments, careful lateral clearances, and the doctrine of "completed staff work." Kennedy left unfilled both the post of The Assistant to the President, in which first Sherman Adams and then General Persons had exercised supervisory authority over other staff members, and the job of Staff Secretary, which had served as a checkpoint for clearances and communications to and from the President. Each of Kennedy's principal aides was to deal directly with him. The functions of several assistants, such as those for press relations (Pierre Salinger), appointments (Kenneth O'Donnell), and congressional liaison (Lawrence O'Brien), were fairly traditional; the office of special counsel (Theodore C. Sorensen) assumed greater importance initially than it had in either the Eisenhower or the Truman administration because of Kennedy's early concentration on messages and legislation. The responsibilities of several other aides, such as Ralph Dungan, Frederick Dutton, Richard Donohue, and Harris Wofford, did not appear—at least from the outside—to be sharply defined, and there was a proclaimed intention to make wider use of all-purpose assistants with shifting assignments. The goal was to keep the new White House staff small and to give such Executive Office units as the Bureau of the Budget and the Council of Economic Advisers increased responsibilities as presidential policy staffs.

Just as important as changes in the structural arrangements were the changes in tone. The President, although decisive and demanding, was informal in his relations with staff. He was said to display a remarkable capacity for absorbing information from his staff, from the reading that he somehow found time to do, and from the stream of visitors that flowed through his office. He preferred to get into all important questions at an early stage of consideration and to wrestle with the details of policy problems. The President's restless energy was shared with his staff, which worked incredibly long hours, paid little attention to week ends, and astounded civil servants and newcomers to the Kennedy group by the audacity of the early deadlines set for completion of staff studies, messages, or other work. The rigor of life on the New Frontier became legendary, a unifying bond among the Kennedyites.

The same direct relations that characterized the President's relations with his personal staff prevailed between the President and his department heads. Instead of having frequent, formal cabinet meetings, Kennedy saw his cabinet members one at a time, or in small groups depending on the problem at hand, and relied on each one for policy initiation and advice in his own sphere. The position of cabinet secretary, which had been an important post in Eisenhower's White House staff, was left unfilled, and the cabinet as such met only three or four times in the first three months of the administration.

At the outset, the National Security Council was handled the same way. Although the President frequently saw the Secretary of State, the Secretary of Defense, the Chairman of the Joint Chiefs of Staff, and other key members of the NSC, he saw them one at a time or in small, *ad hoc* groups. The NSC officially met only three times in the first three months. Problems requiring interdepartmental consideration below the department head level were handed over to temporary task forces or settled by the responsible officials in hasty conferences. The President's special assistant for national security affairs, McGeorge Bundy, and the latter's assistant, Walt W. Rostow, operated as freelance advisers—"a team of Harry Hopkinses," as one newspaper report put it. James S. Lay, Jr., executive secretary of the NSC since its founding, resigned and was not replaced.

The greater emphasis on individual rather than collective responsibility for policy initiative also was applied to policy coordination after decisions. In contrast to the Eisenhower administration's tendency to assume that matters with interdepartmental implications required interdepartmental committees to coordinate them, the Kennedy assumption was that responsibility for interdepartmental coordination rested on the department head or agency primarily concerned. If more than passing arrangements were required, a temporary task force was the preferred instrument. The Operations Coordinating Board, a controversial appendage to the NSC charged with follow-through on policies enunciated in that body, was abolished on March 12, along with 16 other standing interdepartmental committees. On April 8, 41 additional interdepartmental committees, most of them already moribund, were abolished.

The President and the Press

President Kennedy assumed office enjoying excellent relations with the press. In his early weeks, he deliberately and skillfully cooperated with the press in order to dramatize his activities and widen his public acceptance. Although he had been warned of the dangers of the wide-open, on-the-record press conference, he went even further than Eisenhower in making the press conference a public spectacle. Whereas Eisenhower's conferences had always been recorded on tape or film, with the possibility of editing out any dangerous misstatements or indiscretions before release, Kennedy permitted "live" radio and television coverage. Furthermore, his first conference was scheduled for an early evening hour when most of the nation might watch or listen. In his first conferences, there were several minor discomfitures, but his total performance— his forthrightness, self-confidence, command of detail, and steady flow of newsworthy statements—was sufficiently impressive to validate for the moment the decision to use the press conference in this way. In addition there were numerous special news stories and programs using pictures and interviews from "behind the scenes at the White House."

Exploitation of the President's own active person was not all. Mrs. Kennedy, while she did not hold press conferences, appointed a press secretary, gave out a great deal of news and granted special interviews. Her plans for decorating the White House, with the aid of special advisory committees and consultants on art and period furniture, were widely publicized. The President's three-year old daughter, Caroline, also was good for almost daily stories featuring cats, ducks, bright sayings, and unexpected appearances.

The press honeymoon inevitably ran its course in a few weeks. As early as February, some reporters were commenting acidly on the pattern of first a "leak" of a news story, then an announcement that at a given time the President would make an announcement, and finally the announcement itself—thus extracting several stories from a given bit of news. By March, Press Secretary Salinger was losing his temper at reporters who pressed too closely on a story about the planting of more shrubbery on the White House lawn to keep Caroline's play screened from the street. Later it was revealed that one of the White House aides, not Salinger, had taken it on himself to remind the assistants of cabinet officers to make sure that their bosses' speeches and press releases contained appropriate references to the President's "personal interest in, and compassion with, the problems which face the nation."

Strictly personal and "bonus" publicity tapered off rapidly after the first three months, but the President's conduct and image as portrayed by the mass media had the desired effects. At the end of his first month in office, the Gallup Poll reported that 72 per cent of the American people approved of the way Kennedy was doing his job. By the end of April, his approval rate had climbed to 83 per cent, which was higher than Eisenhower's ever had been.[1] In and of itself, this popularity passed no laws and won no battles in the cold war, but it indicated that Kennedy had taken the essential step of establishing in the public mind an image of himself as President.

[1] *Washington Post and Times Herald,* March 1 and May 5, 1961.

The Political Presidency

Kennedy made it clear from the beginning that he would use his position as party leader to reinforce his position as administrative and policy chief. In a post-inaugural transition at the Democratic National Committee, Senator Henry M. Jackson, who had been recognized from the beginning as a caretaker National Chairman, was replaced by a man frankly recognized as the President's choice, State Chairman John M. Bailey of Connecticut. Bailey set out like an experienced professional to pay off the deficit, gird the party for the 1962 struggle, consolidate the President's power in the party, and build up support for his legislative program.

Most Presidents tend to be wary of overt involvement or commitment in factional rows at the state level. Kennedy proceeded, perhaps a little incautiously, to wade into the middle of one in New York, even letting it be known that he was trying, by threatening to withhold patronage, to force the resignation of the State Chairman, Michael H. Prendergast. The President and Robert Kennedy conferred with the anti-Prendergast faction, and on one occasion the President remarked wryly in a press conference that he was sending Mr. Bailey on a mission to "alleviate the distress" in New York. Several months later, however, Mr. Prendergast was still in office, and the disorganization of the New York state party had not been noticeably relieved.

The New President as Chief Legislator

John F. Kennedy had served fourteen years in Congress without adopting that body's traditional attitude toward active presidential leadership in the legislative process. Having campaigned for the Presidency on the theme of strong leadership, he began preparing after election to take the policy initiative. By inauguration day, he and his department heads, aided by numerous consultants and task forces, had reached general agreement on priorities in the most crucial fields of action. Special Counsel Sorensen and Budget Director Bell were well started on the job of reducing the new Kennedy material and the recommendations welling up from the agencies into the messages and draft bills that comprise a presidential legislative program.[2] The first fruit of this endeavor was the State of the Union address on January 30.

The President and the Legislative Party

Meanwhile Kennedy had been taking steps to increase the likelihood that his recommendations would receive favorable action on Capitol Hill. His Senate membership, which he did not give up until the end of December, and close working relationship with Lyndon Johnson made it convenient to participate to a far greater extent than a President-elect normally would in the selection of a successor to Johnson as Senate Majority Leader. The promotion of Senator Mike Mansfield of Montana, already the Democratic Whip, and the elevation to the No. 2 and No. 3 spots of Senators Hubert Humphrey of Minnesota and George Smathers of Florida, were likely to have occurred in any event, but it was noteworthy that these decisions were reached by the Senate Democrats after extensive consultation with Kennedy and Johnson. Mansfield, Humphrey, and Smathers were openly described as Kennedy's "choices," and Mansfield said publicly that, unlike certain Republican Senate leaders of recent memory, he would regard himself as the President's representative in that chamber.

Achieving a favorable leadership situation in the House of Representatives was not so easy. Here Kennedy proceeded cautiously, both in deference to Speaker Sam Rayburn and in recognition of the danger of an unfavorable political reaction to too open an intervention in the internal affairs of the House. But in the end he used his influence, in a way that no President since FDR had dared to do, to bring about one of those decisions that seem to be re-

[2] The Kennedy group's alacrity in this respect, which contrasted with the caution of the Eisenhower team eight years earlier, may have owed something to the advice of Neustadt, who had long been pointing out the utility of the presidential legislative program—and particularly a series of deadlines for messages—as a device for resolving issues within an administration as well as giving timely cues to Congress.

quired to tip the legislative balance and open the way to a period of progressive legislation. At issue was the House Rules Committee, in which a coalition of Republicans and Southern Democrats led by Chairman Howard W. Smith of Virginia seemed likely to continue, as it had in the past, to bottle up liberal measures. While presumably making clear to "Mr. Sam" his feeling that something ought to be done, Kennedy took no public position until Rayburn had proposed and secured House Democratic caucus endorsement of a plan to "pack" the committee by adding three members—two of whom would be Democrats likely to be responsive to the party leadership.

This was a plan that had to be taken before the whole House, and as the "conservative coalition" gathered its forces to block it the outcome was in doubt. Asked about the scheme at his first press conference after inauguration, Kennedy made the inevitable disclaimer that this was really the House's business, but then put himself squarely into the fight with a long statement to the effect that no small group should have the power to deny the whole House the opportunity to express its will on the important measures the administration would propose. In the next few days members of the White House staff and some members of the Cabinet, particularly Secretary Udall, were active in missionary work on members of the House whose votes were doubtful. The proposal was brought up at a favorable moment—the day after Kennedy's powerful State of the Union message—and squeaked through by a 217-212 vote. The closeness of the vote showed that the Kennedy program would have no easy sledding in the new Congress, but the subsequent performance of the reformed Rules Committee in getting Kennedy measures on the floor suggested that the victory had been worth the risk.

Kennedy Proposals

The rules fight out of the way, the President forwarded messages and legislative requests to Congress at a fantastic rate for the next several weeks. On February 2, came a major message on economic policy containing the administration's assessment of the current recession, describing its general approach to budget and fiscal policy, and proposing more than a dozen specific measures to bring the economy out of its slump and back into a pattern of long-term growth. These involved extension of unemployment insurance, increasing the minimum wage, aid to dependent children of the unemployed, and aid to areas of chronic economic distress. On February 6, came proposals for dealing with the balance of payments problem; on February 9, health and hospital care, including the controversial proposal for health insurance for the aged through the social security program; on February 16, a request for a feed grain bill; and on February 20, the administration's controversial proposals for grants to the states for school construction and teachers' salaries. Sprinkled in were several other requests of lesser scope, including additional federal judges and extension of administrative reorganization authority.

At this stage the House was still recovering from the rules fight, and Congress generally was preoccupied with Lincoln's Birthday and Jefferson-Jackson Day events. Most of Kennedy's initial requests had not even been taken up by committees. Amid concern about the growing backlog of presidential requests, Kennedy conferred with the legislative leaders on February 21 and agreed on a sixteen-item priority list. But still other requests were made: a highway program, the Peace Corps, a comprehensive housing program, aid to Latin America, a general farm bill, a general foreign aid bill, and many more. By early May, according to the *Congressional Quarterly* box-score, Kennedy had made 277 identifiable legislative requests.[3]

As in 1953, the new President submitted no single document supplanting the budget submitted by his predecessor but carried on a running revision throughout the session of Congress. Department-by-department modifications were submitted as they were worked out, beginning in mid-March, and most of the presidential messages calling for new programs included financing requests for them. The closest thing to a "new budget" was a March 24 message summarizing the effect of Kennedy's changes and new pro-

[3] *Congressional Quarterly Weekly Report*, Vol. 19, May 12, 1961, pp. 803-11.

posals to date and discussing budgetary prospects generally. The document labored rather heavily to show that Kennedy was not a reckless spender and that any deficits under the current (1961) and proposed fiscal 1962 budgets were at least partly the responsibility of Eisenhower. Eisenhower's estimate of a tiny surplus for the current year was changed to an estimated deficit of something over $2 billion, attributed to diminished revenues and increased spending because of the current recession. Additions to existing programs for 1962 had been held to modest amounts, it was pointed out, and most of the new program proposals included special taxes to finance them or would spread out the spending over several years. Thus, except for defense budget changes, which had not yet been submitted, there would be no deficit in fiscal 1962 if Eisenhower's revenue estimates were correct. But since Eisenhower was said to have been over-optimistic about the state of the economy and had made some other "unrealistic" assumptions about revenue, the prospect was for a $1.8 billion deficit on nondefense items in fiscal 1962.

Kennedy's revised defense budget, submitted on March 28, called for an increase of $2 billion in appropriations but only a $900 million increase in spending in fiscal 1962. Additional modifications continued to be proposed as the session went on, however, and revenue expectations were further revised downward, so that as of mid-June the official estimate was for a $3.7 billion deficit in fiscal 1962. According to the *New York Times* financial reporter, however, "unofficial estimates put the deficit closer to $5 billion."[4]

Caution and Modest Success

The response of Congress to Kennedy's legislative program was neither prompt nor rapid. The committees did not get down to serious business until mid-March. One of the first priority items, extension of unemployment compensation, was held up in the Senate and barely survived a conservative attack, led by Senator Harry F. Byrd, on its financing provisions. The House passed a minimum

[4] Richard E. Mooney, "President Urges Debt-Ceiling Rise," *New York Times,* June 14, 1961.

wage extension bill but only after voting, by a one-vote margin, to substitute a version scaled down from what the administration wanted. The health insurance bill made no progress, the aid to education bill bogged down in a wrangle over aid to parochial schools, and the depressed areas bill was under heavy conservative attack for its proposed financing methods. As of the end of March, only four of the sixteen priority items had been passed.[5]

But if the response was not overwhelming, neither, in a way, was the program. Kennedy's cautious approach to fiscal policy was a little frustrating to some who had been looking forward to an active spending program to take the slack out of the economy, and an end of concern with short-run budget-balancing. The very number of legislative requests, each bearing the presidential endorsement, seemed to blur the impact. The content of the program, furthermore, contained few surprises since most of the proposals had been debated in the previous Congress or were fairly obvious expansions of existing activities. Some of the controversial items, such as health insurance for the aging, were proposed at levels so modest that they disappointed their most enthusiastic advocates in Congress. Where, it was asked, were the bold new programs, the demands for sacrifice, that Kennedy had talked about? And why was he not using his personal popularity and general public approval, which were clear by this time, to arouse the public and drive his bills through Congress?

Having taken the formal initiative and established the legislative agenda, however, Kennedy clearly preferred to use polite but steady pressure rather than an all-out effort that might stiffen backs all over Congress simultaneously and thus lead to a shattering defeat. He continued to make clear his desires to the Democratic legislative leaders and to put in plugs for his measures at press conferences. His legislative liaison staff worked quietly but on the whole effectively, not hesitating on occasion to engage in hard bargaining. As the weeks passed and April wore into May the bills began coming through, often by narrow margins, but usually in a form more or less satisfactory to the administration.

[5] *Congressional Quarterly Weekly Report,* Vol. 19, March 31, 1961, p. 509.

The Bureaucracy on the New Frontier

As transitions go, this was a relatively easy one for the federal bureaucracy. The probity of the civil service had not been a campaign issue, and Democratic program objectives carried no serious threats to the administrative establishment. Only eight years out of power, the Democrats still tended to look possessively on the bureaucracy and to assume that it would welcome their return. The initial statements of President Kennedy and most of the agency heads were calculated to quiet residual fears and stir the enthusiasm of the civil service for service on the New Frontier.

The bureaucracy itself was far better prepared than it had been in 1953 to receive and respond to new leadership. The 1953 experience had left most of the top career men with hard-won wisdom and sophistication about what a change of parties might involve. The briefing arrangements and "black books" of data for the new appointees were handled more deftly this time, although the inevitable volume and density of this material made it difficult for the recipients to digest. There were also some appointees (relatively fewer than in 1953) who were too suspicious of anything emanating from the previous administration to make much use of it.

Most of the high-level holdover officers in 1961 were realistic, even fatalistic, about possible program and organizational changes that might affect them. One Republican innovation, civil service Schedule C, had established a category of several hundred policy jobs just below the presidential appointee level in which the new department heads would have great discretion in firing and hiring, thus providing a welcome element of flexiblity. And it may have been true that many of the top career men, particularly those in social and economic programs that had been restrained by Republican conservatism, privately welcomed the change of party control despite their overt neutrality.

Despite the generally benign climate, there were plenty of cases of misunderstanding and faulty communication between the career service and the new leaders, particularly in departments where the new appointees were inexperienced in Washington or the Executive Branch. In one or two departments these tensions became fairly severe indicating that no new administration is likely to avoid altogether the problem of accommodation with the bureaucracy. On the whole, however, the civil servants and new appointees made a quick adjustment. While the newcomers sometimes were frustrated by the inertia and inherent conservatism encountered in any large organization, they showed few signs of continuing dissatisfaction. The civil servants for the most part responded to the challenge of an administration that openly invited their ideals. Many career men were given increased responsibilities and drawn into the shaping of the Kennedy program. Several months later found them a little winded by the pace, nursing a few bruises, but generally feeling useful, secure, and appreciated.

The issue of staff changes in order to secure policy control was raised only in limited sectors of the government. Even the Bureau of the Budget, which had been attacked as a tool of Republican economizing policy, soon proved its utility to a regime with a different outlook. In a few agencies of acute policy controversy, perhaps most notably the Department of Agriculture, there was a hint of a "purge." But in most agencies, the only personnel replaced were those with fairly clear Republican connections or unusual personal identification with controversial policies. Many career men occupying Schedule C positions were not removed, and some that were found places in other agencies. In the Department of Defense, Secretary McNamara's rapid-fire demands for staff studies, new management methods, and willingness to resolve longstanding issues resulted in charges that he was moving too fast and shutting the career military men out of key decisions, but this seemed almost inevitable, given an energetic secretary determined to make civilian control a reality.

In its first several months, the new administration appeared to be making effective use of the traditional patronage positions to reward friends, influence factional situations, and build legislative support, but there were no charges of major patronage inroads on the civil service. An early order by Secretary Udall freezing civil service hirings except as approved by his office was criticized in the press as a possible prelude to the establishment of a "political clearance" system and was withdrawn after a few weeks. Most of the agencies requested the Civil Service Commission to authorize a few additional Schedule C positions, but the cases involved were not significant. One exception was the request of several departments to have their regional director positions transferred to Schedule C or Schedule A, another exempt category. The commission gave no immediate satisfaction on this, and the issue was unsettled as of the end of June 1961.

Historically, the height of patronage pressure on the merit system usually is not reached until a new administration has exhausted the easily available patronage and is still struggling over its legislative program as the mid-term congressional elections approach. Late 1961 and 1962 may thus bring conflict on this front, and the early record of restraint on patronage therefore cannot be regarded as conclusive.

Administrative reorganization was a less prominent theme than in most new administrations. President Kennedy and his associates tended to concentrate on policy and legislation and spend no unnecessary time or political credit on organizational tinkering.

It was nonetheless essential to secure renewal of the President's authority to submit administrative reorganization plans subject to legislative veto; this had lapsed toward the end of the Eisenhower administration. Congress provided the authority, in the form that Eisenhower had most recently had it, early in the session. Contrary to the advice of some experts, Kennedy made no strong effort to regain the advantage of an earlier form of reorganization authority in which a constitutional majority, rather than a simple majority, of either House of Congress was required to kill a reorganization plan. Once granted, the reorganization authority was not heavily used during the early months of the administration. The principal organizational change to which the administration was committed, upgrading the Housing and Home Finance Agency into a Department of Urban Affairs and Housing, was proposed as legislation rather than a reorganization plan.

In June, Congress killed reorganization plans for the Federal

Communications Commission and the Securities and Exchange Commission. They apparently had been sent to Congress without adequate preliminary discussion with key legislative figures. Congress was suspicious of the influence of James M. Landis, and the FCC plan was jeopardized by a "tough" speech by its new chairman at a critical moment. The action by Congress was a clear defeat for the administration, although the President's personal prestige was only slightly involved.

Old and New Frontiers Abroad

In domestic affairs, the economic recession provided the situation and President Kennedy's experience provided the necessary self-assurance for an early assertion of policy leadership. In foreign affairs, Kennedy had some general approaches in mind but seemed more inclined to a period of cautious study and consultation before making major commitments. But there were crises in being on inauguration day, and the pressure mounted rapidly. By the end of the first hundred days, foreign policy had claimed first place in the President's attention, required several risky stands, and dealt him and his administration some severe blows.

The Kennedy Approach

As revealed in early statements and tentative policy moves, the Kennedy approach to foreign affairs had several main elements. First, it was considered essential to knit up the fraying ends of the Western alliance and to get NATO on a more effective basis. To this end, the President had conferences in Washington with Chancellor Adenauer and Prime Minister Macmillan, made an early promise to visit General de Gaulle, and sent Dean Acheson on an unofficial mission to look into NATO problems. The possibility of giving the NATO command independent control of nuclear weapons was under active discussion as a way to put new life into the alliance.

Second, Kennedy, together with his Secretaries of State and

Defense, launched a reassessment of the military-strategic doctrine inherited from the previous administration. It was suspected that the old policy of building up local military forces and regional alliances on the edges of Communist power, sheltered under the threat of "massive retaliation," had become untenable as Soviet nuclear capability grew to match our own. In a "brushfire war" situation, the United States might have no recourse except to use atomic bombs, with a risk of setting off a world conflagration. In the early weeks of the new administration, steps were taken to strengthen American deterrent forces, while the political and military planners moved toward a new concept in which the United States would have stronger tactical air and ground forces to deal with localized emergencies around the world without having to employ nuclear weapons.

Third, the Kennedy administration proclaimed its intention to identify the United States with the aspirations of the economically underprivileged, newly independent, and ideologically uncommitted peoples of the world. In his early weeks as Ambassador to the United Nations, Adlai Stevenson made progress in gaining the confidence of African and Asian delegates. Several significant votes in the United Nations suggested that the United States was less concerned than formerly to avoid possible offense to the declining colonial powers in the NATO alliance. At the same time, Kennedy sought to establish the legislative and administrative underpinnings of an expanded program of aid for economic and social development abroad. One of his first moves was to establish a Food for Peace office attached to the White House. Soon thereafter he established by Executive Order and asked Congress for continuing legislative authority for a Peace Corps of young Americans who would serve as teachers and demonstration workers abroad. Expanding on the Eisenhower administration's recently increased interest in Latin America, Kennedy proposed heavy United States financial support for an "Alianza para Progresso" in that region. Along with these developments, task forces within the administration studied the perennial question of shaping all these elements into a more effective foreign aid agency.

Fourth, Kennedy proposed to be wary of the Soviet Union but polite and open to all reasonable discussions that might reduce tensions without compromising fundamental interests of the West. His initial communications to Khrushchev indicated no anxiety for an early summit meeting. The most immediate occasion for negotiation with the Russians was the nuclear test ban talks, scheduled for resumption at Geneva in February. Kennedy secured an agreement to postpone the meeting until March, allowing more time to reconsider the American position. John J. McCloy was appointed to direct the preparations, and Arthur Dean was asked to present the proposals at Geneva. It was a sharp disappointment, when negotiations were resumed, to find that the interest of the Russians in achieving a permanent ban on nuclear testing apparently had waned since autumn. They now made a new demand for the so-called "troika" system of inspections, thus guaranteeing a Soviet veto. Kennedy asserted his intention to continue searching for a basis of agreement, but little progress was made, and pressure for a resumption of nuclear testing built up in some parts of the government.

Two Trouble Spots: The Congo and Laos

The Kennedy administration dealt cautiously but fairly successfully with two of the touchiest problems it found on the international scene. Regarding one of these, the Congo, its policy was essentially a continuation of the previous policy of supporting the effort of the United Nations to pacify the country while standing ready to counter any Soviet unilateral intervention. There was a flare-up in the Congo in mid-February, when the killing of Lumumba brought a new threat of Soviet intervention. Under such pressure for the first time, Kennedy did not flinch but sent a direct message warning Khrushchev of the potential consequences of such a course, and the crisis passed. Conditions then improved for several months, as the United Nations poured in economic aid and continued to bring pressure on the Congolese political elements to achieve a workable government.

In another trouble spot, Laos, Kennedy made a cautious withdrawal from what was judged an untenable situation inherited from the previous administration. In his first presidential press conference, Kennedy said that his main desire was to maintain the independence of Laos and that a truly neutral government there would be satisfactory. However, the Soviet-backed insurgents continued their aggression, despite Russian claims that they, too, wished to settle the Laos question peacefully. The situation became critical in mid-March. Kennedy asserted his determination to fight, even under the unfavorable conditions Laos would offer, if necessary to preserve the country's independence. At the same time he joined Prime Minister Macmillan in appealing to the Russians to join in a big-power request for a cease-fire in Laos. Khrushchev eventually endorsed the proposal, but it took another month of fencing before the cease-fire call was officially issued. The Pathet Lao group then stalled for some time before accepting the truce call and continued to violate it during the international conference in Geneva. But having established his desire for a neutral regime and peaceful settlement, it seemed unlikely that Kennedy would take the country to war over Laos.

Adventure in Cuba

The climax of the first hundred days and a major turning point for the new administration was the invasion of Cuba on April 17 by anti-Castro refugee groups financed, trained, and assisted primarily by the United States Central Intelligence Agency. Moreover, in public statements prior to the impending revolutionary effort, the President and the Secretary of State, while making it clear that no armed forces of the United States would participate, more or less associated the United States with the effort. The invasion was speedily crushed, leading quickly to postmortems and recriminations that made the responsibility of the United States abundantly clear. The failure and the revelations were a chilling shock to the ebullient young administration and a serious blow to American prestige abroad.

Apparently the CIA's effort to organize a Cuban refugee army had been started early in 1960 and was well advanced by election time. Kennedy was informed of it, possibly in his CIA briefings during the campaign, and certainly soon after election, either in his talks with CIA Director Allen W. Dulles, whom he had made a commitment to retain, or in his conferences with Eisenhower at the White House. At any rate, Kennedy permitted the preparations to continue after inauguration, the CIA and the Joint Chiefs of Staff developed invasion plans, and pressures built up to force an early decision. According to some reports, most of the newcomers in the State and Defense departments and the White House staff had reservations about the practicality of the scheme, and one or two opposed it on grounds of legality and propriety. However, except for Senator William Fulbright, the doubters hesitated to speak strongly in the face of the assurance of the more experienced military and CIA professionals. Kennedy approved the operation in early April, with the reservation that no United States air or naval forces be directly employed—a proviso that seriously diminished whatever chances of success the plan might otherwise have had.

When the failure became apparent, Kennedy assumed full responsibility for the United States' part in the operation and set out to repair the damage as best he could. He made a showing of national unity and achieved a brief freedom from partisan criticism by conferring with Republican leaders, including Eisenhower and Nixon, and by silencing members of his administration who suggested publicly that the fault was with a plan inherited from Eisenhower. There were the inevitable howls from behind the Iron Curtain, which soon subsided. Britain and France were officially tolerant but privately not very sympathetic, remembering Suez. The denunciations of Yankee intervention in Latin America were perhaps not as violent as expected, and in the succeeding weeks active United States diplomacy and Castro's continued outrageous conduct seemed to heal some of the wounds. The long-range effects in Latin America or among other uncommitted peoples could not be immediately assessed but were clearly not fortunate for the United States.

In the wake of the disaster, and possibly to head off a congressional investigation, Kennedy set up a task force headed by General

Maxwell Taylor, former Army Chief of Staff, to study the errors of military planning and intelligence. He also reactivated a foreign intelligence advisory board headed by James Killian. Reforms in the intelligence agencies were subsequently put into effect, and Taylor was attached to the White House as the President's personal adviser, thus upgrading a function that had been relegated to a White House military aide after the departure of General Andrew J. Goodpaster some weeks before the Cuban affair. The pendulum seemed to be swinging back from the early informality of White House staff work: there were more NSC meetings in the two weeks after Cuba than during the entire administration until then.

There was, however, no escape from the irony that Kennedy, who had criticized his predecessor's formal staff procedures on the ground that they tended to shut the President off from the important questions and commit him to prepackaged answers, had himself come to grief because a plan originating in the military and intelligence bureaucracies was not examined carefully enough. Kennedy had surrounded himself, as he preferred, with more than one set of advisers in a very fluid staff system, but apparently in the pinch he had not asked the probing questions himself or put together all of the pieces essential to a judgment, and no one else had taken it on himself to do so.

Post-Cuba: The Second Hundred Days

The second hundred days were a time of testing and rapid maturing for the new administration. President Kennedy and his associates kept their outward composure but appeared a little grim as they struggled to pull themselves together after the Cuba fiasco. No more was said about how much they were all enjoying their jobs.

The President's personal popularity took no immediate nosedive, but Republican criticism of his administration increased noticeably. The love affair of President and press seemed to be over. Editorial writers, columnists, and cartoonists were no longer pulling their punches, and favorable personal publicity about the President, Mrs. Kennedy, little Caroline, and members of the official family diminished rapidly. Speaking to a group of newspaper publishers on April 27, Kennedy suggested that the press institute a program of voluntary restraint in printing things that might aid the Communists or damage the national interest. The suggestion was coolly received: a committee of editors called on the President to report no immediate need for specific measures. For over seven weeks in May and June, the President held no press conferences, and reporters complained of an unusually tight lid on news from the administration, particularly from the Pentagon.

During this period, the news from abroad was predominantly bad. Prospects for a satisfactory settlement in Laos, which had seemed bright just before Cuba, dimmed rapidly. The successful Russian space flight gave a boost to Soviet prestige that could hardly be matched by our own suborbital space flight several weeks later. The French generals' revolt dramatized the precarious political balance in France. In Korea, where so much American blood and money had been spent, a military coup overturned the government and made the prospects for democracy even more confused. The Russians continued to stall on disarmament negotiations, to attack Secretary-General Hammerskjold's administration of the United Nations, and to make threatening noises about Berlin. Secretary Rusk, who had earlier spoken confidently of staying home and running his department while the ambassadors did the negotiating, dashed from SEATO to NATO to Geneva, making a travel record to match that of John Foster Dulles.

Kennedy in Congress

The area least affected during this difficult period was legislative relations. Congress gave the President no major setbacks, and most of the administration's bills made steady, if slow, progress. As of early May, 10 per cent of Kennedy's requests had been enacted,[6]

[6] *Congressional Quarterly Weekly Report,* Vol. 19, May 12, 1961, p. 803. Comparable statistics were not available, but this was clearly a higher rate of success than Eisenhower's in the comparable period.

and several additional important measures, particularly those with "antirecession" labels, seemed well on their way to passage.

On May 25, Kennedy made another State of the Union address to Congress, explaining that the "extraordinary times" justified the unusual second appearance in a single session. He reviewed the foreign and domestic situations and presented several new proposals to deal with "the host of special opportunities and dangers which have become increasingly clear in recent months." These included such antirecession measures as aid for re-training the unemployed and an expanded small business program; step-ups in civil defense, foreign aid, and Army and Marine forces trained in unconventional ground warfare; and a drastic expansion of the space program, with the avowed goal of a successful manned lunar flight "before this decade is out."

The response was hardly dramatic, but during May and June the Congress continued to grind out significant bills—aid for Latin America, a comprehensive housing program, social security extensions, renewal of excise taxes, and raising the debt ceiling. At the end of June, the administration's aid to education proposal was still snagged on the public-parochial school issue, and health insurance for the aging seemed destined for carryover to the next session. But Kennedy seemed likely to get most of what he had asked for in defense and foreign aid; and it was noteworthy that relatively little time had been spent during the session on investigations of the previous administration or on legislative proposals not on the administration's agenda.

K. Meets K.: A Sober Report

Early in May, Khrushchev renewed an earlier suggestion that he and Kennedy meet. Kennedy had said that he would consider such a meeting if conditions were favorable. Conditions now were hardly favorable, but he decided to go ahead. His purpose, it was reported, was to explain carefully to Khrushchev the American position on such stalemated issues as disarmament, Laos, and Berlin, and to impress Khrushchev with American firmness so that the Russians would not make the mistake of overreaching at a moment of presumed American weakness. After all the Democratic criticisms of Eisenhower's summitry, a full-scale conference was out of the question. However, Kennedy already had plans for a European trip, and it was arranged that he and Khrushchev would meet briefly in Vienna—not to conduct negotiations, but to get acquainted and exchange general views on outstanding problems.

Kennedy flew to Paris, where he met and apparently achieved cordial relations with de Gaulle. Then, on June 3 and 4, he and Khrushchev exchanged memoranda on current issues and had long, informal talks about the future of democracy, communism, and East-West relations. On his way home, Kennedy made an official visit to London.

On his return, Kennedy made a televised report on his trip to the American people, stressing the "very sober two days" with Khrushchev. He stated his conclusion that there was little prospect for substantial improvement in relations with the Communists, although the United States would continue to negotiate and seek ways of relieving the tensions. His talks with Khrushchev had impressed him with the tenacity with which the Soviet leaders clung to the view of history that required the Communist nations to assist in what they considered the inevitable fall of the capitalist nations and the spread of communism to all the world. We could hope that the competition would remain political and economic rather than military, but the West must be prepared for another generation of tension and sacrifice. Kennedy called on the nation to make the necessary sacrifices, and specifically to support the requests he had made for foreign aid and defense.

Kennedy had now confronted the situation in Latin America, Africa, Asia, and Europe and had met the most notable world leaders. He had made some adjustment in foreign affairs programs and approaches, but had come to essential conclusions confirming the main lines of foreign policy since World War II. Berlin, which had been lurking in the background since inauguration, was becoming the key foreign policy problem. The "transition" in foreign affairs could be considered over.

There were unmistakable signs that the transition in domestic affairs also was about over. Republican opposition in Congress be-

came more intense. The Republicans elected a Senator from Texas
to the seat formerly held by Lyndon Johnson, and showed other
signs of organizing vigor at the grass roots. On the eve of Kennedy's meeting with Khrushchev, Eisenhower made a speech to a
Republican gathering, attacking "Government by Big Brother."
The party also elected a new national chairman, who promptly
broke the bipartisan silence on Cuba by charging Kennedy with
bungling an operation that Eisenhower would certainly have carried out successfully. As other Republicans took up variations on
the same theme, it appeared that politics as usual had resumed.

Of This Transition and Others

The 1960-1961 transition can be identified as the one in which
the "transition problem" came of age and received appropriate
recognition. The unsatisfactory experience of 1952-1953 was remembered, and during 1960 scholars, journalists, and conscientious
public servants called attention to the lessons of history and the
facts of the current situation. In the resulting climate of public
concern, political leaders responded with efforts to guard the
public interest during the change of leadership made mandatory
by the Twenty-second Amendment. The transfer of responsibility
from Eisenhower to Kennedy, although by no means flawlessly
executed, was the smoothest such transition in recent times. The
gubernatorial transitions being carried out at the same time also
benefited, for almost the first time, from specific attention to problems of transition at the state level.

An Improving Record

The "presidential common law" covering such events was confirmed and further developed by the Eisenhower-Kennedy transition. Both the incoming and outgoing administrations recognized
the obligation to make suitable preparations and to cooperate with
each other in achieving a smooth transition. The necessity of starting some of these preparations before the election was accepted,

although, unlike 1952, pre-election preparations were more prominent in the out-party than the in-party. However, Eisenhower followed unquestioningly the precedent of giving intelligence briefings to the candidates and, against his own political instincts, permitted some the most essential staff preparations to go on within the administration. He was probably unduly sensitive on this point; in the future there should be a sufficient public understanding of the problem to permit overt preparations and pre-election communication between the administration and the candidates to the extent necessary.

The designation of Clifford and Persons as top-level liaison officers between the incoming and outgoing administrations was an innovation that proved useful and is likely to be used again. The need for such formalization presumably depends in part on the personalities involved and the circumstances. It might become less necessary if the President-elect is ready for early designation of key members of his administration.

Relations between Eisenhower and Kennedy were conducted at a level of dignity and responsibility that their successors will do well to emulate. Eisenhower's offers of assistance to Kennedy were up to the norm for an outgoing President. Kennedy's consideration for Eisenhower, which was especially noteworthy in an incoming President, set an example for other incoming officials and proved its utility soon after inauguration when he was able to consult Eisenhower in the Cuban crisis. Taking their cues from Kennedy, other members of the incoming administration overcame much of the suspicion usually shown by men in their positions and took advantage of the advance information and aid offered by their predecessors.

This transition was notable for the quick assertion of policy leadership by the new President, particularly in relation to Congress. Consciously guided by a tradition and theory of strong presidential leadership, Kennedy took early action to prepare himself, and he and his associates made skillful use of the resources at hand, both inside and outside of the government. The bureaucracy was regarded not as an obstacle but as an instrument through which the new administration could achieve its purposes.

Some Continuing Problems

Despite these and other advances, the transition experience of 1960-1961 revealed the survival of old problems, some of which took on new or more acute forms. One was the problem of recruiting political executives on short notice and in a party system that does not clearly designate a cadre from which top appointees will be selected when the party next achieves power. In this case, Kennedy's creative cabinet-making achieved a result that might be envied in any parliamentary system, and the early "talent search" for lesser appointees was unusually effective for such an operation. The success of the Kennedy approach, in fact, suggests the desirability of continuing a high-level recruiting operation, on a smaller scale, in the White House. Nevertheless, the Kennedy staffing was done with a degree of haste that occasionally appalled even those most intimately involved. There were some costly mistakes and serious delays in filling several of the most important posts; and the work of completing the administration's personnel began to drag soon after inauguration.

This raises the question, which is not new, of pre-election staff work on personnel for presidential candidates. It is probably both impractical and undesirable for a candidate to attempt to reach firm decisions on cabinet and subcabinet appointments before he is elected. But would not a preliminary search for potential appointees of high caliber, and an assembly of dossiers on the obvious prospects, put the personnel operation that much ahead and permit faster and more rational decisions after election?

The obstacle usually cited is that such an operation, if it is to be useful, must be conducted by people in whom the candidate has special confidence, and such people cannot be spared from campaign assignments. This argument has great force. Yet, much of the preliminary spadework in the Kennedy talent search was done by individuals who had been given only minor roles in the campaign, and it appears in retrospect that this would have been a good investment of the time of even one or two who were relatively close to Kennedy during the campaign. Despite the difficulties and the danger of wasted effort, a greater realization of the stakes and the potential benefits may well bring future presidential candidates to the point of authorizing pre-election search for and investigation of potential appointees. A more organized approach to the appointment problems of a future administration might even prove helpful in relation to the problems of campaign strategy.

The scale of the Kennedy post-election preparations magnified what had hitherto been a problem of minor proportions: financing the activities of the President-elect and his staff, including consultants and persons designated for office in the executive agencies. Since it is clearly in the public interest to have the next administration ready to operate as completely as possible on inauguration day, the essential expenses of preparatory work after the election should be covered by a regular appropriation for that purpose. Establishing a proper amount and appropriate limitations on what can be considered reimbursable expenses would be debatable but not insoluble problems.[7]

Although no grave difficulties arose in this turnover, the problem of reconciling policy control and career continuity along the upper edge of the civil service structure is still far from solved. Civil service Schedule C, which has evolved in a way probably unforeseen by either its original founders or critics, seems to have done part of the job of institutionalizing a zone of flexibility in which career and noncareer appointees mingle and in which adjustments can be made at the pleasure of the administration as situations change. Fortunately, the Democrats tended to regard Schedule C as a list of positions in which they could make changes and put in their own appointees if necessary but did not feel compelled to clear out all the incumbents who bore Schedule C labels. Thus many career men who had in one way or another got into

---

[7] The principle of state financing to staff and assist the governor-elect has been accepted in Massachusetts, which in 1960 appropriated $25,000 for that purpose. For a report on this experience, arrangements to the same end in several other states, and the 1960-61 state transition experience generally, see Charles Gibbons, "Transition of Government in Massachusetts," *State Government*, Vol. 34, Spring 1961, pp. 100-01, and Kenneth O. Warner, "Planning for Transition," *ibid.*, pp. 102-03.

Schedule C jobs were retained—at the pleasure of the Secretary, as before. Whether there should be more or less positions in Schedule C is a debatable issue, but it is more than a transition problem.

The important problem yet remaining is that there is no established system or practice giving protection to career men, either in Schedule C or regular civil service positions, who become casualties of policy or leadership changes. In this transition most such displaced persons were picked up and used elsewhere, partly through the efforts of the career executive placement service operated by the Civil Service Commission. However, most such reassignments resulted from personal arrangements and were possible because of the low level of partisan feeling that characterized the period. This might not be possible in a new administration that was reducing the total level of government activities amid suspicions of the bureaucracy in general. Despite the rejection of the Second Hoover Commission's proposal for a Senior Civil Service with rank-in-the-person, we may yet see some arrangement by which high ranking career men can be temporarily assigned to some central pool or reassigned without immediate loss of pay or status.[8]

Shortly before he left the White House, President Eisenhower characterized as "silly" the present requirement that the outgoing President submit a State of the Union message, economic report, and budget to the new Congress. He suggested that these presentations be made the responsibility of the new President in years of presidential change, and that the date of inauguration be advanced to give the incoming President time to prepare them. Embedded in a "package" of reforms proposed by Senator Mansfield is a provision seeking to accomplish this objective. The Mansfield proposals, as noted in Chapter 1, would abolish the electoral college and elect the President by direct popular vote, provide for federally financed and supervised presidential preference primaries in the states, provide federal financial assistance to the campaigns of major party candidates *if nominated after September 1,* and (mak-

[8] For a recent suggestion along this line, see Rufus E. Miles, Jr., "An 'Earned Status' Proposal," *Civil Service Journal,* Vol. 1, April-June 1961, pp. 12-13, 26-27.

ing no change in the present election date) change presidential inauguration day to December 1.[9]

Such proposals raise questions that go far beyond the scope of this chapter, but three brief comments from the viewpoint of transition problems are in order.

First, the present assignment of responsibility for the messages, although anomalous in form, raises no overwhelming difficulties in practice. New messages and appropriate budgetary revisions were prepared and presented in timely fashion by the new President in both 1953 and 1961. The existing arrangement burdens the outgoing administration with work that may be unnecessary but it may be better than a schedule that would give the incoming President full responsibility for the budget but insufficient time to take charge of preparing it. The present untidiness about the budget could be modified either by advancing inauguration day or by delaying the budget submission deadline. But in either course, small changes will not do. A new President should have at least 60 days, and preferably more, before having to assume responsibility for presenting the complete annual budget, for the budget has to be more or less built up from the bottom on the basis of given policies or assumptions.

Second, a strong case can be made for some shortening of the election-inauguration interval because of the inevitable uncertainties of leadership and paralysis of high level policy making in such periods. The relative obligations of the President and Presi-

[9] S. J. Res. 23, S. 227, and S. 228, 87 Cong. 1 sess. Introduced with a statement on Jan. 9, 1961. *Congressional Record,* daily ed., Jan. 9, 1961, pp. 334-37.

In a letter published in the *Washington Post and Times Herald,* June 28, 1961, the editor of this volume proposed a new schedule consisting of shifting election day to the first Tuesday in October, convening the new Congress on the first Monday in November, and inauguration of the President on the following Friday, with the incoming administration then taking full responsibility for the major messages to Congress in January. The plan was intended not only to shorten the campaign period and the interregnum, but also to get rid of the lame-duck budget problem and to facilitate completion of the annual sessions of Congress in early summer, with all appropriation bills enacted by June 30. In testimony before the Subcommittee on Constitutional Amendments of the Senate Committee on the Judiciary, also on June 28, the plan was further discussed, with a draft constitutional amendment for the purpose. See *Nomination and Election of President and Vice President and Qualifications for Voting,* Hearings, Pt. 2, pp. 419-30.

dent-elect have been greatly clarified since the days when Hoover and Roosevelt engaged in futile maneuvering over the 1932-1933 depression crisis. But, as we have seen in the case of Eisenhower and Kennedy, there are stubborn ambiguities in the relationship that are dangerous under present-day requirements for quick decisions.

Third, there is a limit to how much the election-inauguration interval can be shortened without running the equal danger of having a new administration legally installed and responsible but actually disorganized and unready to function. Those who have participated in the process of organizing a new administration under the present schedule shudder at the thought of having to do it any faster. Any advance in inauguration day will require corresponding intensification of pre-election preparations by the candidates, in the realms both of personnel and of policy. There is room for some progress in this direction, but how much room is not clear, especially if, as in the Mansfield proposal, the campaign period itself is to be shortened. Shortening the election-inauguration interval will also require a strengthening and more effective use of the career service, and perhaps a change from the present custom of simultaneous replacement of so large a number of important executive officers on inauguration day. Even under the most optimistic assumptions about earlier preparations by candidates and improvement in relationships between incoming and outgoing administrations, a preparatory period of 30 to 45 days after election seems essential.

In summary, the Eisenhower-Kennedy transition was, from the viewpoint of the public interest, a considerable improvement over other party turnovers of recent times. It established some useful precedents and suggested some lines of improvement for the future. It also suggested some of the inherent limitations on ability to achieve smooth transitions within the framework of the present constitutional and party system. Fundamental constitutional changes from the presidential system seem out of the question, but there is some possibility of useful adjustments in scheduling along lines indicated by the Mansfield proposals. Reforms in the party system tending toward more doctrinal coherence and leadership stability, should they occur, would make a significant contribution to minimizing transitional difficulties. But in the transitions of the foreseeable future we shall be greatly dependent, as in the past, on the quality of the political leadership of the moment, plus an element of sheer luck in regard to the circumstances of the times.

10

The Eighty-seventh Congress

EUGENE J. McCARTHY[1]

In the January 9, 1961 issue of *Christianity and Crisis,* Congressman John Brademas wrote of the special qualities and resources the newly elected President would use effectively in moving his legislative proposals through the Congress. On February 15, a little over a month later, James Reston, writing in the *New York Times,* asserted that the most striking fact in Washington today is the sharp contrast between a vigorous young administration and a cumbersome Congress. President Kennedy is, he said, "cracking his whip. The Executive is bolting along but the Legislature is nibbling at the side of the road." These observations are simply the current judgment about an issue that has been debated since the framing of the Constitution: the relationship of our federal government and the relative importance of each.

Controversy Over Legislative Rules

It is, of course, too early to pass any conclusive judgment on the Eighty-seventh Congress or to predict what kind of record it will make. As of the end of February 1961, major action and major attention in the Eighty-seventh Congress has centered on two political contests each involving rules changes: one in the House and

[1] United States Senator from Minnesota.

This chapter was prepared as a lecture given at the Brookings Institution in February 1961.

one in the Senate. According to the box score, the House controversy has ended in victory for Speaker Rayburn and the President. The result of the Senate rules contest is interpreted as victory for both sides of the controversy.

The Senate Rules

The Senate rules fight is a recurring and rather familiar story. In the last Congress, Rule 22 was modified to provide cloture eventually by vote of two thirds of the senators present and voting, rather than by two thirds of the total membership of the Senate. The battle this year was to be joined over Senator Anderson's proposal to enable three fifths of senators voting to limit debate. Senator Mansfield's motion to refer Anderson's proposal to committee was agreed to by a vote of 50 to 46. Because of the closeness of the vote and because some senators voting for referral, like Senator Mansfield, were believed to favor the Anderson proposal, many have concluded that if it had been possible to force a vote on the proposal itself that day, it would have passed.

My own view is that this conclusion is not wholly justified. On January 11, when the vote was taken, the Anderson proposal probably would have been defeated if it had come to a vote. There appeared to be a desire on the part of some to postpone action until more time had elapsed despite the fact that during the campaign, both presidential candidates as well as many congressional candidates had advocated modification of Rule 22 in the Senate and modification of House rules.

The House Rules Committee

The House Rules Committee fight took place after President Kennedy had been inaugurated. This has been judged to have made a significant difference in the outcome of the vote. Having served for ten years in the House, I must remain somewhat skeptical of the power of the White House to influence individual members in that body. In any case it was a fight that had to be made, and one which has been building up over recent years.

In 1949, at the outset of the Eighty-first Congress, the House adopted the so-called "21-day rule," which permitted a committee chairman to move to take up a bill reported from his committee but blocked in the Rules Committee for 21 days or more. This measure is similar in purpose and effect to the proposal brought before the House this year; it is fair to compare performances on the two occasions. The 21-day rule was adopted 275 to 143; 49 Republicans joined with 225 Democrats and one other member to pass the measure, while 112 Republicans and 31 Democrats opposed it.

In 1950, there was an effort to repeal the rule, but it failed, 236-183. This time 64 Republicans voted against their leadership to maintain the rule, while 85 Democrats voted to repeal it.

In the Eighty-second Congress, with Speaker Rayburn having changed his position, the House repealed the rule in 1951 by a vote of 243-180. On this occasion, 42 Republicans voted to retain it, while 152 of their colleagues joined 91 Democrats in striking it from the rules.

In the Eighty-sixth Congress, when the Democrats outnumbered the Republican members in the House by 283 to 154, there was a demand for a change in the House rules. This move faded, reportedly after Speaker Rayburn assured members that the Rules Committee would report all major legislative proposals.

It was determined after the recent elections that a major assault on the power and prerogatives of the Rules Committee had to be launched. This move was successful, and the committee was expanded from 12 to 15 members by a vote of 217 to 212. In the rules fight in the House this year, only 22 Republicans supported the liberalizing measure; 64 Democrats voted against it. It is interesting to note in passing that Republican support for the two proposals just discussed has declined over the last twelve years. Whereas 49 Republicans supported the 21-day rule in 1949, and 64 voted to retain it in 1950, a mere—but crucial—22 voted to expand the committee in 1961. The two issues are not identical, but they are similar enough to raise doubts for those who believe that the Republican party has indeed been modernized during the Eisenhower years; this evidence points in the opposite direction.

On the other hand, Republicans in the Senate have a rather dif-

ferent record. Fifteen out of 33 voted against referral of the Anderson proposal, a markedly better ratio than House Republicans
displayed during their rules' fight. The best political explanation
is that House Republican leaders hoped that blame for delay, modification, or defeat of the Democratic program might be placed
clearly on a committee nominally controlled by Democrats, since
committee chairmen and control of Congress had been an issue in
the campaign.

Significance of the Conflict

It is easy to make too much of the practical political significance
of the rules controversies in both the House and the Senate. Of
course, the Senate should be permitted to shut off debate after a
reasonable period of time by majority vote, and the House should
not be kept from considering legislation a majority wish to consider. But in practice, the filibuster has been of limited effectiveness. Its use, or the threat of its use, did not prevent civil rights
action in the Senate in each of the last two Congresses, and, in my
view, it is unlikely that stronger legislation would have been
written if the two-thirds rule had been changed to a three-fifths
rule or even to one allowing cloture by majority.

The Rules Committee was truly a road block in the postconvention session, but ordinarily the power of the committee is not as
great as it is under such emergency conditions. It is, however, a
powerful and influential committee and one that constitutes not
only a threat to majority rule, but which has, in fact, been an obstacle to such majority determinations. At the same time, it has
often been used as an excuse by members who are quite content not
to have to vote on the floor on certain issues held up or modified by
the committee. This "scapegoat" function of the Rules Committee
has evidently now been suspended by Chairman Smith who is reportedly anxious to report *everything* to the floor in an effort to
embarrass the Speaker. It will be interesting to see how far this
move is carried. Surely it will elicit other leadershp techniques for
sidetracking such measures. The Speaker of the House, together

with the support he has, will, I am sure, be able to meet this challenge.

Fundamentally, the basic power in the Congress remains with the majority of the members in both the House and the Senate. A committed majority can circumvent or override procedural and personal obstacles. In the face of such a majority, rules or procedure, leadership, and presidential opposition avail very little. The majority in this Congress is clearly a Democratic majority—262 to 174 in the House and 65 to 35 in the Senate—working with a President who is also a Democrat. This is a significant fact and should make for a positive record.

The Problem of Divided Government

Since 1946 all possible combinations of party control have been demonstrated. The Eightieth Congress was Republican, while the President was Democratic. The Democratic Eighty-first and Eighty-second Congresses served during the administration of a Democratic president. The Eighty-third Congress, the first Eisenhower Congress, was Republican, but the Eighty-fourth, Eighty-fifth, and Eighty-sixth were all Democratic Congresses. Now after six years of what is popularly called divided government, the legislative and the executive branches are both of one party.

Divided government in itself is not necessarily bad. It is the consequences of the division that must be considered. Congress is normally a positive force. It may not seek as much as an aggressive administration, but its members never wish to go back to constituents with a blank report. They generally must show either that they have accomplished something or that they have opposed something of significance. But it is difficult for members of a majority party to report that they have headed off threats or dangers. Their need is for positive achievements, and the pressure therefore is on an administration, even of the other party, to go along with congressional demands to some degree.

The Republican Eightieth Congress faced a Democratic president, yet during this period Congress approved the Marshall Plan and economic and military aid to Greece and Turkey. The Truman domestic program, however, fared badly in this Congress.

The Eighty-first and Eighty-second Congresses were Democratic in nominal support of President Truman, yet no significant changes were made in basic economic programs such as taxes, agriculture, and labor legislation. Changes achieved were primarily in the field of welfare legislation such as social security and housing.

The Eighty-third Republican Congress under President Eisenhower was an active Congress. It approved the establishment of the Department of Health, Education, and Welfare, effected a downward tax revision, established flexible price supports for five basic crops, extended social security, approved the St. Lawrence Seaway, and disposed of the tidelands oil question. It did nothing on civil rights, however.

Following that, there was a return to divided government. It is difficult to say whether the last six years of the Eisenhower administration would have been somewhat more constructive or progressive with Republican Congresses. It is possible that they might have been.

When government is divided, one or the other branch is likely to become a negative defensive force. This was the role of the Republican Eightieth Congress and of the Eisenhower administration generally after the elections of 1954.

Influence of the President

The difference in the background and in the experience of President Kennedy and of the men and women whom he has appointed to office should encourage the growth of good relationships between Congress and the Executive Branch of the government in the Eighty-seventh Congress. The Eisenhower appointees were generally men unfamiliar with and somewhat disdainful of public office.

High officers of the government were drawn chiefly from two fields —from big business and from the military. These were men with nonpolitical backgrounds, and the procedures of the military and the procedures of big business are not wholly democratic, nor are they ordinarily conducted under the safeguards of the Constitution. Neither of these two institutions has anything comparable to the "balance of powers" concept. Consequently, the Eisenhower administration took on many aspects of a corporate-military structure. The administration represented the officers of the corporation, or the high officers of the military establishment, who were prepared to set policy and to administer it largely on their own initiative. Any kind of external review was resented. Congress was treated very much like the board of directors of a corporation, or like the junior officers in the military.

The attitude and experience of President Kennedy and of the men and women he has appointed to Cabinet posts and other offices in the Executive Branch of government are quite different, and the possibility of effective presidential leadership has been greatly increased. In the course of the campaign, President Kennedy spoke of presidential leadership of the Congress. It is being said that he will be another Roosevelt in dealing with the Congress, using the full strength of the office of the Presidency. It remains to be seen whether he will do these things and also how successful the attempt may be. The memorable achievements of Franklin Roosevelt took place under the conditions most conducive to effective leadership: depression and war. In the interim, between partial recovery from depression and the beginning of the war, even Roosevelt's leadership faltered. The President does have significant powers both direct and indirect. Of these the latter are, in my judgment, the most powerful.

One of the clearest examples in recent history was the response to President Eisenhower's appeal for support of the Landrum-Griffin version of the labor reform bill. The equal time offered on this occasion to congressional figures by the radio and television networks was an empty gesture. There is no way in which Congress can, in a limited period of time, answer an executive appeal. The

Congress has no one officer, nor does the opposition party have one, who can be thrown into the breach against a presidential appeal on an issue that is new and untested in campaigns. Generally, a campaign during which members of Congress return to their constituencies is the only sure way.

Direct influence of the type so often suggested by the press and emphasized in books like *Advise and Consent*—promises of projects, threats of poor committee assignments—is limited in effect. Most members of Congress have an independent spirit. Most come relatively free of party domination or special influence and consider themselves answerable to their constituents and generally able to explain themselves to these constituents. On the negative side there is a disposition for the Congress to wish to run its own shop and to resent any outside interference or influence that might be expressed in something so obvious as disapproval of public works projects. As long as the President does not have the item veto, Congress is likely to attempt to preserve autonomy in this and other fields and to reserve to itself the power to give and to take away. These factors are likely to be overlooked during the excitement and drama of a change in administrations, especially one as important and promising as this one.

Another limitation on presidential influence in the early days of the Kennedy administration, which is generally overlooked, is the fact that President Kennedy, with a few exceptions, ran *behind* the Democratic candidates for Congress. As the *Congressional Quarterly* put it:

> In contrast to most presidential elections, the victory of the national Democratic ticket did not appear to play an important role in most congressional contests. If "Kennedy's coattails" existed at all, they were probably evident in New York state . . . in Connecticut . . . and in New Jersey. All other Democratic House gains appeared to be the result of special local conditions. Kennedy's electoral victory appeared to have played a negligible role in the 1960 Senate races.[2]

In the House especially, the next election is always just around the corner and the pattern has been for the majority party to suffer in

---

[2] *Congressional Quarterly Almanac,* Vol. 16 (1960), p. 758.

off-year elections like 1962. There will be plenty of incentives for voting in what appears to be the best interest of the locality, rather than accepting presidential directives or threats.

The Future of Coalition Action

There has been some speculation as to the effectiveness of coalitions in the Eighty-seventh Congress. The old coalition of Republicans and Southern Democrats is still operative, although it has lost some of its strength since Republicans in greater numbers have supported civil rights legislation. If the rules fight in the House could have been identified with civil rights, it is quite likely that the Republican support would have been weakened. As it was, the struggle seemed to affect primarily economic issues, and much of the response against rules changes reflected these economic interests and attitudes.

The Republican-Southern Democratic conservative coalition today involves little overt trading of votes. Republicans generally today cannot be indifferent to the civil rights issue and thus are not as free as they once were to support the Southern position, while Southern members increasingly have less and less to offer in exchange for anti-civil rights votes. Many Southern Democrats who during the New Deal, for example, were quite free to vote liberally on economic issues affecting other areas of the country are now called to account by industrial and financial interests in their own states; this reduces the necessity as well as the opportunity for vote trading within the coalition. The coalition has thus become really a bloc holding common views on many issues.

Senator Javits and others have begun to talk of a new bipartisanship and a liberal coalition. Actually, under recent Democratic and Republican administrations, there has been some liberal bipartisanship and a shifting coalition of Republicans and Democrats on some issues. It is unlikely that this pattern or practice will be significantly modified, or that it could be made much more effective.

The Democratic and Republican parties do not divide sharply on ideological grounds. The social welfare programs initiated in Roosevelt's New Deal and long the target of Republican attacks have been accepted to the point that Republicans, not passively or reluctantly or with apologies, claim that they have improved them, made them more effective, and even extended them. The last Republican administration went so far as to support a federal medical aid program to help elderly and disabled citizens meet their medical costs.

Moreover, all evidence points to the conclusion that extreme isolationism is dead among Republicans. Political controversy in this field is concerned more with procedures and prudential determinations, with questions of more or less, rather than basic questions of substance.

Democrats from some areas of the country have retreated somewhat on the issue of free trade and are taking a position closer to the traditional protectionism of the Republicans. At the same time, some financiers and industrialists within the Republican party are most outspoken in advocating free trade policies. Coalition potentialities add no new reason for concern over the President's legislative program.

The Power Structure in Congress

To pass full judgment on the Congress, however, it is important to consider all forces. Personalities, positions, and procedures are very significant. The Speaker of the House is undoubtedly the most influential member of either the House or the Senate. This is a built-in strength, enhanced, of course, or reduced, depending on the personality of the man who is speaker. Senate leaders too are important as are other House leaders.

The Committees

The Ways and Means Committee must be ranked as the most powerful and important legislative committee of either the House or the Senate. Some other committee may temporarily, or on one issue, assume great importance, but consistently the Ways and Means Committee must be ranked first. This is the case in part because of the constitutionally established right of the House of Representatives to originate revenue measures. Moreover, the common practice in the House is to bring revenue measures to the floor under restrictive rules so that the possibility of significant amendment on the floor is greatly limited, and the House in conference has, at least within recent years, stood quite firmly in conference against significant amendments added to tax measures in the Senate. What happens on tax measures in the Eighty-seventh Congress, barring a national emergency that would create unusual revenue demands, will depend primarily on the Ways and Means Committee of the House of Representatives. An additional condition bearing on the importance of this committee is the fact that when a tax is enacted, it is imposed, and when taken off by act of Congress, it is taken off in fact. Appropriations and regulatory statutes, on the contrary, are strained through the Executive Branch and often through the courts before being applied.

The Rules Committee of the House, although somewhat weakened as an obstructive force by the recent action in the House of Representatives, remains a powerful and important committee. And committees in both the House and Senate, such as Interior, Interstate and Foreign Commerce, and Public Works, are effective, but their decisions are somewhat more limited in scope, and when finally in effect have usually been touched and modified by executive and judicial hands.

The Committee Chairmen

Committee chairmen are also important. Their importance varies from one committee to another, depending on the make-up of the committee and the personality of the chairman. Chairmen in the Eighty-seventh Congress are likely to be, on the whole, rather cooperative with the new administration. Of the 13 important legislative committees in the Senate, 8 are chaired by men sympathetic to administration programs within their committee's jurisdiction; only 3 chairmen clearly do not fit this description. In the House, 13 out of 19 important legislative chairmen are favorably disposed toward administration programs coming before their committees; only 3 are unmistakably hostile, and of these only Judge Smith of the Rules Committee is of any great significance.

These proportions do not lend themselves to the kind of gloomy analyses one so frequently hears about the reactionary seats of power within Congress. And it is especially encouraging to note the situation in the House, where it is more difficult to amend bills on the floor and hence more important to get them in good condition from the committees.

This kind of discussion can be misleading, however, because the power of committee chairmen is something less than it is believed to be by the public and much of the press. Committee chairmen are often overruled when they stand firmly against a majority of the members of their committees either in committee or on the floor.

Seniority

The same can be said of seniority. The seniority rule does apply in movement through a committee and in determining the chairman. It is not applied absolutely, however, in the assignment of members to committees, but instead is a kind of rule of convenience or defense for the leadership. The best justification for the rule is that given by Chesterton for the early practice of having the oldest son succeed to the kingship. Chesterton observed that it was unreasonable and without logical defense, but that it did save a lot of trouble.

Leadership in the House

In the House we may expect the same loyal and generally effective leadership from Sam Rayburn that he has given in the past. Rayburn is one of those members of the House who came into prominence during the New Deal and who has great loyalty to the Democratic party and to a Democratic president. This, together with the personal loyalty and devotion he commands, argues that the full measure of Democratic support will be mustered on each issue.

On the Republican side, it is generally accepted that leadership under Congressman Halleck will be more partisan and more effective than it would be under former Speaker Joe Martin. This may be true, although I have some doubts. It will be a somewhat more brash opposition, more open and noisier, but there is reason to doubt that it will be more effective. The Halleck record of opposition leader was made while there was a Republican president in the White House; the Martin record was, for the most part, made while there was a Democratic president. Halleck, failing on many issues, was saved by the power of the presidential veto. Martin in the Eightieth, Eighty-first, and Eighty-second Congresses was Republican leader at a time when major presidential vetoes were overridden—affecting taxes, immigration, and labor-management relations, for example—and efforts to pass legislation in other major areas were blocked or watered down.

Leadership in the Senate

In the Senate questions of leadership generally come back to speculation on the role that will be played by Lyndon Johnson. Undoubtedly, he will exercise some influence on the actions of the Congress. The flurry in the Democratic caucus over the proposal to have Vice President Johnson attend and preside over future caucuses was more shadow than substance. The question of separation of powers does not depend in the United States on whether or not a member of the administration or representative of the President attends a party caucus, as evidently it did in English history when the speaker, as the King's agent, was barred from some parliamentary meetings. To the extent that Lyndon Johnson was an effective leader in the Senate and has the respect and confidence of the senators, he will remain an influence. The Majority Leader of the Senate, Senator Mansfield, is clearly a competent leader in his own right.

Other Influences

Most difficult to evaluate is the possible effect and influence on Congress of other political personalities in the United States. Undoubtedly there will be Republicans who will, for shorter or longer periods of time, emerge as possible candidates for the presidency, either in 1964 or at some later date. Some of these will be in the Congress, others outside. Governor Rockefeller is certainly a potential, although he is likely to be somewhat careful and quiet on national issues for a while. The stands he takes on national issues during the Eighty-seventh Congress will most probably be more closely related to New York politics than to national politics. The two interests may not always be in conflict.

In the Senate today, the most outspoken Republican is Senator Goldwater. Undoubtedly, he speaks for a part of the Republican party. His message is clear and simple. He criticizes both Democrats who won in 1960 and Republicans who lost. The general body of Republicans do not challenge him. They have been silenced by defeat in a campaign in which they attempted generally to reduce and obscure differences between themselves and the Democrats, rather than to broaden or widen the differences. They must wait now for legislative moves on the part of the Democratic majority to provide a platform or a target, or for administration decisions that turn out somewhat short of perfection. In the meantime, Senator Goldwater is the most distinctive performer, and he occupies the center ring.

The Veto Power

The veto power, which in the Eisenhower administration was an important source of strength for the President, will be relatively unimportant in this administration, since it is a power that is generally useful only when a President must deal with a Congress which is aggressively in favor of a program, either progressive or reactionary, that is opposed by the President.

Until the administration of Andrew Johnson, the veto power was used sparingly. All the presidents from 1789 to 1865 vetoed only 52 measures, and during this period the largest number of vetoes of public bills by any president was 12, by Jackson, none of which was overridden. The controversial character of the Johnson administration is indicated by the fact that he vetoed 21 measures and had 15 of his vetoes overriden. President Taft made free use of his veto power during the short session of the Sixty-second Congress, as did President Wilson during the short session of the Sixty-sixth Congress. Wilson described the veto power as beyond all question his most formidable prerogative. He said further that in the exercise of this power, the President acts "not as the executive but as a third branch of the Legislature." Taft also agreed that the veto power was essentially legislative and not executive in nature.

President Franklin Roosevelt in twelve years exercised 371 regular vetoes and 260 pocket vetoes, and 9 of his vetoes were overridden. In seven years President Truman vetoed 250 bills, 70 of which were pocket vetoes, and 12 vetoes were overridden. In eight years President Eisenhower vetoed 181 bills, 107 of them by pocket veto, and only two were overridden.

The evidence is clear that the veto is not merely a negative weapon, but a positive force through which the President can exercise legislative power. Recent presidents have used it with effectiveness. The real influence of the veto power is indicated not only by the number of bills vetoed and in which the veto was sustained, but also by the effect of a threat of veto on decisions of congressional leaders. Legislation is frequently modified or rewritten before passage by Congress in order to eliminate the objections of the chief executive. It remains to be seen how this weapon will be used during the Eighty-seventh Congress, but it is safe to assume that if useful, it will be employed.

Changing Relationships Within Government

There are two additional concerns that must be taken into account in evaluating or in anticipating the work of the Eighty-seventh Congress; that is, the general framework or patterns of trends and relationships within the government. Ours is not a static government. In the years since the adoption of the Constitution, many changes have influenced the structure and the powers of the branches of the federal government. Although constitutional amendments have been few, thousands of laws, administrative directives, and court decisions have given direction and scope to the federal government different from anything that was foreseen by the framers of the Constitution. The balance of power has shifted back and forth in the legislative branch between the House and the Senate. It has shifted between the executive branch of the government and the Congress, and between state governments and the federal government.

Since foreign policy has become more demanding, and since decisions in that field must be made almost on a day-by-day basis, the constitutional procedure of treaty ratification by the Senate has become outmoded. It is still useful in those areas in which long-time arrangements can be agreed on, as in the Antarctic and possibly in space, but the treaty route is far too slow and unresponsive for handling the majority of problems. Summit conferences together with executive agreements are more common instrumentalities for seeking agreement and working out arrangements. These procedures, of course, shift additional power to the President and further reduce the role of the House and the Senate.

In domestic matters, too, the situation has changed. As laws with broad social or economic purpose have been adopted, more and more authority for executive interpretation has been granted. Executive agencies and commissions, primarily responsible to the President, exercise not only executive functions but judicial ones as well and are charged with making administrative policies that have the effect of law.

A second general change that has been taking place should also be helpful to the President and his program; that is, the change in the role of the United States Senate. While upper or second legislative bodies in other countries have declined in importance, some disappearing altogether and others surviving as little more than symbols, the Senate of the United States has extended its jurisdiction and influence.

Membership in the Senate in the early years of our national life carried prestige, but little actual power. The Senators looked on themselves as the assembled ambassadors from the respective "sovereign states," rather than as real powers in the federal government. The House did, in fact, "decidedly predominate," as James Madison stated that it should at the time of the drafting of the Constitution, and membership in the House was generally preferred to membership in the Senate. Madison, for example, refused a Senate seat, saying that he, as a young man "desirous of increasing his reputation as a statesman," could not afford to take a seat in the Senate. He would be surprised today to find that over one third of the members of the Senate formerly served in the House of Representatives.

Many factors account for the growth of power and influence of the Senate. The six-year term in the Senate, the experience of its members, and its continuity as a body stabilize and strengthen the upper house. Then, on a purely arithmetical basis, a senator's vote on a legislative proposal has come to be worth approximately four times that of a vote by a member of the House. When committee assignments and committee votes are considered, the power of an individual senator is greater still. House committees are generally at least two or three times as large as Senate committees, and the importance of a single vote in a Senate committee of fifteen is in reality more than twice as important as a single vote in a House committee of thirty members. In addition, senators may serve on more than one major committee and consequently they have greater flexibility than the House members. Thus when a legislative conflict is clearly drawn between the House and the Senate, especially in conference, this greater flexibility of the Senate, coupled with its concentration of power, gives force to the Senate's side of the argument.

In public debate the Senate again has some advantage because of its rules, which permit any senator to speak to the subject and usually without limitation on time. Changes in the House rules effected under Speaker Tom Reed in the last decade of the nineteenth century prevented obstruction and delay in the general legislative process in the House and accelerated the action of the majority, but these same changes practically destroyed effective House debate. The press finds it easier to cover and report Senate debate, and the debates themselves are more likely to reflect the personal position of individual senators. Public interest in the House, therefore, as reflected in the press is generally concentrated not on what is said in debate or who said it, but rather on the outcome of the vote.

As governmental activities have expanded and presidential appointments have therefore become more numerous and important, the power of the Senate to confirm these appointments, both in the judiciary and in the executive offices, has become increasingly significant. Similarly in the area of foreign affairs, the Senate's power —or at least the appearance of power—has correspondingly increased as foreign policy has become more significant in our national life.

Finally, in the area of legislation, the Senate has gradually, since the end of the Civil War, assumed more initiative in the introduction of legislation and more authority in modifying House bills. The power of the House to initiate appropriations, for example, has become less exclusive than formerly, for it is a matter of absolute necessity to take action during each session of the Congress on major appropriation bills. The Senate can modify these bills by increasing or decreasing the amounts originally set by the House, or by adding new items or deleting those already included. Within recent decades the Senate generally has increased the amounts provided by the House.

Although this is the basic trend and relationship, the House is not without power. This power was demonstrated in the postconvention sessions of Congress last year on significant issues such as aid to education and minimum wage. And it was shown earlier in the session on taxation, agriculture, and labor reform; in all of these areas the House position dominated either positively or negatively.

The greater possibility of administration difficulties in the House of Representatives was accurately noted by Congressman Brademas in the article already cited, when he noted that it is in the House, "more complex and more conservative, that most of the blood will be shed." On the record, the Senate, being more responsive to urban and activist interests, is closer to the administration position and is likely to be the more positive force in this session.

The Over-all Prospects

This picture of the Eighty-seventh Congress is necessarily sketchy and incomplete. Many patterns of forces and personalities interact in any Congress, and this one is no exception.

Much of the work of the Eighty-seventh Congress will involve reworking old ground: federal aid to education, minimum wage legislation, housing, medical aid for the aged, unemployment compensation, a farm program, distressed areas legislation, and possibly civil rights. All of these will be up for consideration again. Some progress undoubtedly will be made in nearly every one of these areas. There will be compromises and some rejections.

As for the over-all prospects, I do not think the situation is quite as desperate as James Reston suggests in his recent reference to the "deep parochialism of American politics . . . [the] fixed regional interests in existing conventions and arrangements, and . . . the system of localized representation." His statement that "the heart of the problem . . . lies in the need of inducing the Congress to think nationally instead of locally," especially now "when the new young administration is looking to the future and the Congress is living in the past"[3] reflects a common but, in my opinion, not wholly justified attitude toward Congress. The Eighty-seventh Congress will make its own record, and I expect it to be a responsive and responsible record.

Nonetheless, I do think there is a need for some modification of the procedures and organizational or institutional relationships, both within the Congress and between Congress and the executive.

The need in very general terms runs in two directions. One is in the direction of giving either more authority or more discretion in the use of authority to the President in such fields as public finance, expenditures, taxation, and foreign trade, and in extending existing programs or new programs over a longer period of time. The other is in the direction of involving Congress more directly and intimately in current policy decisions through possible extension of the idea of the Joint Committee on Atomic Energy into such fields as foreign affairs, intelligence activities, space exploration, and decisions relating to the domestic economy.

Ours is a government of men as well as of laws. Democracy is not self-operating any more than it is self-generating. It cannot work effectively without the continuous attention of thoughtful men, both to the substance of government action and to the institutions and procedures by which policy is determined and judged and executed.

[3] *New York Times,* Feb. 15, 1961.

11

Leadership Problems in the Opposition Party

THRUSTON B. MORTON[1]

YOU HAVE ASKED ME TO DISCUSS the leadership problems that are inherent, under our system of government, in the position of the political party that lost the last presidential election. This is a challenging assignment, particularly since it involves several problems that have not been solved with complete satisfaction by either political party in our lifetime. For the Republican party in 1961, however, the difficulties of the situation, in my opinion, have been exaggerated. We have many able leaders, and they are all on good terms with each other and with the party. We look forward with confidence to the elections of 1962. We shall deal with the longer-term problems of 1964 and more distant years when he have disposed of those that are more immediately before us.

As President John F. Kennedy recently remarked, "The Republican Party is strong and vigorous after the 1960 election." The reasons this is so will become apparent if we look first at what happened in the recent election.

[1] United States Senator from Kentucky and Chairman, Republican National Committee, 1959-1961. This chapter was prepared as a lecture given at the Brookings Institution in March 1961.

A Republican View of the 1960 Election

The events of 1960, while not to the liking of the Republican party, must nonetheless be viewed in perspective. Despite its record narrow defeat for the White House, the party shattered any thought that it plays a minority role in national elections. The party did not suffer a repudiation of its record. Nor was its voice stilled by a one-sided majority that would have called for an immediate and agonizing reappraisal of Republican policies and leadership.

Even in defeat, we were commanded to speak for half of the electorate as we apply our energies and resources to the task of building a better America and easing the crises that threaten the survival of the free world. The fact is, that for a party that lost a major election, the Republican party is in remarkably good shape. This is a tribute to the thousands of loyal workers who fought hard during the campaign. These inspired people—the men and women of the GOP—will continue to fight. All reports indicate that hope and confidence are high in their post-election emotions. This dynamic force is ready-made to spark the victory mood in the years ahead.

The Election Outcome

Vice President Richard M. Nixon ran a tremendously strong race, even in defeat. He carried 26 states to the 23 that provided electoral votes for Senatory Kennedy. The 26 Nixon states, however, gave him only 219 electoral votes while Senator Kennedy's were worth 303. Nixon generally swept the Middle West, the Rocky Mountain states, the Far West, and several southern and border states, while Kennedy's victory pattern covered the remainder of the South, the Middle Atlantic, and the northeastern states. With 50.1 per cent of the major party vote for Kennedy and 49.9 for Nixon, the popular vote made the 1960 presidential contest the closest in percentage terms since 1824, as far back as records have been kept. Senator Kennedy won by a margin of only 112,803 votes, and did not even win a majority of all the votes cast, since minor party candidates received over half a million votes.[2]

Two other factors deserve recognition in appraising the nature of the Kennedy margin. His total popular vote can logically be divided into three separate and distinct elements—the number of votes he received on the Democratic ticket, those he received in New York as the candidate of the Liberal party, and those that were contributed by the cloudy outcome in Alabama. In New York, the Republican presidential vote was higher than the Democratic by 22,510 votes, but Kennedy also received 406,176 Liberal party votes, without which he could not have been elected in New York or the nation. In Alabama, the Democratic voters elected six unpledged electors while also electing five pledged to Kennedy, although Kennedy is credited with 318,303 Alabama votes in the national popular vote totals. In 1960, the Republican party received more presidential votes than any other political party in America, and Kennedy is even more of a minority President than has generally been recognized.

In all of the other major categories of elections, the Republican party made definite gains in 1960—a heartening, general comeback from the low point of 1958. It won two additional seats in the Senate and held all of the seats previously occupied by Republican incumbents. One of the two new Senate seats was lost, however, by the untimely death of Keith Thomson, the Republican victor in Wyoming's senatorial election. In the House of Representatives, 44 new Republican members were elected for a net gain of 21 seats over the number in the previous session. Of the Republican incumbents who sought re-election, just three were defeated.

In the gubernatorial elections, gains were small but nonetheless useful. Republicans now control the executive mansions in 16 states, as against 14 after the 1958 elections. In contests for the state legislatures, Republicans eliminated Democratic control in

[2] These figures credit Senator Kennedy with the highest vote received by a Kennedy-pledged elector in Alabama, but do not credit the minor party candidates with any of the votes received by unpledged electors in Alabama. Final official returns by states as compiled by the research staff of the Republican National Committee can be found in the Committee's publication, *The 1960 Election* (April 1961), Revised Second Printing, Appendix Table 2.

either one or both legislative bodies in 10 states, while losing state legislative houses in only two instances. We gained almost 300 seats in the state legislatures—gains that are highly important in view of the vital re-districting decisions that state legislatures will be making.

This, then, is the over-all picture: an extremely narrow Democratic victory for the Presidency, while at the same time there was a marked resurgence of the Republican party on the congressional and state level. To describe what happened, one must conclude that the Republicans did indeed lose the winning touchdown on a questionable play on the goal line. But they lost, and the loss has been certified. The 1960 election was, as Vice President Nixon contended all along that it would be, one of the closest in history. If, however, the Mundt-Coudert plan for the revision of the electoral college had been in operation, giving effect to the broad geographic distribution of the Republican presidential vote, Richard M. Nixon would have been elected President.

Why the Republicans Lost

A switch of about 12,000 votes in five states—Illinois, Missouri, Nevada, New Mexico, and Hawaii—would have given the Republican ticket a winning margin of electoral votes. Hence a natural question is: Did we fight hard enough? As we rise from the floor, having felt the full impact of the winning blow, we would seem to have reason to reply in the negative. I know my own chin is still sore, and I am sure I am not alone in this respect. Nevertheless, I do not believe there was anything lacking in our ability to trade Sunday punches with the opposition. Indeed we demolished most of the issues—both real and imaginary—but obviously that was not enough.

Clearly, we did not fight hard enough in the centers of mass population where the Democrats did so well. Among the 41 cities with populations of 300,000 or more that participated in the election, Vice President Nixon carried 14. They were all located in southern or western states, except Columbus, Ohio; Indianapolis; and Omaha. The most Republican big city in the nation was

Dallas, Texas, which gave Nixon 63 per cent. At the same time, however, Senator Kennedy was carrying 27 of the big cities. And the Kennedy big cities averaged bigger in size and were also located much more frequently in the swing states with a heavy electoral vote, where the election was really decided. Kennedy racked up a plurality of 2.7 million votes in 13 important big cities. In eight states with 173 electoral votes, it was a big city triumph that put the states in the Kennedy column. In 1956, seven of these states had gone Republican; their swing the other way in 1960 put Kennedy in the White House.

We also paid too little attention to specific segments of the electorate, including, for example, the Negro vote. About three quarters of this group went to Senator Kennedy despite the GOP record of achievements in the field of civil rights. We also lost heavily among Catholic voters, as every election analysis has shown. This may have been inevitable on the first occasion on which a member of that faith was elected President. We strongly believe, however, that many of these voters will return to the Republican party on future occasions. We intend to hold the door open for them.

Some comment should be made on the election recount situation and on the allegations of widespread irregularities that occurred in so many of the closely contested states. Since these allegations came mainly from the Republican side, they drew comments from the cynical minded, as could be expected, that we were poor losers and our motive was nothing more or less than to embarrass the incoming Kennedy administration. Nothing could be further from the truth.

Immediately after the election, the offices of the Republican National Committee were flooded with telegrams and letters demanding recounts in certain areas. The complaints were not confined to any one section of the country. They covered many areas; and within a few weeks after the election, the number of such messages was well in excess of 135,000.

We screened this mass of correspondence with great care and noted that more than generalities were involved. There were hundreds upon hundreds of specific charges ranging from outright fraud to simple errors in procedures at the polling places. We did not rush into this business, but studied carefully the possible courses of action. We felt we had a responsibility not only to the 34 million people who voted for Nixon but to every American regardless of political party. There can be no place in America for election fraud—or even the suggestion of fraud.

We concluded that we had an obligation to take action. As a result, we organized a National Recount and Fair Elections Committee with these purposes in mind: (1) to demand an honest count of this election in every suspicious state; and (2) to investigate and track down the irregularities and fraud wherever they exist. There is no need to recite the outcome of our investigations and actions, which were hampered in many areas by Democratic party control of the election machinery as well as the legal and administrative difficulties in the way of any rapid and effective recount action. The moves we made were amply justified in the light of the character and tone of the citizen complaints we had received. Since the election laws of many states are so unclear and ineffective, we still hope that we may make some contribution to their revision in the public interest.

The Opportunities of 1962

Before leaving the election of 1960, I would like to indicate in some detail the opportunities that provide the targets for the Republican party in 1962. In addition to the opportunities that usually fall to the opposition party at the mid-term election, there are specific reasons we can hope and expect to make substantial gains next year—if we organize and work with that goal in mind.

Two years ago, election analysts were pointing out that the Republican party would have great difficulty in holding its Senate seats in the 1960 elections, in view of the geographic distribution of the states where Senate contests were in prospect in 1960. Despite this handicap, the Republicans made gains. But in 1962, the geographic distribution of the contests for the Senate will be relatively much more favorable to the Republican party. The 15 Republican incumbents who will be up for re-election all seem to stand in a strong posture for victory, judging from the strength demonstrated by the party in their states in 1960. Of the 21 seats held by Democrats that will be up in 1962, six in the deep South are somewhat unpromising, but 15 states, including Florida and Oklahoma, provide opportunities where Republican candidates have a good chance to win.

The 1962 election for the House of Representatives involves a special problem, because 25 states will redistrict congressional boundary lines as the result of the 1960 census, or will be required to elect some or all of their members at large. This speculative aspect of the situation makes it difficult to foretell in detail how party weaknesses and strengths will be affected. But we do know that the 1960 election left 37 Democrats in marginal districts, those where they had won by 55 per cent of the vote or less and could thus be expected to be especially vulnerable in 1962. In addition, there are a considerable number of other Democratic House seats that look like fat targets for Republicans in 1962, because of special situations in those districts or other aspects of their long-term background. On the debit side, 47 House Republican seats, mostly won by newcomers, were won in 1960 by less than 55 per cent of the vote. All will require major efforts in 1962; but by holding these seats and pushing hard in the marginal Democratic districts, there is a definite possibility that Republicans will be able to pick up the 43 seats needed to control the House of Representatives, if the organizational vigor is as good or better than that achieved in 1960.

The governorships also loom as one of the major political battlegrounds in the two years ahead. We warm up in 1961 with two contests, in New Jersey and Virginia. But in the crucial election year of 1962, the battle for the Executive Mansions—with all their state power—will spread across the face of the nation. All but two of the 16 Republican governorships, those in Montana and Utah, will be open for contest. In the Democratic camp, 21 of their governors will be up, and only five of them in the deep South.

Finally, a word about the problems and prospects of the Republican party in the South, and especially in those states and areas where it has been traditional to assume that the party has no chance. In 1960, the Republicans carried fewer states in the South than in 1956, but despite that fact, the party was no pushover. In five southern states—South Carolina, Georgia, Alabama, Mississippi, and Tennessee—Vice President Nixon brought in a percentage of the vote that exceeded the GOP percentage in the Eisenhower landslide year of 1956. The Vice President received about 48 per cent of the southwide vote, just a shade below the 1956 level. We held the line on congressional seats and congressional votes in the South, and made gains that were especially remarkable in four gubernatorial contests. Although we did not win, the Republican vote for governor increased by about one million and nearly doubled from 1956 to 1960 in Arkansas, Florida, North Carolina, and Texas. In Texas, the increase was from 261,283 to 612,963 votes. The Republicans also made a net gain of 20 seats in southern state legislatures, and did well in many scattered local elections, especially in Florida. We look forward with confidence to further gains in all categories of southern state elections in 1962.

Post-Election Discussion of Party Leadership

The drama of the leadership transition in the Republican party began as the election returns were being counted on the night of November 8, 1960. The election was a real "cliff-hanger," as all of us remember all too well. The man we had hoped would be President, Richard M. Nixon, accepted the outcome with dignity and good will, and speculation began at once, as it always does, whether, as the defeated candidate, he would again be his party's nominee in 1964. This broadened out immediately into a general discussion of the leadership problems of the Republican party—a discussion that went on very actively for several weeks, and is still not entirely resolved.

The Nixon Role in Defeat

As the defeated candidate, the Vice President inherited what has come to be known in American politics as the titular leadership of his party. There has been some quibbling about this, but there is no question about the fact that the usage is firmly established. It refers to the person who carried the banner of his party in the last presidential election. During the last eight years, Ambassador Adlai Stevenson was in this sense the titular leader of the Democratic party. But in anything as volatile as politics, the titular leadership can be meaningful, or, as Stevenson proved at Los Angeles, it may not.

So far as his own behavior was concerned, Vice President Nixon made it clear, during the days immediately following the election, that he was deferring any decision concerning his own availability for any race for public office in 1962 or 1964. On the other hand, he also let it be known that he intended to remain active in Republican politics, that he would speak out on the issues of public concern from time to time, and that he would do what he could to assist in the further strengthening of the party in all parts of the country.

His first real test in his new role came when President-elect Kennedy sought a conference with him in Florida on November 14. The objectives of the President-elect in this conference have not been disclosed by either participant, but it has been generally supposed that the Kennedy objective was some form of assistance in giving an appearance of bipartisanship to his administration—perhaps by recruiting one or more eminent Republicans, with Nixon's cooperation, to serve in his Cabinet.

In the press conferences that each man held shortly after the meeting, it became clear that whatever the President-elect had intended, the main thing he had accomplished was a focusing of attention on the status of the leadership in the opposition party. Kennedy, when asked if he had discussed the possibility of using Mr. Nixon in his administration in any capacity, replied, "Mr. Nixon has a definite responsibility as leader of his party, and I think perhaps he can answer how he would define that responsibility more satisfactorily than I can." Nixon, after commenting on Kennedy's courtesy in coming to see him and on the scope of their discussion, went on to say that,

> . . . As the Senator indicated, I have a responsibility as the leader of the opposition at this time, and I would like to say that as the leader of the opposition it is my responsibility to see that our opposition is constructive, that we support those policies which we believe are in the best interest . . . of the nation . . . , whenever the Administration advocates such policies, but that where the new Administration advocates policies that we disagree with, that it is our responsibility vigorously to oppose them. We had such an understanding. The Senator agrees that this is the proper role of an opposition party, of an opposition leader. I trust that both I and my party will be able to provide that kind of constructive opposition to the Administration in these next four years. We need this in our American system. It works better when the opposition is vigorous and constructive, and we trust that ours . . . will meet both of these criteria, in the years ahead.[3]

The Vice President performed his official duties for the balance of his term with propriety and good humor, presiding over the Senate, presiding over the counting of the electoral votes and declaring the outcome, and participating in the inaugural ceremonies. After a few weeks of relaxation, he then returned to his home state of California to resume the private practice of law.

It is merely stating the obvious to say that until the Republican national convention meets in 1964, Vice President Nixon will continue to be the party's most recent presidential nominee. As Governor Rockefeller has put it, moreover, Mr. Nixon will continue to be "one of the vital forces in the Republican party." But this does not mean that he will necessarily be available for the 1964 presidential nomination. It is accordingly important for the future of the party to maintain the equities among all of the possible contenders for the next nomination.

The main asset of any party leader, however, is his personal following in the party. Mr. Nixon has had and still has a very sub-

[3] From the verbatim transcripts of the two conferences, *Congressional Quarterly Weekly Report,* Nov. 18, 1960, pp. 1911-13.

stantial following, as demonstrated by the attention he has been receiving on his speaking tours. His role as the party's titular leader is a personal role, arising out of tradition, it is true, but entirely dependent on the activities of the incumbent in the role for whatever content it may achieve.

The Keating Proposals

Governor Nelson Rockefeller of New York, in discussing the party leadership situation on December 1, 1960, said that what the party needed was "collective leadership." A few days later, Senator Kenneth B. Keating of New York urged the formation of a high-level policy planning committee to advise on the formulation of party programs. He thought this committee should include the party's living former Presidents, Hoover and Eisenhower; its most recent candidates for President and Vice President, Nixon and Lodge; the chairman of the Republican National Committee, currently myself; ten members of each house of Congress; and another ten members from outside of Congress to give diversified representation to the governors and to other leading members of the party around the country. This would be a total group of 35.

In the discussion that followed, the group proposed by Senator Keating was frequently compared to the Democratic advisory committee of the last few years, but Keating himself has said that he considers it more nearly comparable to the Republican group headed by Mr. Charles H. Percy of Chicago, which functioned in advance of the Republican convention of 1960. The Democratic advisory committee undoubtedly served a useful purpose in giving the presidential wing of that party a forum and in getting a lot of publicity, especially by shifting its meetings around among major news centers such as New York, Chicago, and Los Angeles. But the Democratic committee was started in the face of the opposition of the party's congressional leaders, and the longer it functioned the more friction it produced.

In the Republican party, the need for a high-level policy committee is not especially acute at present. We still have the report of the Percy committee and the platform adopted at Chicago, and we have the results of eight years of active effort by the recent Republican administration in hammering out a series of policy positions. We don't have to go to Mackinac Island in order to produce something that we already have. Later the situation may change, and as we approach the 1962 campaign, it is possible that a broadly based committee would become more useful.

The Congressional Leadership Meetings

The congressional leaders of the party were of course as much aware as anyone that the situation in regard to the party leadership would change when President Eisenhower left office on January 20. They were opposed to the Keating proposal when it was first broached, and to a degree still are. But they have felt strongly the need for something to take the place of the weekly meetings of the top party leadership at the White House—meetings that went on regularly, when Congress was in session, throughout the eight years of the Eisenhower administration.

It was accordingly agreed in advance of the meeting of the Republican National Committee in January 1961 and announced at that time that the party's congressional leaders and the national committee chairman would continue to meet at weekly intervals after January 20. The first of these meetings was held in the office of Senator Everett M. Dirksen, the Senate Minority Leader, on January 25, with a full attendance of the party's congressional leaders from each house. It was agreed that the further meetings would be held every Tuesday at 8:30 a.m., and would break up at 10:00 a.m., at which time Senator Dirksen and Representative Charles A. Halleck, Minority Leader of the House of Representatives, would "put out the news."

It is planned that this group will journey to Gettysburg to confer with President Eisenhower, and will meet with Vice President Nixon in Washington. The congressional group may later become the central core of a much larger committee, which would meet only occasionally while the congressional leaders continue to meet every week. The larger committee could concern itself with questions of party policy somewhat more long-range than those involved in the action in Congress from day to day, and should be especially helpful in setting the note for the mid-term campaign in 1962. If the congressional leaders will accept a central place in such an arrangement, as I hope they will, we shall have the basis for a broad representation of party interests while avoiding the difficulties that arose in the Democratic party when its leaders most concerned with presidential politics were pulling in one direction, and its congressional leaders in another.

The National Committee and Its Chairmanship

The national committee of either party has a profoundly different task in defeat from that which it has in victory, with party possession of the White House. In defeat, the national committee becomes the main center for coordination of the party's long-range concerns, and especially those involved in the next oncoming election. Since almost anything can affect an election, the national committee inevitably becomes interested in almost everything that is going on.

From In-Party to Out-Party Status

In shifting over from in-party to out-party status, there is generally some reorganization of the party machinery. Over the hundred years of the Republican party's history, there have occasionally been situations following an election defeat in which one party faction or another attempted to seize control of the national committee in preparation for the nominating struggles of the national convention that would come around again in four years. The more modern conception has been one of avoiding, or at least postponing, this kind of a power struggle as long as possible, operating the national committee in the meantime as a neutral agency genuinely dedicated to the welfare of the party as a whole—the only basis on which it can be completely effective in organizing for the mid-term campaign and in making the preparations for the next convention.

The way in which the party chairmanship is filled is of course a central factor in maintaining this kind of a policy. I have often been asked how I happened to become chairman, and whether I have found it practical to serve as party chairman while also serving actively in the Senate. On the first part of this question, my predecessor, Meade Alcorn, was doing a good job but he had his personal reasons to quit. President Eisenhower was very conscious that we seemed to be orbited in two or three different directions. The national committee was going in one direction, the administration in another direction, the Senate in one direction, and the House in still another.

The President went through the possibilities, and I guess I was the only apple left in the barrel, so it finally got down to Morton. In making his choice, the President had to have someone who supported his programs and had the same political philosophy especially if he were looking to Capitol Hill for someone to take this job. I filled the bill in that regard because I had been a part of his administration and naturally I had been in agreement with it or I would not have been there. And the selection I think, accomplished something. We were able to get going together, because I was an alumnus of the House and had plenty of friends there, and I was presently a member of the Senate, so the situation came out fairly well as we organized for the 1960 campaign.

It was anticipated that my duties would end on the ninth of November, because we were going to elect a President. At the national committee meeting immediately following the election, he would say whom he wanted, and Morton would be relieved of the job. That failed to work out by some 112,000 votes, so I had to stay on the job for the time being. At the national committee meeting in January 1961, I hoped that a successor would be chosen, but the committee unanimously adopted a resolution asking me to remain—a resolution moved by the national committeeman from New York, George Hinman, and seconded by committee members from Arizona, California, Illinois, Kentucky, and Ohio.

But in terms of my own situation as a Senator up for re-election in Kentucky in 1962—a state where no Republican ever expects to have an easy time—it is essential that a new national committee chairman be chosen as soon as possible. I intend to resign as soon as a few problems can be worked out. I will call a meeting of the Republican National Committee probably within three months for the purpose of choosing my successor.[4]

The Immediate Tasks before the Party

The transition in getting the party organized for its present situation will not be completed until a new chairman is on the job, but in the meantime there are many things to do. They are indicated by the nature of the election outcome in 1960. No massive program to rebuild the party is called for, since the party is not at all shattered. Our morale is generally good—we are angry, but not disheartened. But we do have some problems, most notably the "Big City Gap."

Hence at the meeting of the national committee on January 6, 1961, I recommended a specific four-point program of action that the committee approved and that is now under way. This included the following steps.

1. A committee under the chairmanship of Ohio state chairman Ray C. Bliss, to study the practicalities of big city politics and to devise a campaign plan for the maximum Republican impact on these areas. Members of this committee include national committee members who are familiar with big city politics, plus Republican winners who have found the key to victory in metropolitan areas. This committee will work on campaign techniques, not party philosophy. It is analyzing the formulas that have won, interpreting the organizational strengths and weaknesses in various areas, and will tell us what steps have to be taken everywhere to erode the monolithic Democratic big city vote. When this vote is shaved, we can win many of the states lost by narrow margins in 1960.

2. A committee under the chairmanship of New Jersey National

---

[4] Representative William E. Miller of New York was elected National Chairman of the Republican National Committee on June 2, 1961.

Committeeman Bernard M. Shanley to spur the establishment, in every state and every area, of a Republican precinct security program for election day. This is, of course, a major part of our problem in the big cities, one of such importance that it deserves special attention. The committee is charged with investigating and studying election day security procedures beyond the regular staffing of precinct polling places. It will report on the best techniques to make certain that every precinct is staffed on election day by qualified and authentic Republican workers, fully educated and trained in what they can and should do to ensure that only authorized votes are cast, and that they are correctly counted.

3. A committee under the chairmanship of Mrs. Ione F. Herrington, National Committeewoman from Indiana, to make an immediate beginning on a new Republican voter registration program. This committee is surveying registration techniques and plans that have been successfully used, and is serving as a clearing house to make certain that every state has the best registration know-how that can be devised. Most states permit registration now. Its immediate importance is clear, for at least 35 states have municipal elections in 1961. There is little merit in sitting idly by when we could be intensively and systematically registering voters. We need local and state victories in 1961 to maintain the momentum of 1960. Increased registration of Republicans is one way to make victory surer.

4. A committee under the chairmanship of Idaho National Committeeman Harley B. Markham to study state election laws and to develop a model law of full equity that we can recommend to the states where improvements are definitely needed. As we all found out in 1960, it is extremely difficult in most states, and impossible in some, to obtain a speedy recount or even a quick check into indicated irregularities. While this committee is a Republican enterprise, it is also an impartial public service of the highest order. The sanctity of the American ballot is a supreme consideration. It should be guarded by enlightened laws that offer a speedy remedy in suspect instances.

I also made two other announcements at the January committee meeting on which there has since been follow-through activity. One related to the fact that we had found that a very useful tool was the bulletin sent out daily by the Answer Desk at national party headquarters. Initiated in the 1956 campaign, Answer Desk consisted of a staff of research experts and writers who daily punched holes in the Democratic arguments and suggested timely ways in which to capitalize on the positive phases of Republicanism. Their bulletin was sent to all candidates and speakers traveling in the national campaign.

It seemed to me that there was no reason why such an excellent communication should be reserved only for presidential campaigns. We have therefore resumed publication of a fortnightly Answer Desk bulletin that is being mailed to top party leaders, former presidential appointees, and other Republicans who need to keep briefed up to the moment on national issues and party policy. The presidential appointees of the Eisenhower administration have now returned to their home communities in positions of great responsibility—and they are in a perfect position to promote Republicanism and to prepare the way for the next Republican administration, in which many of them will undoubtedly have a part. We intend to see that they and all Republicans have plenty of ammunition.

My other announcement had to do with the increasing usefulness of regional conferences in maintaining a high level of party morale and organizational activity. There are no longer any "off-years" in this business. We therefore decided to hold a series of regional conferences in 1961. At these meetings, we are surveying the state of the party in detail and are laying the groundwork for the campaign of 1962. I am confident that these meetings are helping greatly to forge a Republican organization and spirit that will carry the day in 1961 and 1962.

The Role of the Opposition in Congress

In speaking of organization and leadership, it should not be implied that these are the only factors in party success, although they are the ones for which the national committee has the greatest responsibility. What we Republicans do in Congress is of obvious primary importance in the essential part that the opposition party can play in the growth and development of a free nation.

In America we do not believe that any one man or any one group of men possesses such a monopoly of wisdom that it is capable of governing the whole without question. The ideas of many, freely exchanged, the heated debates of the pros and cons, the business of laying the cards on the table, all fall into a pattern from which the final judgment is determined. Without opposition there is dictatorship. Without dissent, the orderly processes whether they be in government or business lose their rugged strength.

We all agree in the perpetual reaffirmation of traditional American principles, but there is a wide difference of opinion about how these principles should be implemented. This is why we have two major parties, each pursuing common goals but employing different methods to achieve them. Neither holds a monopoly on progress or effectiveness. Both have made lasting contributions to the growth and development of America. Indeed, these many years, they have joined in common causes to build a picture of unity that our nation traditionally displays in matters affecting our security and survival. This phenomenon is not present in countries where splinter parties continually harass government in the pursuit of their selfish and narrow objectives.

When the major areas of disagreement are confined largely to a two-party structure, the chances of a balanced solution of almost any problem are excellent if the out-party remains true to its obligations. I think so long as we accept the out-party as a proper medium of strong and constructive opposition, we have little to fear about our future. Only by absorbing both sides in any controversy can Americans continue to discharge their full obligations as citizens. Lincoln spoke of this freedom when he said: "Our defense is in the preservation of the spirit which prizes liberty as the heritage of all men, in all lands everywhere. Destroy this spirit, and you have planted the seeds of despotism around our doors."

So, in constructive opposition, speaking freely as free men, either in suggesting alternate courses, condemning reckless ones, or in supporting the wise decisions of incumbent leadership, the Republican party's voice will be heard on behalf of the 34 million Americans who support its policies. I do not suggest that the GOP has performance characteristics that would qualify it for sainthood, but I do believe we have demonstrated consistently through history that we are a party of principle rather than of temporary expedience. Witness our sound and workable 1960 platform as compared with the extravagances of the Democratic counterpart.

The Difference Between the Parties

The Republican party thinks of the United States government as one that will offer the greatest opportunity for the growth and advancement of the individual. On the other hand, the Democratic party, retreating from Jeffersonian principles, inclines to think of America and its progress in terms of groups. This is a distinction that should not be overlooked, because it is the great division line of the two parties today.

In foreign affairs the parties generally are firmly committed to world-wide resistance to aggression, support of the United Nations, and sympathetic assistance to newly emerging nations. There are differences in emphasis, priorities, and approaches, but basically the motivation is the same.

On domestic issues the cleavage is marked. There is agreement on what problems face the United States, but sharp disagreement on how to solve the problems. Republicans generally tend to favor reliance on the private sector of the national economy to flourish inside a framework of government partnership, with some regulation and supports that guarantee equality of opportunity to compete. The rights and responsibilities of lower echelons of government—state and local—are stressed.

Democrats are eager to thrust the power of federal government directly into the economy. Democratic proposals almost invariably aim at strengthening and enlarging the federal government and its responsibilities. State and local government are de-emphasized. Democratic planners devise compulsory federal programs, leaving individuals no choice whether they wish to participate or not. Republican programs carefully preserve freedom of choice.

On matters of finance, Republicans are more suspicious of federal deficit financing and inflation than are the Democrats. Many leading Democratic economists not only accept but urge inflationary deficits as a means to drive economic growth at an artificially high rate. Republicans favor sound growth encouraged at a natural rate by sound money, arguing such growth is the only meaningful kind.

Constructive Opposition

The question of guidelines for the opposition party opens broad vistas of thought. Basically, it might be said that the major task of the out-party is to use the interim period in strengthening itself to be a more effective opponent of the party in power. Just how is this objective achieved?

In 1951, Kenneth S. Wherry, Republican minority leader of the Senate, had this to say about out-party functioning:

> The Republican Party has no control over legislation, government policies and operations. Its role in Congress is narrowly limited. No Republican can be chairman of a congressional committee. Republicans are a minority in all committees. They cannot carry through legislation on their own. They cannot take administrative steps to solve national problems or correct abuses in the government of the country. They have no control over the conduct of foreign relations.
>
> But in a two-party system such as ours, the Republican party has a clear and responsible public duty to perform. In the role of the opposition, Republicans can appraise critically the promises and performances of the Democratic Administration. They can call the Democratic Administration to account for its failures in discharging the public trust. They can expose mistakes, corruption and other actions harmful to the public interest. They can press for high standards and principles in the solution of public problems and offer constructive suggestions concerning them.
>
> Finally, by public debate, Republicans can take their opposition to the people who have the power to compel the Administration to safeguard the nation or remove it from office.

The big question is where to draw the line. When is opposition proper and constructive and when is it harmful? An excess of truculence and carping criticism is at once rejected as serving no useful purpose. Yet there is no requirement for the opposition to haunt the public domain as voiceless ghosts waiting for reincarnation. The path we intend to follow as purposeful Republicans, avoiding cynical opposition and shunning negativism, is clearly marked between the two extremes.

Political history has many examples of constructive opposition. In this connection, I would recall a bizarre and moving incident that occurred when Abraham Lincoln was inaugurated. His very eloquent and able opponent in furious campaigning, Stephen A. Douglas, attended the ceremonies deeply in sympathy with Lincoln's resolve to preserve the integrity of the nation at any cost. In this great test Douglas rejected partisanship for the greater good of his country.

When Lincoln rose to speak, Douglas moved swiftly to relieve him of that horrendous hat of the times—the stovepipe—and hold it until the address was completed. This simple gesture of support by the leader of the opposition was widely noted. Not only did Douglas do this, but he was the first to congratulate the new President when he returned to his seat.

Arthur Vandenberg of Michigan too, was a classic example of dedication to the national interests. This great Republican senator as you know, was a militant foe of New Dealism. He was Republican to the core. At the same time he was an extreme isolationist. During World War II he courageously re-examined his thinking and accepted the inevitability of internationalism as a new posture for the United States.

He plunged into the implementation of this new concept with all his vigor and persuasiveness, pressing for a bipartisan foreign policy for the postwar era. In the Republican Congress, he fought for the Democratic administration's Marshall Plan for saving free Europe. Without his efforts, it is doubtful the plan would have been adopted. Fully aware that Harry Truman, the Democratic President, would one day claim full credit, Vandenberg nevertheless pushed through his famous resolution of 1948 that gave the administration the mandate of the Republican-controlled Senate for the negotiation of the North Atlantic Treaty. The same resolution also gave Senate sanction to American participation in military and political alliances in defense of the free world.

We Republicans should be inspired by this and other comparable examples of responsible opposition and keep them in mind as we continue to exert an influence on national affairs. As in the case of Senator Douglas, there will be occasions when we would hasten to hold the Kennedy hat in the interest of national unity. But we will not volunteer for such cavalier duty if he seems to be moving in the wrong direction.

For example, we don't have to wait and see whether the new federal spending authorizations will add to the size of the budget. They will.

We don't have to wait and see whether lower interest rates will increase, not stem the flow of gold from the United States. They will.

We don't have to wait and see whether policies which further tend to price American goods out of world markets will widen, not close the so-called dollar gap. They will.

We don't have to wait and see whether payment of teachers' salaries by the Federal government would be followed by Federal intervention in the operation of our public schools. It would be.

We don't have to wait and see whether pump priming, boot-strap-lifting policies, which failed so miserably two decades ago, will meet the demands and challenges of the sixties. They won't.

We don't have to wait and see whether Mr. Khrushchev has "softened" toward the United States and is now eager to reach a settlement on such far reaching items as atomic testing and inspection, disarmament, and the cold war in general. He wants no firm and lasting settlement short of unconditional surrender.

As members of the out-party, we recognize our responsibility to approach all problems with the same zeal we would exercise in office. The unfavorable situations that worry all of us are challenges that all Americans must face. In the national interest, wise, bipartisan action, free of panic and distortion, and free of extremist influences, must be pursued at all levels—federal, state, and local. With all these essential factors converging on the problem, each in its proper role, steady progress should be possible.

Finally, I would say that Republicans, in meeting the problems of an age in which there is so much unrest and confusion, should always have the courage of their convictions. The millions more we seek as supporters in future elections will elude us if we display less than full allegiance to our traditional policies and programs. Our mission is to win on merit as we appeal to all segments of the population, not as separate groups but as part of the whole with equal but never superior claims on the progress we can generate. The overriding challenge in this task is to build so effectively that no one in the fifty states will ever have to ask: "What is Republicanism, what can it do for me?"

12

The Political Changes of 1960-1961

PAUL T. DAVID[1]

PREVIOUS CHAPTERS OF THIS BOOK have dealt with various segments of the presidential election and transition of 1960-1961. In this final chapter, the whole flow of the action is relevant, but those aspects that in one way or another reflect some kind of a break with the past are especially relevant. The purpose is to review highlights of the experience, not merely for its importance as history—although that importance obviously is great—but rather for what it may show of the potentialities for continuing and further changes in political habits and customs.

The operational perceptions of an active new generation of leaders, in combination with the pressures from abroad and long-term shifts within America itself, can be expected to result in a series of adaptations in the political system. Those adaptations seem likely to take place initially more often as changes in operating patterns and procedures than as changes in the formal institutions of politics and government. This does not necessarily lessen the importance of such changes as may occur, but it does increase the difficulties of cognition and assessment.

We can speculate about what some of the adaptations may be even while they are still in prospect. Some probably have already occurred, although it is too soon to say which will be permanent. To begin the review, we can return to the subject of the first two

[1] Professor of Political Science, University of Virginia.

This chapter was prepared initially as a lecture given in March 1961, and was rewritten for publication in July 1961.

chapters, the events and activities of the presidential nominations and the party conventions.

The Nominating Campaigns and the Party Conventions

Long-standing precedents were broken in choosing the candidates of 1960, although typical patterns of party decision were maintained in doing so. Nationalizing forces were clearly at work throughout the process.

Candidates Trained in National Affairs

Both presidential nominees were remarkable exceptions to past practice in the selection of candidates. Kennedy was the second Roman Catholic in American history to receive a presidential nomination, the other being Al Smith, who was not elected. Kennedy was also the first incumbent senator since Stephen A. Douglas in 1860 to receive the Democratic nomination, and the only incumbent senator, other than Warren G. Harding, to win a presidential election at any time. Nixon, in turn, was the first Vice President since Martin Van Buren in 1836 to achieve a major party presidential nomination without having previously succeeded to the higher office through the death of his predecessor. Both men were younger than average as presidential candidates.

These oddities, however, were associated with something almost as unusual and much more important: the extent to which each man had been trained for the Presidency through relevant experience in national affairs. Both, after war service, had been elected to the House of Representatives on the same day in 1946 and had thereafter served continuously in federal elective office. Nixon's experience as Vice President was claimed as a major campaign asset, despite the limitations of the Vice Presidency as a post in which to acquire either legislative or administrative experience. Kennedy had his own offsetting assets, made apparent in the campaign through the quality of his personal performance and the background it revealed.

A pair of presidential nominees, each of whom could claim as much experience in dealing with federal government problems, is a phenomenon so rare in American history that one must go back more than a hundred years for any real counterpart. If these nominations reflect a new assessment of the requirements of the office—as indeed they may, judging by the differential aspects of the treatment accorded other candidates for the 1960 nominations—they may be as precedent-setting as those of 1876, when each party nominated an incumbent governor for the first time.

In making the nominations, each party followed the patterns of decision most compatible with electoral success. The Republicans, as the party in power, stayed within the ranks of the previous administration, avoided a party-splitting fight, and nominated their heir apparent with a minimum of overt conflict. The Democrats, with no executive record to defend, conducted the kind of contest that is normal when an out-party scents victory, and then nominated the front runner on the first ballot at the convention—again indicating the irrelevance, in recent decades, of dreams of victory for a dark horse candidate.[2]

Nationalizing Influences at the Conventions

The national party conventions were not consciously used in 1960 as instruments to strengthen national forces within their respective parties, but they undoubtedly had their effect, as Paul Tillett noted in "The National Conventions," Chapter 2. The 1960 conventions seemed to complete the subordination of sectional and other dissident elements that had been under way in 1948, 1952, and 1956. The boredom of the 1960 conventions was itself evidence that the dissident elements of former years, still present,

[2] On harmony in the in-party and conflict in the out-party as the respective roads to victory, cf. Arthur N. Holcombe, *Our More Perfect Union* (Harvard University Press, 1950), pp. 82-87; Paul T. David, Ralph M. Goldman, and Richard C. Bain, *The Politics of National Party Conventions* (The Brookings Institution, 1960), pp. 156-57, 467-75.

were no longer fighting very hard, and least of all when the national party was on public display.

Platform drafting made further gains as a convention function, as it has in both parties since World War II. Obviously, the point had not yet been reached where many could agree with Paul Butler that a party platform is the most important product of a national convention, but it was a novel experience to see a national party chairman stand up in public and say so, as Butler did in opening the platform hearings at Los Angeles. The involvement of the candidates indicated that platform provisions have become increasingly strategic in the party struggle, with consequences that may harass the winning candidate and his party when the platform is overtly disregarded.

The campaign rally aspect of the conventions was again emphasized in response to the opportunities of television and radio, but with obvious room for further improvement in 1964. This is a point that will undoubtedly receive the earnest attention, in due course, of the new leaders of each party. The basic question in this area is whether the further reforms, if any, will be merely superficial, or will instead extend to some substantial restructuring of the conventions to meet their responsibilities more adequately. In the latter case, the conscious use of the conventions to strengthen national forces within the parties might become more of a possibility.

The General Election Campaign

In the campaign that followed the conventions, Nixon and Kennedy occupied contrasting positions. With Nixon, the Republicans offered the voters the opportunity to continue the kind of conservative government the Eisenhower administration had been providing, but with younger, more vigorous, and more adaptive leadership. With Kennedy, the Democrats offered the voters the opportunity for a much more complete break with the previous administration, and for a new and more aggressive approach to the entire range of problems awaiting attention. Each candidate was an able exponent of the kind of change he symbolized, as became increasingly apparent as the campaign progressed.

There were several major respects in which the 1960 campaign was new or unusual, of which six may merit thought for the future.

The Religious Issue

First of all was the importance in the campaign of what Stanley Kelley has called the silent issue—whether a member of the Catholic faith *could* or *should* be elected President. This issue seems to have generated at least as much disreputable behavior in the political underworld in 1960 as it did in 1928. With Kennedy's election, however, the *could* part of the issue has been settled. Future potential candidates of his religion will no longer face as great a handicap. The number of such candidates will probably increase, with the result that the religious issue will be more persistent, even if less intense when present.

The question whether a Catholic *should* be elected will thus continue to be a factor in presidential elections, including, presumably, that of 1964. In 1964, unlike 1960, the evidence of experience will be available. It may cut in both directions even within the same groups. Some Catholics who voted for Kennedy may discover that they would rather not have him as President, while some Protestants who were opposed to him in 1960 may discover that they would be for him in 1964. This would be consistent with what usually happens when a first-term President is up for reelection, by which time the cross-cutting effects of his program are likely to shift the composition of his electoral support. The net shift cannot easily be predicted, however, and it will undoubtedly produce uncertainties of major importance for the strategists in the White House as 1964 approaches.

Khrushchev and Foreign Policy

Foreign policy again dominated the issue debates of 1960, as it had in 1952 and 1956 and may into the future in presidential campaigns as far as one can see. The presence of Nikita Khrushchev at the United Nations in New York for a number of weeks was, however, a new feature of the 1960 campaign. The coincidental timing of this event may have been fortuitous, but the limited ability of the Eisenhower administration to engage in political reprisals during its final days may have inspired an unusual degree of boldness on Khrushchev's part. By his presence and provocative behavior, Khrushchev was a constant reminder of the U-2 incident, the abortive summit meeting, and the canceled visit to Japan.

The whole episode underlined the growing impact of foreign affairs on domestic politics. This has been apparent in many ways since the end of World War II, but the potentialities of debate at the United Nations during a campaign period had not previously been given so dramatic a form. One can only wonder what further occasions of this kind will occur to test the stability of the American people in future campaign years.

The Debates

The television debates of 1960 were a third notable feature of the campaign. President Kennedy has indicated that in his view, he could not have been elected without them. Many election postmortems have suggested that Vice President Nixon made a mistake in agreeing to take part, but he himself seems to have believed that he had no choice. Certainly he needed some positive means of reaching and influencing independents and Democratic voters who were virtually unavailable in any other way.

After the debates had been authorized, in the circumstances prevailing in Congress and the White House in August 1960, it would have been difficult for either candidate to hold back completely. The drive back of the legislation, as recounted by Charles Thomson, had essentially a public interest motivation, although with many overtones involving the special interests of the television networks and the misgivings of their critics in both parties. Presumably, in advance of the event, both parties and both candidates had concluded that the debates could be used to their advantage; but all concerned had been boxed in to some extent by a developing concept of what the public was entitled to have from the candidates by way of personal confrontation.[3]

For the future, President Kennedy has already indicated that he will be willing to participate in similar debates in 1964, thus opening the way for a precedent from which future incumbent Presidents may not easily escape. That the experience will be a testing process for an incumbent, as well as for any challenger, would seem certain. Yet any form of confrontation by which the candidates can be tested against each other before a bipartisan audience would seem in the public interest, whatever it may do to the candidates. In addition to such educational effect as it may have for the electorate, it will inevitably give a higher status to the candidate of the party out of power than he has usually been accorded when running against an incumbent. This is a change that could be important in maintaining effective levels of competition between the parties under modern conditions.

The Fifty-State Campaign

A fourth aspect of the campaign that could be considered both novel and important was the geographic spread of the campaigning, made possible in part by the extensive use of the newly available jet aircraft. Nixon pledged himself to campaign in all fifty states, and did, on the theory that not one should be conceded in advance to the Democrats. Kennedy concentrated somewhat more on the major industrial states, but campaigned almost as widely as Nixon. This is demonstrated by the statistics in "The Presidential Campaign," Chapter 3.

Why was there so much emphasis in 1960—a year in which network television reaching national audiences was used more intensively than ever before—on going everywhere and being seen and heard in person? The answer seems to reside in two factors: so many states had become so close in presidential politics; and in so many states there had been a new integration of presidential and

[3] On Nixon's attitudes see T. H. White, *The Making of the President, 1960* (Atheneum, 1961), p. 178. Nixon thought Kennedy would be an easy victim in the debates, after watching his acceptance speech at Los Angeles.

state politics. Campaigning could no longer be confined to a few pivotal states when so many states had become pivotal. In both parties, local party officials who could not be sure of carrying their states were demanding appearances.

Kennedy and Johnson felt their own need to enlist the active work of state and local organizations, most of all in those states where the local Democratic organization could expect to win local races, whatever happened to the national ticket. Nixon and Lodge had an opposite problem: the need to help Republican organizations all over the country in pulling themselves up by their bootstraps, in order to win the presidential race if possible, and to continue strengthening the party in Congress and in the state capitols as an obvious necessity for party survival. In view of the narrow outcome and mixed verdict of 1960, it would seem certain that similar forces will again be operating in 1962 and 1964.

The South in National Politics

In 1960, the South was recognized as a pivotal area in presidential politics, and on a basis much more enduring than Eisenhower's personal popularity in the region. Signs of the readjustment in southern politics were evident in the attitudes of the southern delegations at the Democratic convention; in the Johnson nomination as a successful appeal to the moderate element in the southern Democracy; in the kind of attention that the candidates of both parties gave the South during the campaign; and in dramatic increases in southern voter turnout.

Neither party made any important concession to southern conservatism on civil rights. Kennedy not only stood firm but dramatized his position by his personal expression of sympathy in the Martin Luther King case. Despite this, the party held most of the South, and it provided an essential portion of the Kennedy-Johnson victory. But Republican gains were noteworthy in major areas, as the party's former chairman, Senator Thruston B. Morton, has pointed out in his lecture in this series. In the spring of 1961,

Republican gains were climaxed by the election of the Republican senator from Texas, John G. Tower. Safely in office for six years, Tower quickly became a new rallying point for southern conservatives in the Republican party.

Registration Drives and the Turnout Problem

A final aspect of the campaign that deserves notice was the national emphasis on registration drives and on the effort in each party to secure a higher turnout. Both efforts are standard political operations. What was new in 1960 was the kind of attention given these operations at the highest levels in each party, and by national leaders of business and organized labor. As Herbert Alexander (Chapter 5) suggests, labor muscle may have done as much for Democratic turnout in key states as anything the party did for itself.

Of the estimated 107,000,000 Americans who were old enough to vote in the presidential election, over 64 per cent did so, as against 63 per cent in 1952, the high point of recent years. But if indeed "it is easier to bring a new voter into the system than to induce an old partisan to change sides," both parties still have major opportunities.[4] The problem is to find patterns of national party organization that will permit the effective exploitation of these opportunities in national politics. Labor's crash program in 1960 was an illustration of an effort generated centrally that seems to have had some effect in critical localities.[5]

[4] The quotation is from the discussion of such opportunities in E. E. Schattschneider, *The Semisovereign People* (Henry Holt & Co., 1960), Chap. 6, p. 112.

[5] In a recent column, Roscoe Drummond has suggested that the Republican National Committee needs paid party workers in every critical congressional district. Presumably, these would be workers on the national party payroll, resident in districts where the party has no incumbent member of Congress, and concerned with the long-term efforts required to build party strength for congressional and presidential elections, including voter registration, precinct organization, and candidate recruitment. "Memo to GOP," *Washington Post and Times Herald,* July 3, 1961.

The Narrow Outcome and Its Effects

Most of the presidential elections of this century have been settled by wide margins. There were the noteworthy exceptions of 1916 and 1948, but the general statement holds for every election since 1896 that produced a party overturn in the White House. We find ourselves mentally ill-adapted to deal with a situation in which so narrow an electoral margin has produced so sweeping a change in the administration. Moreover, although the Democratic party won the congressional election by somewhat greater margins than the presidential, it nonetheless lost seats rather than gained them in both Houses of Congress.

Reasons for the Close Outcome

In developing expectations for the future, it is important to discover why the outcome was so close in 1960. The voter motivations that produced this curious pattern of election returns have already been the subject of much research, but more is still to be published. A few points can be noted, as well as issues still unresolved.

Obviously, there was no Eisenhower in this election. Each candidate was meritorious, but the choice was not foreclosed by any overwhelming preference for one candidate over the other on personality grounds. In a somewhat similar way, the issue positions of the candidates and of their parties seemed incapable of pushing the electorate decisively in one direction or another. The differences in issue positions were substantial, and by the end of the campaign, they had been rather clearly elucidated—more so than is often the case. But the result established no preponderant majority on one side or the other.[6]

The Republican party could have been expected to have an ad-

---

[6] On these matters, cf. the summary by Stanley Kelley, Jr., in Ivan Hinderaker (ed.), *American Government Annual, 1961-1962* (Holt, Rinehart & Winston, 1961), pp. 72-73.

vantage, because it was incumbent; on the other hand, the Democratic party could have been expected to have an advantage, because of its much larger following in the total population. In the event, these generalized types of advantage not only offset each other but were individually neutralized by special factors. Eisenhower could doubtless have been re-elected on his record, but it was not good enough to make a Nixon victory a certainty. The record was damaged on the foreign affairs side as the election approached, and the mild downturn in economic conditions did nothing to help. The Gallup poll evidence suggests that Nixon could have won easily if the election had been held in the fall of 1959. By mid-1960, the race had become a dead heat and stayed so through the election.

Kennedy was doubtless helped by the Democratic majority in the population at large, but there were several limiting factors. More Democrats than Republicans are nonvoters; they split their tickets more often; and despite the party's predominant appeal for Catholics, it also has its share of anti-Catholics. The incompatible elements that have recently given the party its large and somewhat fictitious majorities in Congress could not all be expected to vote for the same presidential candidate, and especially one like Kennedy.

Religion as a Factor in the Voting

All analysts agree that the religious factor was of overwhelming importance in shifting votes in the 1960 election, but there is controversy over the character of the net effect, and on whether it was helpful or harmful to Kennedy. V. O. Key (Chapter 6), using the election returns for state and local areas, has shown the dramatic increase in the Democratic vote in Catholic areas of the Northeast and Middle West. The election returns for Protestant areas are more difficult to interpret, but there were areas, notably in the South, where Kennedy ran behind Stevenson's vote in 1956. Yet Key concludes, unlike many of the experts of the immediate post-election period, that Kennedy probably won *in spite of* rather than *because of* the fact that he was a Catholic.

Further evidence bearing on the issue is provided by the recently published research of the Michigan Survey Research Center.[7] By survey methods, it was found that among the voters active in both the 1956 and 1960 elections, 17 per cent shifted from Eisenhower to Kennedy and 6 per cent from Stevenson to Nixon. Among the Eisenhower-Kennedy changers, 40 per cent were Protestant and nearly 60 per cent Catholic. The Stevenson-Nixon changers, however, were 90 per cent Protestant and only 8 per cent Catholic. These changes left Nixon with 63 per cent of the Protestant vote, against Eisenhower's 64, but gave Kennedy 80 per cent of the Catholic vote, against Stevenson's 50. Hence it might seem that the increase in the Catholic Democratic vote elected Kennedy.

But, the Michigan group contends, the Stevenson vote in 1956 is an exceptionally poor measure of a normal Democratic vote, and hence a poor yardstick against which to measure the 1960 vote. They contend that if Kennedy had polled a normal Democratic vote, defined on the basis of the survey evidence of the last ten years, he would have carried fifteen southern states 2-to-1 and would have polled 49 per cent of the popular vote elsewhere, for a total of 53 per cent of the popular vote nationwide, against his actual 49.5. Hence, they conclude, Kennedy was hurt rather than helped by his Catholicism, because of his inability to exploit the full potential of that portion of the Protestant vote that is normally Democratic; and this is why he barely squeaked through, although he was "the candidate of a party enjoying a fundamental majority in the land."[8]

By themselves, these computations remain unconvincing, for two reasons: First, there is the question concerning how the defined normal popular vote would convert into electoral votes, on which the Michigan group offers no opinion.[9] Second, there is a more

[7] Philip E. Converse, Angus Campbell, Warren E. Miller, Donald E. Stokes, "Stability and Change in 1960: A Reinstating Election," *American Political Science Review*, Vol. 55, June 1961, pp. 269-80.

[8] *Ibid.*, p. 279.

[9] The fifteen states defined as the South by the Michigan group had 163 electoral votes in 1960; the other states 374. If each of the southern states had given the Democratic candidate a 2-to-1 popular majority and each of the other states had given him 49 per cent of the popular vote, in accordance with

fundamental question whether any conceivable presidential nominee of the Democratic party could reasonably have been expected to poll a normal Democratic vote in all parts of the country at the same time. A candidate acceptable to a majority of the party's voters nationally would seem inherently unacceptable to a considerable number of southern voters who normally vote Democratic for most purposes. At each election, they may decide not to vote for the party's presidential candidate because of "short-term forces," but after substantial portions of the southern Democratic electorate have defected for short-term reasons in each of four successive elections, the problem of defining a normal presidential vote for the Democratic party in the South would seem virtually insoluble. This is the reason major portions of the area have become so pivotal in presidential elections.[10]

The Michigan group, however, obviously does not pin all of its faith on the statistics just reviewed, arguing that there are several reasons for thinking that their figures underestimate the anti-Catholic vote of 1960, especially outside the South.[11] Many observers, including most members of Congress, have undoubtedly pondered

---

the specified regional norms in each case, he obviously would have been defeated by 374 to 163 in the electoral college, even while bringing to the polls the party's "fundamental majority." Alternatively, if one assumes that the fifteen states should be treated as solid but the others not, the conversion might take the form of 163 southern electoral votes plus 49 per cent of the others, 183, for a total of 346—a good working majority in the electoral college, but one usually exceeded in all but the closest elections.

[10] By a coincidence not entirely strange, the figure of 346 electoral votes, reached at the end of the previous footnote, is almost the same as the number of senators and representatives in Congress who were elected as Democrats in 1958: 347. The coincidence results from the definition of a normal Democratic vote, which seems to consist of the total of those voters who normally turn out and vote Democratic—for any office.

It would be remarkable if the constituencies that elect the Democratic members of the "conservative coalition" in Congress could be expected to vote indefinitely for the Democratic party's presidential nominees. In recent years, many of them have obviously found a series of reasons for not doing so. For data on the composition and voting strength of the coalition see *Congressional Quarterly Almanac,* Vol. 16 (1960), pp. 117-42.

[11] James A. Michener reached a similar conclusion on the basis of his observations as a participant and his study of the election returns in Pennsylvania and elsewhere. *Report of the County Chairman* (Random House, 1961), pp. 267-69.

the implications of the fact that in vote percentage on the basis of
the two-party split, Kennedy ran behind his party's candidates for
the House of Representatives in 198 nonsouthern congressional
districts, whereas Nixon ran behind his party's candidates in only
127.[12] On the total showing, Kennedy ran behind his party in
1960; and it is difficult to believe that he would not have run better
if he had not been a Catholic.

The Kennedy victory of 1960 is thus not likely to encourage any
automatic seeking out of Catholics for the Democratic party's
nominations in the future, even though it can be expected that they
will receive fair consideration in accordance with their other qualifications for availability—which is more than could be said when
Kennedy started down the long road.

Election Effects at Home and Abroad

The election over, Kennedy received his mead of welcome as
the victor, marred only by partisan allegations that his victory had
been stolen. These in turn were quieted when the recounts were in,
and Kennedy had been welcomed at the White House as the President's legitimate successor. The immediate effect of the election was
to restore prospects for a more unified and active government than
had existed for some years, with a President dedicated to concepts
of active leadership and with majorities of his party in both houses
of Congress. This view began to be somewhat modified as the consequences of party losses in Congress were faced, but the new
administration nonetheless entered office with high hopes and with,
on the whole, a cordial welcome from the country.

The effects of the election abroad were more important than has
been generally realized, for reasons discussed by John Hightower
in Chapter 10. The campaign had been reported abroad more fully
than ever before, including the exportation of the television debates, shown full length in many other countries. The response had
been one of close attention; and while widely divergent elements
had seemed prepared to welcome either candidate in advance of the
election, they showed surprising evidences of relief at the choice.

[12] Conversely, of course, Nixon ran ahead in 198 and Kennedy ran ahead
in 127. *Congressional Quarterly Special Report,* March 10, 1961, p. 1.

Kennedy's underdog position as a Catholic running for President of the United States had apparently established a bond, not only with his religious compatriots in Europe, but also with the submerged masses of other religions and races around the world. The breakthrough in the election of a Catholic seems to have done much to refurbish the reputation of the United States on matters of religious and racial tolerance. In the Communist bloc, where some deference is still paid to the memory of Franklin D. Roosevelt, Kennedy was welcomed initially as an heir to the Roosevelt tradition; and in the anti-Communist centers of the free world, there was welcome for a new promise of vigor in the leadership of the western alliance.

An aspect almost frightening, however, was the extent to which Kennedy's campaign statements had been accepted abroad as solid commitments. As Hightower remarks, possibly no other President ever carried into office the burden of so many hopes from so many parts of the world—a measure of the danger and the opportunity before him.

Transition, Transfer, and the New Frontier

The election over, the Nation entered on the problems of an interregnum in the form in which it occurs in this country. Partly because of the efforts of the Brookings Institution, the process that has been christened transition was more self-conscious than ever before.[13] The processes of transition were also more effective than formerly in a number of ways. For this, credit must be given the main protagonists in the transfer of power, the President and the President-elect. Both men displayed attitudes that were noticeably more mature in some respects than those of their predecessors in similar situations.

---

[13] In November 1960, the Institution published Laurin L. Henry's *Presidential Transitions,* a five-year study of the major presidential transitions of this century; and throughout much of 1960 and 1961, the Institution was engaged in a study of the contemporary problem, of which Henry's two chapters in the present volume are among the products.

The Formation of the New Administration

The formation of the new administration went on concurrently at three different levels: staffing the White House, forming a Cabinet, and recruiting a subcabinet. The three categories of major appointments differed noticeably from each other, but each was replete with distinction. The White House staff was built around the previously existing Kennedy congressional and campaign staffs, and could begin with long-established and highly personal working relationships with the President. The Cabinet choices lacked this quality of previous intimacy in most cases, but reflected a combination of political, administrative, and intellectual qualifications. The subcabinet choices were more flamboyant and more controversial in noteworthy instances, but seemed well calculated to add both energy and a diversity of points of view.

The administration as a whole was a new creation; in no sense was it a previous shadow government transferred as a body from the opposition to a position of operating responsibility. But the new administration was impressive for the amount of governmental experience that it contained; and it was this that led one journal of opinion to remark: "For the first time in remembered history, the formation of an incoming Administration resembles the formation of a new government under the parliamentary system of England and France; many of the incoming officials are already known to each other, most have had some previous governmental experience."[14]

There were at least three reasons for the kind of success that President Kennedy achieved in putting together his administration. One was the simple fact that the Democratic party had been out of office in the Executive Branch of the federal government for only eight years, and had meanwhile retained great strength elsewhere. The party had ample reserves of skilled man power, able and willing to accept governmental appointment. The experience tends to confirm the view of those who have argued that party overturns at intervals of no more than eight or twelve years can be absorbed

[14] *New Republic,* Feb. 6, 1961, p. 5.

much more readily than those that come at longer periods.

A second reason was the incoming President's fourteen years of experience at the national capital, a period long enough to overlap the last previous administration of his party. Kennedy had a degree of personal acquaintance with potential appointees and with sources of information about them that has rarely been matched at a time of party overturn. This may be a point of long-term advantage in going to the Senate for a presidential candidate, by contrast with selecting a governor—unless he is one, like Franklin D. Roosevelt, with relevant federal experience in a previous administration.

The third reason was personal to President Kennedy. Without his competence, energy, and concept of the office, it would have been possible to get into as many recruiting difficulties as those encountered by President Harding—who also came out of the Senate and entered the White House as the leader of a party that had been out of office only eight years.

Relations with Eisenhower and Nixon

Kennedy's call at the White House on December 6, 1960, may have been delayed by Eisenhower, who seems to have been unwilling to go through with the gesture as long as there was any doubt of the outcome of the election. But the occasion, when it did come, had the effect of silencing partisan discussion and confirming the legitimacy of the succession. Eisenhower retained full responsibility up to the time of the transfer, and then made the transfer handsomely. His military training and experience in the transfer of command posts were relevant.

Kennedy's call on Nixon at Miami on November 14, 1960, was an innovation in relationships between a President-elect and the defeated candidate of the other party. Whatever Kennedy's initial intentions were in making the visit, it had the effect of publicizing Nixon's claim to the titular leadership of the Republican party, and of giving it sanction as a fact of which the President-elect had taken cognizance.[15] It was after this had occurred that the discussion

[15] See the remarks quoted in Chap. 11.

took place in which Governor Nelson Rockefeller challenged Nixon's claim to the titular leadership; and it was still later that President Eisenhower toasted Nixon at the White House as the incoming leader of the Republican party, with the Governor and many other Republican leaders present and joining in the toast.[16] Whether this symbolism has had any permanent effect is doubtful, in view of the limited recognition accorded Nixon by his party after he left the Vice Presidency, but it was a new ceremonial and an interesting process of investiture for the new leader.

Furthermore, insofar as President Kennedy's place in the chain of events is concerned, it may be worth noting that the present position of the opposition party leader in Britain is due about as much to the recognition he is accorded by the government as it is to his relationships within his own party. The reasons a succession of British governments have participated in developing the status of the opposition leader are undoubtedly apparent to President Kennedy, and it is possible that he may continue to assist in making them apparent to the country.

The reasons include the contribution to national unity that can be made when the top leaders of each party are in visible agreement with each other, especially on matters of foreign and military policy in times of crisis. Partisan conflict can also be kept within bounds in campaign years more easily if there has been a degree of courtesy and comity between the party leaders in previous years. Under American conditions, moreover, there may be occasions when the leaders of the presidential wing of each party have an interest in making common cause with each other in dealing with the leaders of the two parties in Congress.

Program Development and Congressional Relations

Part of the folklore of American politics is the contention that a new President should get what he wants from Congress during his

---

[16] President Eisenhower was quoted as saying, "The Vice President will be the head of the Republican Party for the next four years, and he will have my support and the support of all those who are here tonight." *Washington Post and Times Herald*, Dec. 1, 1960, p. 18.

first hundred days, or he may not get it at all. With the Roosevelt model in mind, this view seems to have been influential with Kennedy when he was still only a candidate. In the light of the election returns, however, it was obvious that the Kennedy relationship to Congress, in terms of available congressional working majorities, would be much more akin to that of Harry S. Truman after his upset victory in 1948 than to that of Franklin D. Roosevelt after the landslide of 1932.

The record of the new Kennedy administration in preparing and submitting its initial legislative program was nonetheless comparable to that of the Roosevelt administration, as Laurin Henry makes clear in Chapter 9, and in sharp contrast to the slow start of the Eisenhower administration. As the messages accumulated in a sluggish Congress, however, it became apparent that the new President would have to utilize all of the opportunities of his office if his program were to prosper. He could work through the congressional leaders, which he did with great deference and persistence from election day onward. He could help the congressional leaders in lining up the votes they needed to meet their own commitments, as was demonstrated in the conflict over the House Rules Committee. He could go to the public to educate, to dramatize the issues, and to build up public sentiment for action in Congress.

By all of these means, President Kennedy was able to demonstrate, as others had done before, that a President who works at his job can obtain much from Congress even when the situation is sticky and there is a lack of committed majorities in Congress for his program as a whole. At the end of the first six months, the President had withstood and survived the backwash of the Cuban affair, had returned from his meeting with Khrushchev in Vienna, had maintained his personal prestige at a high level, and, as Henry says, had confronted reality in Latin America, Africa, Asia, and Europe. The period of the transition was substantially over, with domestic affairs and the legislative program doing reasonably well, but with continuing anticipations of further crises abroad.

Transition in Congress and the Party Organizations

Congress and the party organizations are the most tradition-bound parts of the political system; and much of the time they seem to reinforce each other in resisting change. Yet the pressures of transition resulting from the party overturn in the White House were not confined to the Executive Branch. In Congress, there were changes in roles, leadership relations, and power equations; while in the party organizations, there were some genuine innovations, as well as the curious transformations that usually result from a reversal of in-party and out-party statuses. The headquarters of the Democratic party was no longer a center of autonomous free-wheeling initiatives; it had become a subsidiary enterprise of a party in power. Conversely, the Republican headquarters was no longer an appendage of the White House and was instead free to exercise leadership and show initiative to whatever extent it could.

The Democratic Advisory Council, created after the election defeat of 1956, was liquidated soon after the victory of 1960. In effect, this was a concession by the President-elect to the congressional leaders whose cooperation he needed. Certainly, it was contrary to the wishes of former Chairman Paul Butler, who had believed that the council should be continued regardless of the election outcome and had obtained a resolution at the national convention approving the council and directing its continuance. It was agreed on all sides, however, that the function of the council, if continued, would be different with the party in power. Many of those who valued it highly for its previous services were dubious of its potential value in a new role, although disposed to argue that something like it should be reinstituted whenever the party again found itself in the opposition. Meanwhile, many of the council's alumni were absorbed into major positions in the new administration.

The Eighty-seventh Congress

For the first time in this century, as *Congressional Quarterly* pointed out, a party winning the Presidency from the opposition failed to gain seats in Congress.[17] Numerically, the Republican gains were not large—2 seats in the Senate, of which 1 was shortly lost by death, and 19 seats in the House—but the Republican gains increased the strength of the conservative coalition in Congress, and seriously impaired the working majority of Democrats in the House of Representatives who could be expected to support the party's program. In the House, the apparent majority of 262 Democrats to 174 Republicans was available in its entirety for virtually no purpose other than the election of the Speaker. On the basis of the form sheet, as computed, for example, by *Congressional Quarterly* early in the session, it could have been expected that the minimum wage bill would be rejected 240-192, the school bill 227-201, and the area development bill 220-197.[18] The later adoption of some of these bills was made possible only by some shifting of votes in the direction of the administration.

The strength and composition of the conservative coalition in the new House of Representatives was shown most clearly in the vote on enlarging the Rules Committee. As Senator Eugene J. McCarthy said (Chapter 10), this was a fight that had been building up for years and that had to be made. Speaker Sam Rayburn chose the least offensive of the plans for reform, but one also that avoided a fight in the party caucus by risking a vote in the whole House. After massive pressures on both sides, in which the administration became fully committed, the vote was carried by the narrow margin of 217-212. Under the embattled leadership of Chairman Howard W. Smith of the Rules Committee, a majority of southern Democrats had voted against the Speaker's plan, 63-47. On the other hand, anti-coalition Republicans deserted their party leaders to provide the margin of victory.[19]

In the voting on other issues later in the session, the administration frequently gained somewhat larger majorities, but usually at the cost of program concessions, and with a frequent dependence on a few Republican votes to provide the margin of victory. Rarely could it be assumed in advance that a dependable majority would

[17] *Congressional Quarterly Special Report,* March 10, 1961, p. 1.
[18] *Congressional Quarterly Weekly Report,* Feb. 10, 1961, pp. 223-24.
[19] *Ibid.,* Feb. 3, 1961, pp. 170-71.

be available in the House for the administration's proposals.

The Senate continued to be a more liberal body than the House of Representatives. Its top-heavy Democratic majority included a few Democrats who typically voted Republican,[20] but there was a majority in the Senate in 1961 for most of the Kennedy program, and occasionally an actual or near majority for proposals going further than those sponsored by the administration. On issues defining a "pro-labor" versus an "anti-labor" position, 51 senators could be counted as pro-labor, 49 as anti-labor, although in the House the anti-labor group appeared to have a solid majority.[21] As Senator McCarthy remarked, the Senate has become more responsive to urban and activist interests than the House and is thus closer to the position of the administration.

The long-term role of the Senate as it has clarified in recent years reflects a number of factors. Unlike the House, no Senate seat can be made safe by any contemporary process of gerrymandering in a state legislature. The consequences of the direct election of senators have become more important as the states have become more populous, more urbanized, and in most cases more exposed to the full sweep of a competitive two-party politics. Senate constituencies have thus become much like the presidential constituency; and the results are apparent in the voting and other behavior of the Senate.

The Houses also have their characteristic differences in leadership tenure and succession. In recent years, Senate leaders have come to their posts relatively young in their Senate careers; and lengthy tenure in the leadership posts has not been common. Opposite tendencies have prevailed in the House and have undoubtedly decreased the adaptability of the larger body. Eventually, however, a new generation of leadership will come to power in the House, with consequences not as yet predictable.[22]

---

[20] Cf. note, p. 323.

[21] *Congressional Quarterly Weekly Report,* Nov. 11, 1960, p. 1856, reported the new Senate as 50 pro-labor and 48 anti-labor before selection of the replacements for Senators Kennedy and Johnson. The figures in the text credit the Kennedy replacement to the labor side, and the eventual Johnson replacement, Tower, to the other side.

[22] A recently published article on the qualifications and operating techniques of one of the least publicized members of Congress, Richard Bolling of

The Leadership Crisis in the Republican Party

Soon after the election defeat, there began a discussion of leadership problems in the Republican party that continued into the meeting of the party's national committee in January, without being completely resolved even then. The precedents created by the Democratic Advisory Council as a medium for out-party leadership were undoubtedly responsible for much of the discussion. Three alternative kinds of proposal were actively considered.

One involved building up the status of the defeated candidate as the titular leader of his party. This is a proposal that has been supported at times by various political scientists, including the present writer.[23] Various forms of the proposal apparently attracted more interest in the transition of 1960-61 than ever before, but were given no encouragement by Vice President Nixon.

The second proposal came from Governor Rockefeller when he said, on December 1, 1960, that what the party really needed was "collective leadership." This was spelled out more fully in a proposal by Senator Kenneth B. Keating of New York, as noted by Senator Morton in his lecture (Chapter 11). The proposal attracted considerable support, but also met the immediate opposition of the party's congressional leaders.

A third alternative, less clearly developed in public debate, was for a different kind of collective leadership modeled on the weekly meetings at the White House of the party in power. In modified form, the party leaders in Congress accepted this alternative, and began meeting with each other and the party chairman at weekly intervals.

Missouri, was of particular interest in relation to the problems of the succession in the Speakership. William S. White, "The Invisible Gentleman from Kansas City," *Harper's*, May 1961, pp. 83-87.

[23] Previous discussion included a letter by the writer, *Washington Post and Times Herald*, Nov. 24, 1952; an article by Norton E. Long, "Patriotism for Partisans: A Responsible Opposition," *Antioch Review*, Winter issue 1952-53; an article by Frederic W. Collins, "What Adlai Stevenson Can Do," *New Republic*, July 25, 1955; many letters of comment in following issues; Paul T. David, "A New Role for the Opposition Party Leader," *New York Times Magazine*, Sept. 18, 1955; Clinton Rossiter, "Let's Not Lose the Losing Candidate," *ibid.*, Nov. 6, 1960; letter commenting on the Rossiter article by the writer, *ibid.*, Nov. 20, 1960.

The central role of the party chairman, Senator Morton, in hold-ing his party together during two months of debate over leadership arrangements was noteworthy. He had much to do with the origins of the new leadership meetings, and consistently advocated expand-ing them on occasion to make them more broadly representative of the whole party. When he left the chairmanship to prepare for his forthcoming Senate race in Kentucky, he was succeeded by Repre-sentative William E. Miller, a 47-year-old Republican congress-man from Buffalo, New York, with a conservative voting record.[24]

Chairman Miller was apparently acceptable to Vice President Nixon, Governor Rockefeller, Senator Barry Goldwater, and their respective groups of followers in the party. He was expected to occupy a position of neutrality in the party's choice of a nominee in 1964. After he had been in office a few weeks, it was reported that, like his predecessor, he also favored some form of collective leader-ship for the party and was advocating the creation of "a Republi-can Forum" to make special studies of developing domestic and international problems and outline what the Republican party would do about them.[25]

Preparations for 1962—and 1964

In the reorganization of party activities after the election, un-usual attention was given in both parties to an early beginning of preparations for the congressional and state campaigns of 1962. In the Republican party, Chairman Morton advocated postpone-ment of any power struggle over the party's presidential nomina-tion in 1964, suggesting that it would be worthless unless the party made gains in Congress in 1962. As recounted in Chapter 11, he initiated a series of activities to increase the Republican share of the big-city vote, to register more Republican voters, and to make sure

---

[24] *Congressional Quarterly Weekly Report*, June 2, 1961, pp. 933-34.

[25] Roscoe Drummond, "A GOP Forum? Council Could Give Party Focus," *Washington Post and Times Herald*, July 17, 1961, p. 13. According to Drummond, the early opposition to the council idea among Republican leaders was shifting to positive support for some such action, for two reasons: dis-enchantment with the party image conveyed by the "Ev and Charlie show," and the evident tendency of the party's disparate elements to race off in all direc-tions, in the absence of any central forum to pull them together.

that all Republican votes are counted. The party also began making greater use of regional conferences, as the Democratic party has in recent years, in order to plan more intensive activities in groups of adjoining states with common problems.

In the Democratic case, party reorganization was dominated for some months by the 1960 deficit and the problems of party and campaign finance. Decisive action occurred on these fronts, as Herbert Alexander reported in Chapter 5, with major fund-raising events, the initial successes of a revised state quota system contemplating much larger payments from the states, and a consolidation of the financial operations of the two congressional campaign committees with those of the national committee—an act of party centralization that would not have seemed possible in the Democratic party a few months earlier, although it had occurred on the Republican side some years ago. The durability of these changes will have to be viewed with some skepticism until they have survived for a longer period, but they suggest that the new management at Democratic party headquarters is not only vigorous, but relatively well able to secure cooperation from the state parties and from congressional elements. Firm White House backing was presumably a major factor in securing the new arrangements for party finance.

The expectations created by the outcome in 1960 have led both parties to look forward to a most intense struggle in the campaigns of 1962, as well as those of 1964. The outcome in 1962 may be affected by a number of technical factors that deserve notice, but most of all by the evolving record of the Kennedy administration in the light of world events. President Kennedy will presumably lead his party's national campaign in 1962, as his predecessors have in recent years.[26] He can be expected to seek not merely to withstand the mid-term losses in Congress that are typical for a party in power, but also to work for an increase in the number of Democrats in Congress who will vote with their party.

As for 1964, comment after the 1960 election generally tended

[26] On the new doctrine of presidential leadership in mid-term campaigns, see Paul T. David, "The Changing Party Pattern," *Antioch Review*, Fall 1956, pp. 333-50.

to assume that President Kennedy would be unbeatable in seeking a second term. This assumption was widely re-examined in the first few months of the Kennedy administration, and particularly after the unhappy affair in Cuba, with a corresponding increase in the hopes of Republican partisans. The Republican party, without necessarily wishing adversity for either the President or the country, has every reason to nourish its hopes for future elections; and this is one of the major factors tending toward a higher level of tension in the domestic political system.

Problems of Electoral Reform

Interest in certain types of electoral reform seems to rise with every presidential election, then dwindle away with no permanent result. In the past the dwindling of interest has usually reflected the absence of any organized pressure group to supply the necessary factors of persistence and leadership. In the present case, congressional sentiment in the winter of 1960-61 seemed to reflect an unusual amount of constituency interest in the reform of the electoral college, the party conventions, and the presidential primaries. Interest in these issues has undoubtedly subsided under the pressure of other concerns, but a more persistent leadership for electoral change may be in the making.

The announced interest of the Republican National Committee in securing a general reform of state election laws was a noteworthy innovation, one that can perhaps be credited in part to the excellence of the research staff at the party's national headquarters.[27] President Kennedy has his own score to settle with state laws permitting the election of presidential electors who will vote against their party's candidate. In addition, several other factors are present in the situation that will undoubtedly generate pressures for various kinds of electoral reform in the relatively near future.

The most explosive potentialities are probably those inherent in

[27] On this subject, with invidious comment on the Democratic counterpart, see White, *op. cit.,* pp. 386-87.

the congressional redistricting that has been going on in the states as the result of the 1960 census. An estimate by *Congressional Quarterly* indicates that the most likely net effect of changes in some 25 states would be a Republican gain of about five seats in the House of Representatives in the elections of 1962. But several state legislatures have deadlocked over redistricting, with the probable result, as of July 1961, that all members of Congress from Illinois, Minnesota, and Pennsylvania will be elected at large, and with similar possibilities in several other states.

If the Illinois and Pennsylvania elections are held at large, with 51 seats at stake, the outcome in these states could be decisive in the control of the House after 1962. A Republican sweep would solidify the control of the conservative coalition, even if it fell short of a Republican party majority in the House. A Democratic sweep, conversely, would probably come close to providing a solid working majority of Democrats who usually vote Democratic.[28] In either case, the turmoil resulting may improve somewhat the prospects for national legislative action on the problems of congressional districting—action long overdue, but in a field that has been as sticky in Congress as it is in the state legislatures.

Meanwhile, there are the further possibilities of another sleeper situation—the pending Tennessee case in the Supreme Court. In November 1960, after the election, the Court reversed its practice of recent years and agreed to hear argument on appeal in a case involving the inequities of representation in the Tennessee legislature. The argument occurred on April 19 and 20, 1961, with the Department of Justice participating and strongly urging action. Two weeks later, the Court postponed decision and announced that it would hear further argument at the October term.

Any action by the Court to bring state legislative districting within the scope of judicial review under the federal Constitution would soon have profound effects on state politics—and on congressional districting. The same doctrines, once enunciated by the Court,

[28] *Congressional Quarterly Weekly Report,* July 14, 1961, pp. 1231-33.

would probably also soon be applicable directly to congressional districting, reversing the decision by which the Court declined action in *Colegrove* v. *Green* in 1946. In this, as in other matters, it can be supposed that the Court is becoming more responsive to the needs of the presidential constituency—a consequence that could be expected from the President's closer relationship to his own constituency in recent decades, since members of the Court are appointed by the President. State legislative districting is a subject on which President Kennedy has long held strong views, as evidenced by his article on "The Shame of the States," in the *New York Times Magazine,* May 18, 1958—cited by the Solicitor General, Archibald Cox, in his brief in the Tennessee case.

Both parties have interests, not necessarily the same, in the extension of the franchise to groups currently deprived or disadvantaged. Both national parties cooperated, despite opposition mainly from southern members, in the drive to give the suffrage in presidential elections to residents of the District of Columbia. This was done by means of the Twenty-third Amendment to the federal Constitution, approved by Congress on June 16, 1960. It was ratified by the necessary number of state legislatures, now 38, more rapidly than any amendment since the Twelfth in 1804, and came into effect on March 29, 1961.[29]

Similar action may soon become possible on the proposed constitutional amendment to outlaw the poll tax as a qualification for voting in federal elections. Approved by the Senate in 1960 by a vote of 72 to 16 as one element in the proposal that also contained suffrage for the District of Columbia, the anti-poll tax portion of the measure was bottled up in the House of Representatives under conditions of late session complexity. The proposal has the support of the administration in the present Congress, can be expected to move through both Houses in due time with bipartisan support, and should find relatively quick approval in the requisite number of states. In conjunction with the work already in progress under the federal civil rights act of 1960, a further long-term broaden-

[29] *Ibid.,* March 31, 1961, pp. 535-36.

ing of the voting electorate can be expected in a number of southern states.

Party and campaign finance is the other field affecting elections in which significant federal legislation is a near-term possibility. President Kennedy has repeatedly indicated his interest in measures by which the financial burdens of campaigning might be relieved by public contributions. Another major possibility, as suggested by Herbert Alexander, would be a change in the federal tax laws by which millions of voters might be encouraged to make financial contributions up to $20 a year to parties and candidates of their choice, receiving a credit against their federal income tax of half the amount of the contribution, for a maximum tax credit of $10.

The financial problems of the parties have become so acute under traditional patterns of organization and finance that some form of breakthrough to a new pattern is clearly needed. Whatever form the action takes in the circumstances now prevailing, it seems likely to strengthen the national parties as organizations, and to strengthen the nationally oriented interests within each party.

Intensified Competition Between the Parties

Many signs indicate that the party system as a whole now occupies what is probably the most highly competitive position it has ever reached in national politics. The narrowing margins of victory in all the major arenas in 1960—elections for President, Congress, the governors, state legislatures—are a major factor in this assessment, along with the close votes in both Houses of Congress on most of the critical legislative issues this year. In both respects, the recent situation has reflected an intensification of trends operating most of the time since the end of World War II.

The competition between the parties for the control of the national government, as well as that of the state governments, has become a matter of vast importance to all of the major interests in the country. The results were shown in the number of states in which the election was fought hard to a close outcome in 1960, in the speed with which the professionals in each party turned to the problems of preparing for 1962, and in the aggressive characteristics of the leadership that has come to the top in each of the national parties.

The parties may not remain as closely balanced as they were in 1960, but the general long-term outlook is for a continuation of a highly competitive relationship. It is difficult indeed to visualize a set of factors that could return the country to a sectional imbalance in politics as extreme as the one prevailing from 1896 to 1928. A different kind of imbalance might occur along social class and economic lines if the Democratic party could become more successful in bringing to the polls the population elements that are allegedly attached to it. But, as noted earlier in this chapter, a normal Democratic vote in terms of turnout, outside the South, has actually been less than a majority in recent years. The Kennedy administration has the strategic advantages of incumbency in building party strength in most parts of the country, but the Republican party will be an effective competitor for many years to come if it exploits its available opportunities.

World Politics and a More National Politics

The pressures of international affairs and their various impacts on domestic politics have been noted throughout the book and throughout this chapter. It seems inevitable that all aspects of American political life will continue to be affected by world conditions, and that a more national politics will be the result.

One can suppose that the stresses and strains of domestic politics must be quite different in a country that constantly faces an external threat from what they are in a country that need not concern itself with external affairs. The United States began its life as a nation during a period in which the external threat was serious, was then free of any serious fear of external aggression for most of a century, and has in recent decades been compelled to adjust to a situation in which the danger from abroad seems ever greater. It seems more than coincidental that broad characteristics of American politics, including the primacy of national issues and the characteristics of national political leadership, were of one kind from Washington to Jackson, of another kind from Jackson to McKinley, and have shown a noteworthy tendency to revert to some aspects of their first form in recent decades.

The change that has come in politics has come along with a maturing of our economic and social order—a maturing that has been accompanied by the development of a somewhat greater degree of bipolarization in the two-party system. The increasing differentiation between the parties is a change that has been received with regret by some, but one that seems inevitable in a modern industrial order. It does have the advantage of giving the voters a more discernible choice between two major alternatives. It also establishes a system of countervailing power that seems to have advantages comparable to those contemplated by the Founding Fathers in their tripartite division of the government—as long as the two-party system is sufficiently balanced to make the opposition party a constant threat and a genuine alternative.

The present balance between the parties may be somewhat fortuitous, but since we have it, we could well cultivate its advantages. Competition between the parties puts each on its mettle, and tends to make each party somewhat intolerant of dissentient elements that seem to be mainly engaged in the practice of trading with the enemy. On the other hand, each party tends to develop a more tolerant attitude toward the elements that it must regard as peculiarly its own, because they have nowhere else to go. Withal, each party must continue its competition for the uncommitted elements in the center of the spectrum, without which it would have no chance of winning at all.

Hence each party tends to develop its interests over a wide range, and yet a range that runs from the center of the total spectrum to one end or the other, with only a limited overlap between the parties in the middle. This is the basis on which each party can seek to become representative of half or more of the total population, while still maintaining a sufficiently clear identity to give a distinct direction to the national life, when it does happen to find itself in power.

A vigorous competition between the parties tends to make each party more cohesive than it might otherwise be. The effects of this tendency may come slowly and be long delayed, yet it would seem that in the end they may overcome the excessive localism that has been so characteristic of the American parties throughout their history. The special characteristics of the South as a region are the main factor currently standing in the way of this tendency, but even the South seems to be giving ground under the pressures of the present era. It seems likely that having the Democratic party in power with the kind of President now in office may expedite the development of a two-party South even more than a Republican administration would have done. The cleavage between the southern Democrats who are prepared to go along with their northern brethren and those who are not has certainly been sharpened in the last twelve months.

These shifting forces within the party system are in themselves a reflection of the factors that move us in the direction of a more national politics—a tendency that has been visible to almost every observer of the political scene for the last ten years. So far the tendency has shown itself, not in major changes in the institutional apparatus of the political parties or the government, but in a disposition for issues formerly deemed local to become recognized as national, in the new primacy of the issues of survival that have always been posed in national terms, and in a stronger position of influence not only for the President, but also for other political leaders who hold national political responsibilities. All of these aspects of a more national politics were clearly present in 1960 and 1961, and it seems unlikely that there will be any retreat on such essentials in the kind of world in which we now live.

Index

Acheson, Dean, 251
Adenauer, Konrad, 186, 187, 251
Advertising media in campaign, 62-63, 85
Advisory Council to Democratic National Committee, 33-34, 142, 330, 333
AFL-CIO, campaign activity, 23n, 64, 137
Africa: Kennedy policy toward, 252, 253; reaction to U.S. election, 196
Agricultural issues at conventions, 23, 70
Airmen, release by Soviet Union, 237
Alcorn, Meade, 301
Alexander, Herbert E., 116, 319, 335, 339
Allen, George V., 104
Almond, James L., Jr., 47
Americans for Constitutional Action, 132
Americans for Democratic Action, 132
Anderson, Robert B., 229
Anderson Senate rules proposal, 269, 271
Argentina, reaction to U.S. election, 192
Auchincloss, Mrs. Hugh D., 121n

Bailey, John M., 33n, 144, 242
Balance of payments problem, 228-30, 231
Balance of power, federal government, shifts in, 283-86
Ball, George W., 216
Balloting at Democratic convention, 11-13
Bean, Richard, 62
Belknap, George, 61
Bell, David E., 220, 243
Bennett, John B., 92
Bennett, John C., 79
Benson farm program, 70
"Big city" vote, 302, 334
Bipartisanship, 178, 276-77, 308, 310
Bliss, Ray C., 302
Boggs, J. Caleb, 172

Bolling, Richard, 332n
Bolton, Frances, 38
Bowles, Chester: as chairman, Democratic platform committee, 32, 34, 35, 36, 40-41, 52, 95; as foreign policy adviser, 74, 194; as liaison with White House, 210; as Under Secretary of State, 191, 204, 220; foreign appraisal, 191, 194, 196
Brademas, John, 268, 286
Brandt, Willy, 187
Brazil, reaction to U.S. election, 181, 192
Briefings for presidential transition, 208, 209-10, 212, 214-15, 223-25, 229, 231, 233-34, 248, 261
Brightman, Samuel, 61
Brinkley, David, 95
Broadcasting (see also Television debates): campaign costs, 29, 126-30; convention and election coverage, 40, 51, 52, 54-55, 95-98, 101, 108; free time for candidates, 91, 118, 127-30; legislation and public policy, 89-93, 94, 112, 114-15; role in political campaigns, 88, 91, 95, 108-10, 314
Brookings Institution, project for facilitating presidential transition, 207, 208, 211, 212, 219, 325
Brown, Edmund G. (Pat), 6, 9
Budget: Eisenhower, 226, 227, 265; Kennedy, 245-46, 265; proposed changes in timing, 264-65
Bundy, McGeorge, 239
Burns, Arthur F., 62
Bush, Prescott, 32
Business, political support, 23, 125, 136, 138-40
Business and Professional Men and Women for Kennedy-Johnson, 128
Butler, Paul, 42-43, 44, 45, 46, 49, 91, 136, 143, 314, 330
Byrd, Harry F., 150n, 246

Cabinet, Kennedy, 211, 215, 219-20, 221-22, 233, 234, 239, 262, 326
California primary, 9

343

Campaign, presidential, *1960* (*see also* Election, presidential, *1960*; Nominating conventions; Nominations, presidential; *and* Primaries), 57-87; duration, 180, 203; financing (*see* Financing presidential election); geographic spread, 70-72, 317-18; innovations and new aspects, 62-63, 85-87, 88, 311-20; issues, 22-24, 59-60, 69-70, 75-79, 81-83, 87, 100, 102-03, 104, 105; organizations and staff, 60-63, 126, 141-42; phases, 74; pledges, implementation, 40-42, 56; preconvention campaigns, 2-10, 21-22, 25-26, 30, 93-94, 110; registration of voters, 63-64, 303, 319, 334; scurrilous literature, 79, 118, 132; strategies (*see also under* Kennedy *and* Nixon), 24-27, 63-74; voter turnout, efforts for, 319

Campaign Associates, 62-63, 85, 127

Candidates, presidential and vice presidential, experience and training, 4-6, 312-13, 327

Cannon, Clarence, 43, 44

Carlino, Joseph F., 37, 38, 39

Case, Clifford P., 171

Castro, Fidel, 199-200, 230

Catholic vote (*see also* Religious issue), 7, 153, 154, 155-61, 174-75, 292, 322-24

Central Intelligence Agency, role in Cuban refugee invasion, 254-55

Century Club for Symington, 121

Chayes, Abram J., 34, 62

Chicago convention *1960. See* Republican national convention.

China, Communist: reaction to U.S. election, 197-98, 200; U.S. policy toward, 194-95

China, Nationalist, reaction to U.S. election, 192

Chou En-lai, 197-98

Christian Nationalist Crusade, 132

Citizens for Kennedy-Johnson, 120, 121, 126, 128

Citizens' Research Foundation, 116*n*

Civil rights issue, 22, 73, 74, 84-85, 276, 318, 338-39; planks, 32*n*, 33-36, 37-40, 41, 44, 53, 56, 70

Civil service, career (*see also* Personnel recruitment *and* Schedule C

jobs), 263-64, 266

Clifford, Clark M., 210-11, 212, 213, 214, 223, 225, 261

Cochrane, Willard, 62

Collins, LeRoy, 44, 45-46

Committees, interdepartmental, abolishment, 240

Communications Act of *1934:* Lar Daly amendment, 90-91, 93, 94; relaxation of requirements under Section *315,* 91-93, 112, 114

Congo: as campaign issue, 59; Kennedy policy toward, 253

Congress (*see also* Congressional elections): balance of power shifts, 283-86; bipartisanship, 178, 276-77, 308, 310; committees and leadership, 277-81, 332; Eighty-seventh Congress, prospects, 286-87; party control in, 272-73, 299; postconvention session, 25, 60, 73-74; presidential influence and relations, 269, 273-76, 287, 329; redistricting for, 336-38; role of opposition party in, 304-10; rules controversies, 243-44, 268-72, 276, 278; seniority in, 279

Congressional election campaigns: financing, 143, 147; prospects and preparations for *1962* and *1964,* 293-94, 334-36

Congressional elections, *1960,* results, 168-72, 275, 290, 320, 330-31

Constitutional amendments regarding suffrage, 338

Conventions, nominating. *See* Democratic national convention; Nominating conventions; *and* Republican national convention.

Cox, Archibald, 62

Credentials at national conventions, 46-48, 52

Cuba: as campaign issue, 59, 82-83; reaction to U.S. election, 199-200; refugee attempted invasion, 254-56, 261, 336; U.S. postelection policy, 228, 230-31

Cushing, Cardinal, 83

Daley, Richard J., 90, 104

Daly, John, 101

Daniel, Price, 47

David, Paul T., 1, 311